THE WORLD ACCORDING TO
MIKE LEIGH

Michael Coveney is the theatre critic of the *Observer*. He was born in the East End of London in 1948, raised in Ilford, Essex, and educated at a Jesuit grammar school (where Alfred Hitchcock had been an earlier pupil) and at Oxford. He began reviewing plays in 1972, edited *Plays and Players* magazine in the late 1970s, and was theatre critic and deputy arts editor on the *Financial Times* during the 1980s. He joined the *Observer* in 1990.

His books include *The Citz*, a study of the Glasgow Citizens' Theatre; *Maggie Smith: A Bright Particular Star*; *The Aisle is Full of Noises*, a theatrical journal of 1993; and, with Robert Stephens, *Knight Errant: Memoirs of a Vagabond Actor*.

From the reviews of *The World According to Mike Leigh*:

'Should rivet anyone who has ever been captivated by, or just interested in, Mike Leigh's unique body of work'
CHRIS SAVAGE KING, *New Statesman and Society*

'Coveney has done a thorough and often brilliant job of researching Leigh's dramatic cv, and of seeking out former collaborators to record their insights into the man and his famous working methods' COLIN DONALD, *Scotsman*

'Detailed and meticulously researched'
LOU STEIN, *Financial Times*

'Affectionate and definitive' *Comedy Review*

'Excellent . . . never less than absorbing' *Film Review*

THE WORLD ACCORDING TO
MIKE LEIGH

Michael Coveney

HarperCollins*Publishers*

HarperCollins*Publishers*
77–85 Fulham Palace Road,
Hammersmith, London W6 8JB

This paperback edition 1997
1 3 5 7 9 8 6 4 2

First published in Great Britain by
HarperCollins*Publishers* 1996

ISBN 0 00 638339 4

Set in Linotron Bembo

Printed in Great Britain by
Caledonian International Book Manufacturing Ltd, Glasgow

For Toby, Leo and Thomas

CONTENTS

CONTENTS

ILLUSTRATIONS

Leigh's paternal grandfather Mayer Liebermann in Mogilev, near Moscow, c. 1900, before emigrating to England.

Abe and Phyllis Leigh at their wedding reception in the Grand Hotel, Manchester, in August 1941.

Abe and Phyllis with young Michael, aged twenty months, in Salford.

Michael, aged six, pretending to be a statue – or directing traffic? – at Blackpool, on holiday in 1949.

Family group in 1956.

Family group drawn by Leigh in 1955, showing the influence of Ronald Searle.

Michael aged eleven, at North Grecian Street County Primary School, Salford, in 1954.

Leigh borne aloft by his Habonim friends on a portable lavatory, Wirral peninsula, 1959.

Two pictures taken around the time Leigh left RADA in 1962.

Leigh as Costard the clown in *Love's Labour's Lost* at RADA, 1962.

From Leigh's sketchbook: in the Camberwell School of Art life-drawing class in 1964 . . .

. . . and in the theatre design department of the Central School of Art and Design in 1965.

The future film director in Birmingham in 1966.

Anne Raitt as the repressed and lonely Sylvia in the film of *Bleak Moments* (1971).

Leigh's original poster design for the stage play *Bleak Moments* in 1970.

After Mike Leigh and Alison Steadman's wedding ceremony, September 1973.

Leigh's poster for his RSC production of *Babies Grow Old* on its transfer from Stratford-upon-Avon to the ICA in London in 1975.

Toby Leigh, aged several months, on the kitchen table in Wood Green, 1978.

Alison Steadman, Roger Sloman and Geoffrey Hutchings in *Wholesome Glory* (1973) in the Theatre Upstairs at the Royal Court.

Nuts in May (1976) was the film that grew out of *Wholesome Glory*: Steadman and Sloman as Candice-Marie and Keith entertain Anthony O'Donnell as Ray, their fellow camper. (*BBC Photograph Library*)

Angela Curran, John Wheatley, David Threlfall and Kay Adshead in the discotheque scene in *The Kiss of Death*, 1977. (*BBC Photograph Library*)

Alison Steadman as the monstrous Beverly, with Janine Duvitski as Angela and Harriet Reynolds as Susan, in the legendary *Abigail's Party* at Hampstead Theatre, 1977. (*John Haynes*)

Ecstasy at Hampstead Theatre, 1979: Stephen Rea, Julie Walters, Jim Broadbent and Sheila Kelley in a baleful bedsit boozerama. (*John Haynes*)

Segregated neighbours in the BBC film *Grown-Ups*, 1980: Lindsay Duncan and Sam Kelly, Philip Davis and Lesley Manville. (*BBC Photograph Library*)

Goose-Pimples at Hampstead Theatre in 1981: Jill Baker, Jim Broadbent, Marion Bailey and Antony Sher. (*John Haynes*)

Timothy Spall, Eric Richard and Tim Barker as the three hopeless postmen in another notable BBC film, *Home Sweet Home*, 1982. (*BBC Photograph Library*)

Tim Roth and Gary Oldman in *Meantime*, 1983. (*British Film Institute*)

Mike Leigh on the Great Wall of China, May Day, 1985.

Alison, Leo, Toby and Mike (*Tim Douglas, Camera Press*)

The Short and Curlies (1987): David Thewlis as Clive, a rubber-purchasing customer in Joy's (Sylvestra Le Touzel) chemist's shop . . .

. . . and Joy, a rubber-wearing one at Betty's (Alison Steadman) hairdressing salon, 'Cynthia's'.

The writer/director on location with producer Simon Channing-Williams during filming of *High Hopes*, 1988. (*Blowup*)

Ruth Sheen, Edna Doré and Philip Davis in the last scene of *High Hopes*. (*Blowup*)

Saskia Reeves and Greg Cruttwell in *Smelling a Rat* (1988), Leigh's fourth Hampstead Theatre play, a rabid anti-farce in a pink boudoir. (*John Haynes*)

Stan Kouros and Evdokia Katahanas in *Greek Tragedy*, Leigh's play for the Belvoir Street Theatre, Sydney, in 1989.

Timothy Spall as Aubrey tries to enthuse his kitchen assistant, Paula (Moya Brady), before the opening of the Regret Rien restaurant in *Life is Sweet*. (*Simon Mein*)

Jane Horrocks as the anorexic Nicola, and Alison Steadman as Wendy, her mother, in *Life is Sweet*. (*Simon Mein*)

Paul Trussell and Wendy Nottingham in the grisly first-act climax of *It's a Great Big Shame!* at Stratford East (1993). (*Alastair Muir*)

On location with *Naked*: Leigh, director of photography Dick Pope, boom operator Loveday Harding and focus puller Garry Turnbull. (*Simon Mein*)

David Thewlis as Johnny in *Naked* (1993). (*Simon Mein*)

Greg Cruttwell as Jeremy, the repellent landlord, and Katrin Cartlidge as Sophie, the victimised punk Goth, in *Naked*. (*Simon Mein*)

Leigh and Dick Pope on location in east London during the filming of 'Untitled '95', which was to become *Secrets and Lies*. (*Simon Mein*)

Mother and daughter getting to know each other after years of separation. Marianne Jean-Baptiste and Brenda Blethyn in 'Untitled '95' (*Secrets and Lies*). (*Simon Mein*)

ACKNOWLEDGEMENTS

MIKE LEIGH'S CAREER is a typical British success story. A growing international and domestic reputation, eminence in his field of idiosyncratic British movies, and recent European acclaim, have all been achieved against a backdrop of critical, cultural and financial indifference at home. Like so many great maverick artists – Robert Altman, the late Derek Jarman, Peter Brook, Joan Littlewood, Steven Berkoff, Ken Campbell – Leigh has prospered in spite of the system and the establishment, not thanks to it. His work is testament to his courage, tenacity and belief in his having something to say.

The idea of writing a book about Mike Leigh was first put to me by Nick Hern, who had invited Leigh to write one himself. Leigh, whom I have known slightly for ten years on a personal basis, and for twenty, more intimately, as one of our most distinctive and controversial film and theatre artists, suggested that I might be interested. My initial qualms were defeated by a National Film Theatre retrospective in May 1993 which confirmed what I already suspected: that Leigh's work, in depth, range and homogeneity, is unsurpassed by any other comparable *auteur* (is there one?) currently at work in the British cinema and theatre.

The subsequent enthusiasm of Richard Johnson and his colleagues at HarperCollins clinched my resolve. Leigh's story is one of the most interesting in the British film and theatre culture of the past thirty years, and the telling of it for the first time in full seemed to be a great opportunity of documenting not only an almost classic biographical journey, but also of charting the temperature of the times in the artistic and political life of the country.

Leigh's plays and films – which amount to a wonderful, distinctive *oeuvre* achieved against all sorts of odds – tell the story of a major artist and the story of a nation unrepresented, on the whole, elsewhere in British film and theatre. Leigh celebrates the ordinary lives of ordinary people in the heightening process of his true, vigorous and appreciative art. His work teems with a gallery of national characters who are brilliantly drawn, pungently alive and broadly humorous, and it is not inappropriate, I feel, to invoke the achievements of Hogarth and Dickens in discussing them.

I am grateful to the following for providing facilities, tapes, photographs and other material: Deborah Reade and Simon Channing-Williams at Thin Man Films; Brian Robinson at the British Film Institute; David Fraser at BBC Radio 3; Shelley Simmons and Bobby Mitchell at BBC TV (pictures); Genista Streeten at Hampstead Theatre; Martin Coveney at the Theatre Royal, Stratford East; Mrs Phyllis Leigh (Leigh's mother) and, especially, Alison Steadman (Leigh's wife), both of whom were generous with time and hospitality in discussing Leigh's life and work.

My biggest thanks are to Leigh himself, who cleared his diary and his desk for a series of extensive, exhaustive interviews between April and November 1994. Our many hours of taped conversation were supplemented with a long interview Leigh had granted me for an *Observer* feature article in 1993, a memorable 'location' trip to Salford in November 1994, and further conversations subsequent to an early draft of the book in February 1995. Leigh has kept full records of his career in press cuttings and personal memorabilia, all of which he made available to me without condition. And his supply of tapes, publications, contacts, photographs and drawings has been both stimulating and generous to a fault.

The following of Leigh's friends and colleagues spared time to be interviewed: Eric Allan, David Aukin, Stephen Bill, Les Blair, Chris Blundell, Mike Bradwell, Bríd Brennan, Jim Broadbent, Kathy Burke, David Canter, Katrin Cartlidge, Alison Chitty, Colin Cina, Shane Connaughton, Phil Daniels, Carl Davis, Philip Davis, Andrew Dickson, Janine Duvitski, Tony Garnett, Jon Gregory, David Halliwell, Terry Hands, Lindy Hemming, Jane Horrocks, Philip Jackson, Marianne Jean-Baptiste, Anthony Jones, Sheila Kelley, Sam Kelly, Ruth Lesirge, Jeff Lipsky, Gary McDonald, Adrienne Mancia, Lesley Manville, Wendy Nottingham, Dick Pope, Bob and Dizzy Quaif, Stephen Rea, David Rose, Paul Rowley, Lesley Sharp, Ruth Sheen, Claire Skinner, Timothy Spall, Heather Storr, Paul Trussell. In addition, I enjoyed a lively, to-the-point telephone conversation with David Thewlis; and received some interesting details from Anthony O'Donnell and illuminating letters from Antony Sher and Julie Walters.

For other gestures of support and companionship I am grateful to my wife Sue Hyman, and to Penelope Dunn and Caradoc King at A.P. Watt

Acknowledgements

Ltd. I need hardly add that my conclusions are in some ways provisional. Leigh works slowly and meticulously, but we must hope that he has many more films and plays to give us in the coming years. My task is to tell the story so far and to try to indicate why Leigh's ever-increasing popularity, and especially his appeal to young cinema and television audiences, is a cause for celebration and pride not only in his talent, but also in the talents of the actors and technical colleagues with whom he has worked so painstakingly and so fruitfully over three decades.

M.C., London, 1995

PREFACE TO THE
PAPERBACK EDITION

THE FILM REFERRED to at the beginning and end of this book as 'Untitled '95' was shown at the Cannes Film Festival in May 1996 as *Secrets and Lies*. It won instant and almost universal acclaim, and the Cannes jury awarded the film the Palme d'Or – the top prize – and Brenda Blethyn the Best Actress award.

This was an extraordinary triumph in a festival that also showed films by Robert Altman, Michael Cimino, Bernardo Bertolucci, Chen Kaige, Joel Coen, David Cronenberg, the Chilean Raul Ruiz, and Leigh's compatriot Stephen Frears. Leigh had won the Best Director award at Cannes in 1993 for *Naked*, a film which can now be seen not only as a real breakthrough but something of a watershed; *Secrets and Lies* confirmed for many Leigh's arrival on the international scene as a master European director of our times. Much of this book is devoted to telling the story, and the struggle, of how he got there.

The significance of the success of *Secrets and Lies* was not lost on its director. The hostility Leigh instinctively feels towards the homogenisation of the culture, the systematic dilution of social concerns and shared responsibility in political life, and his unfashionable campaign to reflect the sheer monotony and hardship of most people's lives in a self-serving, envious and triviality-obsessed media climate of comment and reportage, was well expressed in his acceptance speech at the awards ceremony: 'It is wonderful and delightful and terrific, and what more can I say? It is wonderful for there to be this recognition of films about ordinary people. That's not to say the banal films of the world, but those of us in the international cinema who are making films about the essence of what it is to be alive. I hope it is an encouragement to all kinds of personal cinema.' He added that his prize would stimulate independent spirits who made films about people and relationships, real life and all the things that really matter.

At a subsequent press conference, he insisted that he was still as pessimistic as ever and that life, as usual, was hilarious and tragic. This blend, which he is wise enough not to claim as an original diagnosis, has never been caught in mellower, or more poignant, vein than it is in *Secrets and Lies*. At the same time, critics such as the estimable Adam Mars-Jones in the *Independent*, who acclaimed the film as one which eschewed cruel caricature at last and gave humanity back to 'Mike Leigh' characters, were both missing the point (there's still plenty of healthy caricature in *Secrets and Lies*) and belatedly justifying their past calumnies, while Mark Steyn in the *Spectator* laboured under the illusion that an outside loo was an anachronism – well, he does live in New Hampshire – and sourly reiterated the old objections about Leigh patronising his characters. These were minority reactions.

Cinema audiences lapped up the film, which did bigger and better business in Britain than any previous Leigh movie. The narrative is engagingly developed over three strands in the early stages: the mysteriously arid, dangerously poised marriage of a High Street photographer, Maurice Purley (Timothy Spall), and his distressed wife, Monica (Phyllis Logan); the embattled domesticity of Maurice's partly estranged, and partly deranged, sister, Cynthia (Brenda Blethyn), and her street-sweeping, sulky daughter, Roxanne (Claire Rushbrook), and the campaign of the bereaved Hortense (Marianne Jean-Baptiste) – the film opens with the funeral of her adoptive mother – to touch base with her blood mother. Who turns out to be Cynthia.

Hortense is black, Cynthia white. Colour blindness, and difficulty of same, is a pressing theme behind many of the social transactions. Over the phone, Hortense tells her 'new' Mum that her name is Hortense Cumberbatch. 'Hortense Clumberbunch?' asks an incredulous Cynthia. There's one great moment, inconceivable in any film other than one made by Mike Leigh, when Hortense arrives at Maurice's house. Monica answers the door and almost slams it in her face with a 'Sorry, no...' and the clear implication that Jehovah's Witnesses (and black people) are unwelcome. Hortense sticks her foot in the door and explains that she is Cynthia's guest. The 'ways of seeing' imagery is further enriched by Hortense's occupation as an optometrist. As Peter Conrad succinctly expressed it in the *Independent on Sunday*, 'she corrects and cleanses vision; Spall, as her befuddled uncle, does the opposite'.

When the action draws to a classic Leigh climax at a barbecue-cum-birthday party (for Roxanne), all sorts of truth-telling take over as Maurice explodes in frustrated rage against the veils of representation his profession typifies, the resentments and antipathies that inform all of our daily lives. The three people he loves most, he says, hate each others' guts: 'Why can't we share our pain?' Spall's outburst is the pay-off to his quiet, soft, underplayed and beautifully gentle performance. When his assistant (Elizabeth Berrington), overcome with her boss's heroism – are they by any chance having an affair? The idea flits across the film and is gone – blurts out that she wishes she had had a Dad like him, a warm 'Aaagh' rises like steam from the cinema stalls.

It emerges that Maurice and Monica cannot have children. They've tried everything for fifteen years. Their marriage, nonetheless, is renewed. Cynthia has found her first daughter, but will not as yet divulge the identity of her father. The camera pulls away from Cynthia's little back garden, with its shed and its creaky garden furniture, as Cynthia basks in the prospect of her two girls getting along together: 'This is the life, innit?'

We cut to black, and the credits roll. At every public screening I have attended, the audience bursts into spontaneous applause. Partly this is due to the bravura tenderness of the finale, but chiefly, I feel, because we have recognised so much of our own lives in these brilliantly delineated parlour and sitting-room war games. The film is suppurating with emotion. And as in *Life is Sweet*, probably the film of Leigh's that most prepares us for this one – *Naked* stands monumentally alone in the *oeuvre* as an intellectual and cinematic *tour de force* – there is fantastic comedy.

Most of this emanates from Blethyn's amazing performance as Cynthia. With her, as with so much in this film, you laugh and you cry. Sad, silly and locked up in her parents' pokey terraced house, like some crazy suburban offspring of Dickens's Miss Havisham, she has not seen her brother for a year. Monica has been busy stencilling the wallpaper and decorating the bedrooms and toilets for the large family she will never possess. 'What's he need six bedrooms for?' Cynthia asks unkindly, unwittingly. She nags Roxanne about safe sex, even offering to help out: 'I've got a Dutch cap floating around somewhere upstairs.'

The pivotal scenes are those where Cynthia and Hortense get together. The sequence of scenes is handled with magisterial deftness and aplomb, even Andrew Dickson's music blossoming from careful keyboards and cellos to polyphonic trumpetings and busy, rushing melodiousness. This is the 'coming alive' of Cynthia, tentatively embarked upon in a desolate Holborn café where the mother and daughter first sit down together.

Interestingly, Adam Mars-Jones questioned the plausibility of two people who had never met before sitting next to each other (and not opposite each other) in a deserted café. The question could only be asked if you had been so drawn into the reality of these characters that you were prepared to overlook the fact that they were appearing in a film. The scene is memorable precisely because they *are* sitting next to each other, the delicate counterpoint of their raw, touching dialogue unimpeded by a moving camera. The mood accelerates into the burgeoning relationship of mother and daughter. They meet for supper in a bistro. 'Where's this food, then? I'm ravishing!' exclaims Cynthia in a wonderful malapropism, to a burst of Hortense's supportive amusement: she really does look more attractive.

The use of a static camera is one of Leigh's mature skills. His confidence in knowing exactly how long to hold shots for is a crucial symptom of his mastery acquired over the years. There are two signifcantly long 'takes' in the film, one of nine minutes (mother meets daugher in the café) and one of six and a half minutes (at the family barbecue). Philip French in the *Observer* noted how seven people at a garden table are allowed to interact without any one of them being especially favoured: 'The cinematographer Dick Pope uses deep focus so that Maurice, who is at the barbecue behind them, is vividly of the group yet standing apart. After that long take, we cut to the inside of the house for truth-telling and blood-letting, and here Leigh cuts between big close-ups and shots in which a foreground figure is in focus and a second person behind them slightly out of focus. This is masterly movie-making that never draws attention to itself.'

One sequence in Maurice's studio has already acquired classic status. In rapid, almost rollercoaster, succession, a stream of clients is encouraged and cajoled by Maurice into giving a little smile, and a whole series of complete lives and relationships flashes past: the snarling boxer; the shy boy from India who needs a wedding photograph for someone he has not yet met; a giggling, toothy couple; an amiable beanpole and his glum wife; a young mother and her baby; a small boy who picks his nose; triplets; businessmen; a dog-owner played hectically by Alison Steadman. The effect is not only richly comic in itself, but also indicative of Maurice's deftness with his subjects and the gentle indentation each of them makes on his own appreciative consciousness.

On the question of how Leigh has treated the tricky subject of adopted children tracing their blood parents: two separately adopted women of my acquaintance have assured me that Leigh's treatment of this subject is faultless. The problems and complications always arise when the child finds his or her real mother, a right which adopted children have enjoyed since the passing of the 1975 Act of Parliament. The blanking out of Hortense's adoptive family is absolutely spot-on, they say; that isn't the area of difficulty.

And Marianne Jean-Baptiste's performance – quietly-spoken, measured, dignified – conveys perfectly the odd resignation to, and then growing enthusiasm for, the quandary of a black middle-class career girl adjusting to a peculiarly alien white lower-middle- and working-class ambience. By the end, and without any false crashing of gears, we really can believe that Jean-Baptiste's Hortense and Claire Rushbrook's fraught, tetchy, quite beautifully played Roxanne, are sisters under the skin.

I have encountered the same general approval of the treatment of the hasty social worker, whom Lesley Manville plays with broad brush-strokes as a busy professional quite keen to display the inconvenience to herself of all that caring. Her two scenes with Hortense, however, are more 'controversial' in a characteristic Leigh manner.

This delicious little cameo decorates a film that has received full recognition for the overall quality of the acting. Every frame is bursting with life and detail: watch, for instance, Roxanne's boyfriend, Paul, as the domestic chickens come home to roost, clenching his face in disbelief as if to say, 'What on earth are this lot going to hit me with next?' Paul's a scaffolder. That can be dangerous, can't it, Maurice asks? 'Can be mate, yeah, cheers.'

Another keenly discussed episode was the return to Maurice's shop of the former owner, Stuart (Ron Cook), a bitter drunk whose father has died and whose attempt at starting a new life has been a total failure. It is a wonderful scene and serves the important function of contextualising Maurice's professional success ('There but for the grace of God...').

Sadly, Leigh's marriage to Alison Steadman, which constitutes such a large theme of this book, was revealed shortly before Cannes to have broken down after twenty-three years. It emerged that Alison had begun an affair with the actor Michael Elwyn while filming a BBC series about families during the last war, *No Bananas*. The couple have now separated. Alison has left the family home in north London, where Leigh continues to live with their two sons.

As an artist, Leigh has gone through all sorts of fires, but the split from Alison will undoubtedly be the one that singes him most. The peak of critical and public approbation that the success of *Naked* seemed to indicate has been gloriously confirmed in the new film, and Leigh has already completed his latest work – 'Untitled '96' – a feature film for Channel 4. The life, and the work, goes on.

THE WORLD ACCORDING TO
MIKE LEIGH

PROLOGUE

In Soho

Soho, London, the last Monday morning of November 1994. The first cast and crew get-together on the new Mike Leigh film. Sixteen actors gather for coffee and mineral water in an upstairs room in Kettner's restaurant, Romilly Street. Also present: the producer Simon Channing-Williams, the designer Alison Chitty, the art director Eve Stewart, the director of photography Dick Pope, the film editor Jon Gregory, other members of the production team. And Mike Leigh. There is no script, no title, no knowledge of what the film will be about, no preconceptions, and (apparently) no panic.

The film ('Untitled '95') will be created in discussions, improvisations and rehearsals in Stoke Newington, north London, over the coming eighteen weeks, and will be shot on location in London over thirteen weeks between April and July 1995. It will cost about £3 million, twice as much as Leigh's biggest project to date, his last film, *Naked*, but approximately a twelfth of the budget on Kenneth Branagh's version of *Mary Shelley's Frankenstein*. The money has been wholly raised from a French company, CiBy 2000 (the name is clearly a homage to the pioneer Hollywood director and producer Cecil B. De Mille), which made a fortune in building and concrete and financed Jane Campion's *The Piano*.

Leigh, unlike Branagh, does not have Robert de Niro in his cast. And would not want to have him. But he does have the flower of young British character acting. Nine of this company have worked with him before, and old friendships are being merrily renewed: Michelle Austin and Marianne Jean-Baptiste,

1

both black, and Joe Tucker, were in Leigh's last stage work, *It's a Great Big Shame!* (1993); Elizabeth Berrington was the slinky waitress in *Naked* (1993); Brenda Blethyn, a pathetic, unloved relation in *Grown-Ups* (1980), one of the most memorable characters in the Leigh canon; Ron Cook, small and dangerous, exploded alongside Julie Walters and Stephen Rea in the stage play *Ecstasy* (1979); Janine Duvitski, bright-eyed and brilliantly funny, was the bespectacled nurse, Angela, in *Abigail's Party* (1977) and a quieter foil in *Grown-Ups*; Bob Mason, lugubrious and Lancastrian, appeared in a short early TV play, *The Permissive Society* (1975); and the inimitable Timothy Spall, most Dickensian and Falstaffian of young actors, not yet forty, slobbered variously in *Home Sweet Home* (1982), *Smelling a Rat* (1988) and *Life is Sweet* (1990).

One senses this might be a comedy. After the preliminaries, the company sits on chairs in a large circle and Leigh introduces each cast and crew member by name. His domination, lightly applied, is total; some directors at such gatherings – Hal Prince, for instance, or Trevor Nunn – invite the participants to introduce themselves. Not Leigh. He explains that this is the first film he has made which is not partly or largely financed by a television company. The money is in place with no strings attached and complete guarantees of freedom. It is, he says, 'a landmark'. Leigh has struggled in the margins of British film and theatre for thirty years because he has insisted on working in the way he does, without a script and without any conditions of casting or content imposed by anyone else. He's a true maverick.

'I have no idea what we are going to end up doing,' announces Leigh, confidently, 'though of course there are a series of notions and possibilities floating around in my head. We are going to go out on location and make up a film. It will be a story with a beginning, a middle and an end. The next few months are the preparation so that we are saturated with our world when we start shooting.' The Scottish actress Phyllis Logan looks both intrigued and bemused. Emma Amos, a rising young blonde actress lately at the National Theatre, lights another cigarette.

Leigh, now fifty-one, is small, hunched and bearded, dressed

in a casual jumper and black corduroy jeans. He swings lightly
forward on his chair like a mischievous monkey. He pokes
at Simon Channing-Williams's well-upholstered stomach, and
pinches at a modest roll of fat round his own waist, by way of
explaining why their company, formed in 1989, is named Thin
Man Films Ltd. 'Untitled 95' will be his forty-sixth piece contrived
in this 'starting from scratch' mode; and his thirteenth full-length
film since a remarkable debut with *Bleak Moments* in 1971. His
next feature film was *High Hopes* in 1988.

The intervening work of one of this country's most original
and gifted film-makers was made for television. And in order to
get going, and keep going, there was the theatre. The British film
industry, or the government arts policy, in whatever manifestation
they appeared, simply did not know how to recognise, or accommodate, one of their own greatest talents. And as only the British
establishment could, they endowed Mike Leigh with a celebratory
honour, the OBE, 'for services to the British film industry' in
1993. At the time, I expressed surprise that Leigh should have
accepted this honour. His response was typical: 'If I hadn't, how
would anyone know that I'd been offered it?' Was he chuffed?
'You bet.' He regards his acceptance as an amusing act of subversion. I have written to him with his gong attached to his name
on the envelope, as required by etiquette, and he writes back
dubbing me in the same unexpected style.

In Kettner's on this dank and chilly November morning, Leigh
confronts his colleagues as they embark on another voyage into
the unknown, and promises 'a mad, wild scream of a time'. He
outlines the rules. He will work one-to-one, initially, with each
actor, developing a character who is based, in the first place, on
someone he or she knows. Each actor will treat this character
objectively, but will not be apprised of any knowledge of the
other characters beyond what he or she would know of them as
that character at that particular point in the story. The story will
be developed chronologically. The characters will meet each other
only in situations of Leigh's devising. Utter secrecy on this is
essential: 'You have to be free as an actor from knowing what
your character wouldn't know; the centre of the world is your

character,' is Leigh's message to each actor, and his eyes scan the room, decisively.

Leigh explains how the 'one-to-one' principle will apply all the way through the film. He takes an actor on one side, works separately with him or her: would this really happen; or might not this happen instead? Improvisation and 'making it up' are tethered continuously to objective critical appraisal and directorial manipulation.

One of many rehearsal techniques is the 'come out of character' instruction, which signals the end of an improvisation and the opening of objective discussion. Leigh always knows more than his actors about what is going on. Paradoxically, they are inventing the circumstances, and the narrative possibilities, where this dominance – the ultimate condition of 'making a film' – can take place. And it is only at that crucial stage of shooting, after three months' rehearsal, that the script is finalised, the writing nailed right down on the characters. There is almost no 'improvisation' on camera.

Leigh revels in the apprehensive atmosphere in Kettner's: 'I've had everyone checked, before and behind the camera, to make sure you are all stark raving bonkers and totally mad.' The laughter is general but tinged, at last, with anxiety. The company disperses into the Soho lunchtime. Spall is still cavorting in his chair. Blethyn and Duvitski are plotting the next instalment of their friendship dating from *Grown-Ups*. I ask Bob Mason if he feels like someone jumping out of a plane without a parachute. He says he does. But he also knows that Leigh will be alongside throughout the descent, holding his hand and softening the impact.

ONE

The World According to Mike Leigh

> 'My ongoing preoccupation is with families, relationships, parents, children, sex, work, surviving, being born and dying. I'm totally intuitive, emotional, subjective, empirical, instinctive. I'm not an intellectual film-maker. Primarily, my films are a response to the way people are, the way things are as I experience them. In a way, they are acts of taking the temperature.'
>
> MIKE LEIGH, *International Herald Tribune*, 2 February 1994

It is proof of making your mark as an artist that people know exactly what you mean when your name is invoked. 'Like a Mike Leigh film, or play' has become shorthand for a certain kind of grungey domestic scenario, with pop-up toasters and cups of tea, fake-fur coats and rugs, pink bobble carpet slippers, bad haircuts, domestic arguments on leatherette sofas, and adolescent anxieties. Welcome to the slump, the outer London *anomie*, the china animals, the flying geese on brown wallpaper, the smoky pub, the cold light of dawn and the cheerless laundrette.

But if that were all there was to Leigh's work - the physical material of parody and imitation, a sort of downmarket sodden-ashtray Philip Larkin suburbia - I would not be writing this book and you would not be reading it. Leigh's pictures of ordinary life are given extraordinary resonance by the thoroughness of their presentation, the brilliance of the acting, the sureness of the atmospheres and the classical structure to which most of his work aspires, often successfully. Imagine *Così fan tutte*, said Clive James, without the music, and without the words, plus cheap furniture:

you have a Mike Leigh film. It's the Mozart invocation that is both apt and poignant.

Kenneth Tynan said that, in fifty years' time, even the youngest of us would know what is meant by 'a very Noël Coward sort of person'. (He said that in 1953; the point is still valid forty years on.) The mention of 'a Pinter play' today carries the same easy power of connotation, as does 'Jonsonian comedy' or 'an Alan Ayckbourn scenario'. The work of Mike Leigh relates in various ways to each member of that distinguished quartet of English (the 'English' is quite important) dramatists. All four, like Leigh, have a wonderful ear for dialogue and the rhythms of natural speech.

Like Coward, Leigh uses words and phrases for rhythmic effect, not aphoristically. 'Little' is a qualifying commonplace for both writers, as in 'have a little sandwich', or 'a nice little cup of tea', or 'have a little go at the patio'. His characters 'pop the Beaujolais in the fridge', or claim to have seen 'Keith Chegwin in W.H. Smith', or order someone to 'stop standing on the rug; you're *squashing* it', or hope that they don't have 'a kid that's a bit thick'. Their speech is a halting, compendious deposit of lower-middle-class and working-class argot, much of it rescued with poetic bravura, carefully orchestrated into dramatic patterns and character delineation.

Language cascades gloriously from the mouth of Leigh's most articulate and unsettling character, Johnny in *Naked* (1993), but quite a lot of his creations are fumbling for words, struggling to express inexpressible feelings and catching at phrases like drowning men looking for rafts. Words are important, but rarely enough. Clive James, reviewing *Home Sweet Home* (1982), averred that Leigh was 'conducting the most daring raid on the inarticulate yet. Harold Pinter is Christopher Fry beside him.'

The art of evasion and failure in communication certainly comes from Pinter, whom Leigh acknowledges as an important influence. He especially admires Pinter's earliest work, and directed *The Caretaker* while still at RADA. Jonson's comedy of humours lies behind the fact that Leigh's characters are wound up and unleashed on the world; they don't change or develop all that much, but the situation around them does, farcically and sometimes catastrophically. And Ayckbourn's increasingly dark and wry middle-class chronicles of social unease and embarrassment are comparable to Leigh's rougher, noisier essays in snobbery and violence and misguided social aspiration.

But the world of Mike Leigh reaches even deeper into the contemporary cultural consciousness for two reasons: he makes films, and so takes those theatrical elements of class comedy and speech patterns into the popular mainstream; and those films, for an audience now extending way beyond the enclosures of *cinéastes* and critical trend-setters, define, in a peculiar and disturbing manner, the way we live today.

Leigh was born in 1943 in Salford, Manchester. His father, Abe, was a doctor ('the whistling doctor', on account of his, well, whistling), a general practitioner, and rated a very good one, who died in 1985. He has a younger (by three years) sister, Ruth, to whom he is not particularly close. His mother, Phyllis, still lives in Salford. Leigh went to Salford Grammar School, whose alumni include the actor Albert Finney and the director Les Blair, Leigh's friend and immediate contemporary, who produced Leigh's first feature film, *Bleak Moments*, in 1971. Leigh astonished and alarmed his family by devising an escape route to London in 1960, aged seventeen: he won a scholarship to the Royal Academy of Dramatic Art. After RADA, he took further courses in stage design and film technique, in life drawing on a foundation course at art college, and then served an apprenticeship in the theatre simply because it was easier to break into than the cinema.

There are three important aspects of Leigh to emphasise early on: he is a brilliant, naturally gifted, satirical cartoonist, and could easily have made his living by the broad-nibbed pen, or brush; he is an unreconstructed northerner who came south to 'make it' in London, slightly chippy, fiercely proud (and critical) of his roots and his Jewish background, an instinctive maverick and non-joiner; and he is a child of the 1960s, the decade of the first British teenagers, of the Beatles and student unrest, and of the explosion of interest in the European cinema and the possibilities of television.

In his formative young-adult years (1965–70), Leigh worked in drama schools, in an arts centre in Birmingham and a youth theatre in Manchester. During this time he gradually evolved a rigorous and scientific method of working and writing with actors in rehearsals which is unique, unprecedented and frequently mis-understood as a form of random, or casual, 'improvisation'. He also worked as a small-part actor in films and on the stage, and as an assistant director to both Peter Hall and Trevor Nunn at the Royal Shakespeare Company.

Between 1971, when he made *Bleak Moments*, and 1988, when he made his second feature film, *High Hopes*, Leigh's career oscil-lated between the theatre (the Royal Shakespeare Company, the London fringe, Hampstead Theatre, the West End) and BBC Tele-vision. His films for the BBC, which included *Hard Labour* (1973), *Nuts in May* (1976), *Grown-Ups* (1980) and *Four Days in July* (1984), taken together with such memorable stage plays as *Babies Grow Old* (1974), *Abigail's Party* (1977), *Ecstasy* (1979) and *Goose-Pimples* (1981), comprise a distinctive, homogeneous body of work which stands comparison with anyone's in the British theatre and cinema over the same period. Recognition, however, even among his peers, has been slow coming. There was an *Evening Standard* Theatre Award in 1982 for *Goose-Pimples* as the year's Best Com-edy. *High Hopes* was named Best Comedy in the *Evening Standard* Film Awards of 1989. And *Naked* won Leigh the Best Director award at the 1993 Cannes Film Festival. Shortly afterwards, he was awarded the OBE. But the British Academy of Film and Television Awards, BAFTA, consistently ignores his claims on its attention in its annual junketings and gong-dispensing rituals.

The price of Leigh's artistic integrity – there's no way round this statement – has been high. Like one of his heroes, the film director Robert Altman, he has never sought Hollywood's approval, so has never minded not going there. He works on his own terms, and no one else's. Every project, on stage or film, is a blank page until he starts casting and piecing together his ideas with what the actors bring him. He rehearses all day and all night for two or three months. He does not have an outline, or a script, to show any producers or potential backers. He makes life very hard – interesting, exhausting, demanding, but hard – for almost everyone who works with him. But he makes it hardest of all for himself.

He does not work with stars. He tends, rather, to help create them: Liz Smith in *Hard Labour*; Alison Steadman in *Abigail's Party*; Brenda Blethyn in *Grown-Ups*; Antony Sher in *Goose-Pimples*; Gary Oldman and Tim Roth in *Meantime* (1983); Jane Horrocks and Timothy Spall in *Life is Sweet* (1990); most spectacularly, perhaps, David Thewlis in *Naked*. In addition, the roster of actors who have worked with him over the years – Julie Walters, Stephen Rea, Jim Broadbent, Phil Daniels, Lesley Manville, Claire Skinner, Sheila Kelley, Lindsay Duncan, Lesley Sharp, Eric Allan, Kathy Burke, Anne Raitt, Eric Richard, Paul Jesson – comprises an impressive, almost representative, nucleus of outstanding British acting talent.

It is one of my major contentions that Leigh's method of work, far from exploiting the contribution of the actors by using them to make up his scripts for him – an accusation often levelled at him – in fact liberates them into a condition of creative artistry rarely available to them elsewhere in their profession. Critical comment comes a serious cropper whenever it broaches this subject, though one local Leatherhead paper, incorporating a literal, once came unwittingly close to the mark while aiming well wide of it: 'Mike Leigh's plays are largely improved by actors.'

One London critic, hailing a pleasant but flaccid comedy imitatively composed in the style of Mike Leigh (Les Blair's *Bad Behaviour*), said that Leigh himself would make this kind of film if he liked people more. This comment contains another gross misunderstanding about Leigh. He likes people more than anyone I know; but he is also more alive to their frailties and inadequacies, and his work rejoices in those shortcomings and quirks. In this respect, and given that his feature films – albeit for economic reasons – have been made in London, there is an almost Dickensian quality about them. Indeed, the novelist and Dickens biographer Peter Ackroyd, reviewing *Meantime* in *The Times*, described the brothers played by Phil Daniels and Tim Roth as 'Magwitch and Smike growing up in Tower Hamlets'.

Ackroyd also thought that as Leigh's work became bleaker (like

Alan Ayckbourn, Leigh could justly claim that it started off pretty bleak), so it became less convincing. This was to do, he felt, with the work's similarity to Racinian tragedy, 'since the women are all monsters and the men pathetic victims of circumstance', an interesting allegation in the light of exactly the opposite being alleged (with equal wrongheadedness, as it happens) over the controversial narrative in *Naked*.

But the ongoing critical dispute surrounding issues of portraiture and of sympathetic representation of character lies very near the heart of Leigh's work, and is one of the main topics of this book: what *rights* does a fictional character possess independently of his creator; who is patronising whom, and how does a writer/director become 'condescending', and to whom, if he is dealing in fictional creations; and who is laying down the rules, and setting the agenda, for writers and actors in this post-modern, post-structural, post-feminist age? There is tension with the middle-class, politically correct lobby, and Leigh is in no mood to make allowances for fashionable queasiness in the class war, the sex war, or any other war.

The success of *Naked* suggests that Leigh is poised on the brink of a new phase in his career. His critical reputation, always a matter of keen contention, has never been higher, and he is becoming increasingly admired in Europe and America. There is also a bit of a Mike Leigh cult, which is both a good thing and a bad thing. Many people know whole scenes of *Abigail's Party* and *Nuts in May* by heart. That sort of fanzine adulation among ordinary punters attaches to very few leading writers and is in itself an interesting phenomenon: there is no doubt that people recognise themselves in Mike Leigh's films and plays without taking offence and without the sort of anguished difficulty that afflicts some middle-class commentators and critics. A newer sort of cultism dates from the showing of *Meantime* at the London Film Festival and on Channel 4 at the end of 1983. The film touched a nerve in its discussion of unemployment and disaffected skinheads and no-hopers in east London. Long articles about Leigh and his actors began to appear in such widely read youth publications as the *New Musical Express* and *The Face*. A decade later, new rock idols such as Brett Anderson of Suede and Damon Albarn of Blur would consistently invoke the films of Mike Leigh in their interviews with the music press.

There had been a major BBC retrospective of Leigh's television films in 1982. And an important season of British films at the San Francisco Film Festival of 1986 – five of Leigh's films were shown alongside Chris Barnard's *Letter to Brezhnev* (1985), Stephen Frears's *My Beautiful Laundrette* (1985) and Julien Temple's *Absolute Beginners* (1986) – was prefaced in the brochure with a significant imprimatur for Leigh from the film historian and critic, David Thomson: 'No one has come so close to filming the core of Britishness today, or made films more funny or desperate . . . they are timeless, too, as unique and valuable as the films of Michael Powell, the only other English film-maker whose strength of character – so different, and so based on triumphant individualism – seems equal to Leigh's.'

This is an important point. Leigh's career, like Powell's, has been one of struggle, commitment and purpose in the face of considerable discouragement and disparagement. At the same time, his sense of humour is at the root of everything he does, and informs every shot. His most fêted contemporaries among English film directors – Stephen Frears and Mike Newell – are far more eclectic and dilettante in their choice of material. You would never know, for instance, that Frears's brilliant made-in-America film noir *The Grifters* (1990) was the work of a British film-maker, nor would you wish to ask too many incisive questions about characterisation, settings and plot plausibility when considering Newell's runaway comedy hit confection *Four Weddings and a Funeral* (1993). More crucially, neither is a writer or instigator of his own material. They are, in the best sense of the phrase, jobbing directors. Leigh, you could argue, is a bit more than that.

A wilfully extreme view of what Mike Leigh does was expressed by Peter Greenaway, the film-maker who prefers to think of himself as 'a painter in cinema'. Although Greenaway misunderstands the nature of acting on film, and confuses having something to say about the world at large, through a detailed examination of one quarter of it, with little Englander parochialism, he did express an interesting contempt for British cinema in an interview with John Walsh in the *Independent* magazine in September 1993: 'The main centre line is *Saturday Night and Sunday Morning*, on to *My Beautiful Laundrette*, on to something by Mike Leigh. It's British cinema taking over Italian neo-realism and following it through. Making no doubt acerbic and acute Real Life movies whose political circumstance is particularly germane to England, especially south-east England. I can respect that kind of cinema, I can see its heart is in the right place, but frankly I find it very boring.'

Well, Leigh has always cited Jean Renoir and Satyajit Ray among his favourite film-makers, and both are specialists in making the real in life more heightened, hyper-real, in effect, on film. But it is absurd to suggest that Leigh is a boring *auteur* because he is stuck in some kind of aesthetic rut. The camera work in his films is characterised by what David Thomson calls 'a detached, medical watchfulness', and has justly been compared, thinks Thomson, to the sensibility of the Japanese maestro Yasujiro Ozu.

The cramped domestic interiors of Ozu find many echoes in Leigh's scenes on stairways and in corridors, and on landings, especially in *Grown-Ups*, *Meantime* and *Naked*. And two wonderful little episodes in Ozu's *Tokyo Story* (made in 1953 but first shown in London in 1965), in a hairdressing salon and a bar, must have been in Leigh's subconscious memory when he made *The Short and Curlies* (1987), one of his most devastatingly funny, and tightest, pieces of work, and the pub scene in *Life is Sweet*, where Stephen Rea (an Arsenal supporter, as it happens) litanises the great double-winning side of Tottenham Hotspur, Arsenal's deadly north London rivals, in 1961.

Leigh eats, breathes, sleeps and smells cinema. He would almost certainly win any quiz show competition among his fellow directors, though Martin Scorsese, a notable director buff, would probably give him a good run for his money. The sense of lives being lived in Ozu is what he aims for all the time. Which is why the sort of 'neo-realism' referred to by Greenaway in a film such as Ermanno Olmi's *Tree of Wooden Clogs* (1978) makes such a deep impression: Olmi's three-hour epic of turn-of-the-century peasant life in Lombardy is, in Leigh's words, 'the ultimate location film', telling several stories among the tenant families on a large farm near Bergamo, with masterly control and precision, and with a cast of non-actors. It is indeed an amazing, unforgettable piece of work, and Leigh remains dazzled by it still, years after he first saw it: 'Directly, objectively, yet compassionately, it puts on the screen the great, hard, real adventure of living and surviving from day to day, and from year to year, the experience of ordinary people everywhere . . . the camera is always in exactly the right place . . . you never see the same shot twice . . . but the big question, arising out of the paradox of these truthful and utterly convincing performances achieved by non-actors, always remains: how does he really do it?'

Greenaway's sloppy generalisation occurs again whenever Leigh is compared, negatively or positively, with Ken Loach, the director most often thought to be similar to Leigh, probably because his characters are working class and wear anoraks while generally rummaging around at the bottom of the social heap. Loach's *Cathy Come Home* (BBC TV, 1966) brought the poignancy of house eviction, and of children separated from their parents, into the nation's living rooms and was a contributing factor to the establishment of Shelter, an organisation for the homeless. Right through to his 1994 film, *Ladybird, Ladybird*, which also focuses on children in care, Loach has often used amateur actors and a very free form of improvisatory filming. But whereas Olmi's amateur actors look anything but, and irradiate a profound sense of spiritual grace and integrity, Loach's actors are deliberately rough-edged, untutored, anti-actorish. They exude great vitality, but they are continually drawing attention to the fact that they are not really actors. In addition, Loach has a political agenda and his purpose as a film-maker is avowedly socialist, propagandist and confrontational.

Although Leigh's career in the BBC was at first smoothed by Tony Garnett, Loach's producer, and although both directors benefited from that golden period of patronage in hard-hitting, innovative television film which has now been resurrected at

Channel 4, the differences between them are much more marked than are the similarities. Loach works initially from the issue, Leigh always from the character. Loach cherishes roughness and spontaneity on film. Leigh cherishes those same qualities in rehearsal and works towards heightened, concentrated and entirely finished performances when the camera starts to roll. Loach knows what's good for us and doesn't provide too many laughs. Leigh is, on the whole, a pessimistic philosopher, a social cartoonist, an idiosyncratic writer, with a pronounced penchant for good (and bad) jokes.

The one broad area of similarity is the canvas of the nation's housing estates, pubs, small shops, churches, building sites and social security centres. But whereas Loach wants realism at all costs, a quest which sometimes results in a curious, stilted form of artificiality in his films, Leigh wants to take the real in life, and the realism, and to recreate that realism on film by glorying in the artificiality of the medium. This aesthetic divergence of method means that Loach's films, many of them superb, are not necessarily identifiable as the work of one particular artist. Leigh's are. Ian Buruma, writing in the *New York Review of Books* in January 1994, summed it up thus:

> It is hard to get on a London bus or listen to the people at the next table in a cafeteria without thinking of Mike Leigh. Like other wholly original artists, he has staked out his own territory. Leigh's London is as distinctive as Fellini's Rome or Ozu's Tokyo. These are of course products of the imagination, cities reinvented for the movies. Mike Leigh's England is personal as well as a local product. And yet it is universal too.

Leigh lives modestly and unostentatiously in Wood Green, north London, in the house he bought in 1976 on a joint mortgage with Alison Steadman. The couple, who were married in 1973, share the address with their two teenage sons, Toby and Leo, and a gormless floppy dog. At home, as at work, Leigh is hunched, wary, rebarbative and extremely funny. He has been compared to a rabbinical hamster, a bearded polytechnic lecturer, a bloodhound in mourning, and a garden gnome in a woolly hat. Clothes are merely functional. He needs pockets for pens and notebooks (he is a complete stationery freak, ordering special requirements in bulk). His shoes are always from Clarks and, as he cheerfully admitted in an *Observer* fashion survey in February 1994, 'Everything I have ever worn has been beige or black. I'm afraid I have worn an awful lot of corduroy trousers over the years.'

There is a history of heart disease on his father's side of the family, so he takes good care of himself, avoids starchy foods and dairy produce, eats and drinks moderately, works out on a rowing machine, doesn't smoke, and uses public transport or Shanks's pony whenever possible. One not uncommon legacy of an upbringing in the grimy North is chronic catarrh, which Leigh has endured all his life, taking homoeopathic treatment in latter years.

He builds his own bookshelves and would certainly survive on Sue Lawley's Desert Island were he ever invited to select his discs with her. His office at the top and the back of the three-storey house is a superbly equipped den with a huge wall map of the world, a vast collection of videos, tapes, books and stationery, a comprehensive filing system of press cuttings, a small television and many drawings and mementoes. His large desk is usually seriously cluttered. But each time we sat in this office to discuss his life and career, the surface was entirely clear except for a telephone, a blank sheet of paper and a pencil.

Leigh is an excellent mimic and receives news of others' disasters and vanities with a deadpan, mocking acceptance of how the world and its inhabitants are. His life swings between quite lively, often half-yearly, stretches of preparation and slopping around, and working periods of intense purdah and total immersion. There are certain characteristics that spring from his working method. Although he was never on time for anyone or anything at school and at RADA, he is nowadays punctual, in the sense of never being late (in the sense of actually being really rather early) for any appointment. He has matured into associating being late with being rude. His natural inclination towards total disorganisation is combatted by his hard-working tendency for being organised; he can only operate once this state is achieved. To work, and to speak to the media, he is always well prepared. He is never going to be caught out by an actor or technician, let alone by a journalist.

He has a sometimes rather terrifying way of knee-capping his inquisitors and colleagues with such pre-emptive strikes as 'I would have thought it was obvious to you that . . .' or 'Far be it from me to suggest how you should be going about this, but . . .' But he mostly cajoles his actors with jokes, comic asides and throwaway banter. In rehearsal, he addresses the actors and crew as 'Ladies and Gentlemen of the Depicting Profession and Allied Trades'. Before each take the actors are simply instructed to concentrate, or 'warm up' (that is, 'to get into character'), his particular way of bringing the floor to a state of total silence and readiness. When an improvisation needs to be stopped, he says to the actors: 'Come out of character,' before they discuss what's happened or what might have happened in this situation. He often says, 'This might be a question with no answer.'

In April 1993, Leigh responded to a questionnaire in *City Limits*, the London listings magazine. His perfect night out? Food, film, fuck. The one film he would choose to see again? *Les Quatre cents coups* (Truffaut's delightful 1958 'new wave' film about adolescence and schooldays). If he was a pigeon, who would he crap on? Whoever wrote this questionnaire. Epitaph? 'Mike Leigh. Warmed up 1943. Came out of character (sometime in the next century).'

Leigh likes to get his own way and has been more or less self-sufficient since the age of ten. His father used to say: 'If Mike got lost in the middle of the Sahara desert, he'd find his way home.' Everything about his physical demeanour and social outlook is practical and to the point. I once suggested having lunch in a fashionable Soho restaurant and he responded, bleakly, 'Well, if that's the road you want to go down . . .' shaming me into conforming to his much better suggestion of sharing dim sum from the mobile trolleys in one of his favourite Chinese haunts. The food was better, the occasion was more fun, the price was right (i.e. dead cheap), and we were not likely to bump into Melvyn Bragg or any of the Ivy and Caprice crowd.

The family have no second home or country residence, but

they did keep a caravan in Battle down on the Sussex coast near Hastings for several years until it was destroyed in a storm, during the rehearsals of *Life is Sweet*. Leigh says it was the most derelict caravan on the site, but they used it for weekends away, and for making trips to Beachy Head and Hastings. He loves holidays, and travel's most certainly his bag, or suitcase. In the summer of 1986, with Alison and the boys, he took an upmarket package trip to Sardinia.

As chance would have it, my family and I were on exactly the same flight, and staying in the same hotel and villa complex. We spent many happy hours talking about his films: on the beach, in the sea (Leigh does not swim; he wades in up to his waist and starts talking), in each other's rooms. The off-duty director, not really one of God's gifts to shorts and beachwear, may have proved only a marginally competent ball boy in our inter-family tennis matches, but he was certainly a dab hand at the beach barbecues. I still dread some future fictional pay-off with a cur-mudgeonly critic portrayed on holiday with a suspect backhand and an embarrassing array of less than state-of-the-art leisurewear.

Alison Steadman does not think Leigh has changed all that much over the years, but she concedes that he may have mellowed a bit. He will not tolerate a lack of punctuality. When the couple were filming *Life is Sweet* together – Steadman has appeared in only seven of her husband's projects since 1973, more than some of his regular actors, but not that many more – she says that, while grabbing a quick banana at the breakfast table, Leigh would be standing by the front door, shouting: 'Come on, we can't be late . . . if I'm late because of you this is the last time I ever give you a lift . . . you can find your own way to the bloody place . . .'

She first met Leigh when he went to teach at E15 Acting School in Loughton, east of London in Essex, where she studied, and she retains an image of him turning up in a little old black car, a Riley 1.5, peeking over the wheel and looking like a little boy driving into the school: 'He's always been tremendous fun and tremen-dously funny. What made him jumpy and frustrated was those early years of not being able to get a film. It used to colour every-thing in his life and he is quite volatile anyway. If he had to mend a plug he would suddenly explode, shouting at "the fucking plug" and "Why am I mending plugs and not making films?" It used to upset me and life could be very difficult. But over the years, things have got slightly easier from that point of view. And so our private life has got easier.' On the other hand, the work is never easy, and the person Leigh drives hardest of all is himself. After that first Soho meeting of cast and crew, the long days and nights begin all over again, and Leigh drives on to his next and only objective, the wonderful adventure of getting ready to go out and make a movie.

Leigh is Jewish, though he has never made a great song and dance about this. He is proud of his background, but not flamboyantly so. It has been one of the revelatory aspects of working on this book that Leigh has, for the first time, fully expressed the pride, ambivalence and frustrations he takes in his boyhood domestic environment. This background is clearly of fundamental importance in his work. Alison Steadman is not Jewish, nor are their sons, Toby (born in February 1978) and Leo (born in August 1981).

Two more personal, not too personal, details: in March 1967, while working at Stratford-upon-Avon with the Royal Shakespeare Company, Mike Leigh stopped shaving his face and has not shaved it since; when Alison Steadman married Leigh in 1973, she decided to call him 'Flea' and has done so ever since, as do their two boys, and no one else is allowed access to that intimate soubriquet.

TWO

Naked as Nature Distended

'Each time a butterfly flaps its wings in Tokyo, this old lady coughs in Salford.'

JOHNNY in *Naked*

Naked has been described as Mike Leigh's breakthrough film, and although it summarises and relates to his other work in many ways, there is something about *Naked*'s scale, ambition and power that sets it apart. In Johnny, the central character, a Dostoevskyan drifter from Manchester whose spiritual disgust, fuelled by sexual violence, is the film's main theme, Leigh and the actor David Thewlis created a touchstone character for a generation. Johnny isn't nice, but he is appealing. And he captures something of the day's anxiety about date rape, rootless cynicism, big-city defeatism and trying to make sense of it all. Sheridan Morley's phrase for Johnny, 'Alfie in the grips of Thatcherite depression', cross-fertilising Bill Naughton's chirpy, unapologetic 1960s cockney Lothario, immortalised on film by Michael Caine, with the dark, sinister disaffection of the new underclass, was a neat way of indicating that the Swinging Sixties had degenerated into the Nauseated Nineties.

The film also sparked a critical controversy that highlighted many of the arguments that surround Leigh's work and demonstrated how contemporary criticism can dribble into proscriptive political correctness. Johnny is a shit who is vile to women; therefore, crowed the proscribers, Mike Leigh is a misogynist. You might as well say that, on the evidence of *King Lear*, Shakespeare is a heartless ageist, or of *Saved* (the 1965 play with a baby-stoning incident) that Edward Bond is a child abuser. About the same

19

time *Naked* was shown in Cannes, Saul Bellow found himself pilloried in New York as an elitist, a chauvinist, a reactionary and a racist by the 'petty thought police' of politically correct multi-culturalism. He derided the fallacy of assuming that fictional characters represent the author's views. 'In this new climate of multi-cultural McCarthyism,' he wrote in the *New York Times*, 'no writer can take it for granted that the views of his characters will not be attributed to him personally.'

This is exactly what happened to Leigh in some quarters over *Naked*. The film is an anti-odyssey, a bad-news chronicle, a journey to the heart of one man's sickness and despair while registering his damaging effect on the women he meets. *Naked* has a mobility and a dynamic that is unprecedented in Leigh's work. Yet Nigel Andrews of the *Financial Times* accused Leigh of creating pawns in a 'Great Miserablist Plot. Those who are not villains are victims. Those who are not DIY philosophers . . . are birdbrains [sic] like Sophie or Louise. Put more bluntly, those who are not men – the bio-determinist thesis almost seems to amount to this – are women.' On the other hand, a female critic on the *Village Voice* in New York opined that 'Leigh has the temerity to present . . . a terrible sexual dynamic: men hurting women and women relishing the hurt.' Even in Britain, at a safe distance from the metropolitan clamour of fuming feminists, William Parente of *The Scotsman* coolly observed that the sexual adventurism of the film was by no means 'jollied over', as it had been in Bertrand Blier's *Les Valseuses* (1974), a clammy sex/road movie that achieved belated and spurious notoriety due to the participation of Gérard Depardieu and the posthumous myth of his co-star, Patrick Dewaere.

The title of *Naked*, which carries connotations of both sexual activity and spiritual emptiness, conveys, too, an idea of Shakespeare's bare fork'd animal and his intellectual struggle with his own primeval condition. A new underclass of the peripheral and underprivileged was represented by Edgar in *King Lear* ('poor Tom's a-cold'), the unclothed 'Bedlamite' on the blasted heath, who deliberately adopts a manic identity in order to join the ejected monarch and his Fool. And in *Hamlet*, the hero's intended action is delayed by talking incessantly to the audience and assuming a dominance over other characters through expressions of mania and rapid, witty speech.

In *Naked*, the first shots by a hand-held camera reveal a blurred, vicious sexual encounter against an outside wall in the backstreets of Manchester. The woman, possibly a prostitute, yells abusively as Johnny runs off, steals a car and heads out of town for London. From this point, Johnny is spinning, and talking, free, a loose cannon of critical articulacy heading for the London flat of his old girlfriend, Louise, in Dalston, a scrawny, unpretentious area in the East End of London. Thewlis as Johnny immediately makes the film compelling and watchable: he's a tall, lanky, manky Mancunian (the actor comes from the smaller Lancastrian town of Blackpool), chain-smoking, wrapped like Hamlet in a black and inky coat (and one that has seen better days), dribbling through his unkempt, undernourished moustache, toothy, gimlet-eyed, socially untethered but burdened with useless knowledge and a vicious, bullying line in repartee. He's a walking time-bomb waiting to be detonated.

Louise is flat-sharing with Sophie, an addled, spaced-out, loping, punky Goth in black leather, and Sandra, a nurse, who has gone on holiday to Zimbabwe with her useless boyfriend ('a wanker'), and who does not return, or show up in the film, until the last couple of reels. Sandra found the flat through her devious yuppie friend 'Sebastian Hawks', who is known in his non-landlordish life as 'Jeremy'; under English law, it is possible to form companies under different names, and to go bankrupt any number of times. Jeremy's revolting characteristics and predatory sexuality form a parallel distraction to Johnny's exploits, and trigger a catastrophic climax in the flat.

There are several ways of looking at the impact of *Naked*. In strict chronological terms, it is made as a complete contrast to *Life is Sweet* (1990), a bittersweet, but totally delightful, comic idyll set in Enfield. Leigh is not an upfront 'state-of-the-nation' artist like David Hare in the theatre, or a social issues proselytiser like Ken Loach in the cinema. But there is a rich penumbra of political atmosphere even in his comedies: the recession is beginning to kick in as early as 1976, when Finger, the Brummagen motorbike-toting plasterer in *Nuts in May*, who disrupts the vegetarian quietude of Keith and Candice-Marie Pratt on the Dorset camping site, predicts a slump in the building trade. The point emerges sharply, but only as an aside, not a political speech. Leigh's instinct is to goose speech-makers, or anyone self-important, even while agreeing with the gist of their message. Thus 'Bollocks to the poll tax' is a sentiment with which he would have concurred at the time of making *Life is Sweet*. But the slogan is sported on the T-shirt of the bulimic twin played by Jane Horrocks, and twisted into a comic parody a) metaphorically, as Horrocks's defensive armoury of received feminist ideology is gently ridiculed by the film developing around her physical plight; and b) literally, as she scrunches up her emblazoned proclamation with tight little fists pounding away within her own garment.

Nuts in May is an antecedent of *Life is Sweet*, just as the darker, more overtly 'politicised' films of the 1980s – *Meantime* and *High Hopes* – are precursors of *Naked*. But the articulate egomaniac, the critical motormouth, the dissident yelper at what happens to other 'inadequate' people, is a character very close to Mike Leigh's creative centre, and the archetype thrives just this side of insanity. We meet him first in Trevor, the apprentice undertaker in *The Kiss of Death* (1977), brilliantly played by David Threlfall. Trevor's a bit of a joker who is never the same once he's paid a professional visit to the scene of a cot death. He has a sloping walk and a nervous, twitchy smile that ices over into scathing expressions of sarcastic disapproval. And we meet him again in the dominating presence of Mark, another coruscating performance, this time by Phil Daniels, in *Meantime*. Mark has the gift of the destructive gab, both egging on his younger brother, Colin (Tim Roth), against their parents, and hardening up his attitudes to everyone else around them in the East End of London. Colin's aunt, who has been upgraded to suburban life in Chigwell, Essex, offers him a decorating job as a well-meaning gesture. Mark destroys this pathetic 'chance', or opening, for his younger brother for two reasons, one ideological, one pitiful: he doesn't want Colin to have anything to do with that dead suburban life out there; he really wants everything to stay as it is, even though the static depressiveness of it all is, he says, 'doing my brain in'.

Meantime caught a national mood on the wing, four years into the Thatcher government, of despair and disenchantment, of dole queues and scratchy, aimless hanging around in pubs, on street corners and in a decaying council estate where the lifts smell of urine and litter blows chest-high through the urban wasteland. Apart from Daniels and Roth, the cast also contained Gary Oldman as the useless, vaguely psychopathic skinhead Coxy, last seen in the film rolling around inside a tin drum while bashing his head, legs and arms against the echoing interior in a pointless, almost Japanese, ritual of anger, pain and frustration.

One of the quick, cliché-bound methods of describing Leigh's work – apart from invoking Alison Steadman as Beverly in *Abigail's Party* passing round her cheesy cocktails and nipping out to pop the Beaujolais in the fridge – is to suggest a grubby interior with people in cardigans picking their noses and not saying very much to each other on a sofa. But all Leigh's films, from the very first, *Bleak Moments*, with its pregnant, poetic exterior shots of Tulse Hill (for God's sake), are imbued with a lingering compositional intensity. What people say, or don't say, to each other is endemic to their geographic, as well as domestic, location.

In *Naked*, this particular quality accumulates through Johnny's various encounters. He turns up at Louise's flat and almost immediately seduces Sophie (although 'seduces' is too soft a word). She is a pathetic creature, both fascinated and frightened by Johnny's mesmerising, dominating chat. In one of Leigh's best gags, and one that characteristically derives from the details of costume, she diverts Johnny's attention from a bewildering profusion of black laces and punkish buckles to the simple, but concealed, zip: 'You've tried the stairs; I think we should take the escalator.' When you see the couple having sex a few scenes later, Johnny is violently bashing Sophie's head against the sofa. Obviously no one could approve this tactic as a model seduction, but the fact remains that this is how sex is for some people, and violence is part of sexual expression, to a greater or lesser extent, for all of us. The actress who plays Sophie, Katrin Cartlidge, avers that Sophie is so dumb and numb most of the time that any strong feeling is worth having: 'Even pain is better than nothing.'

In a remarkable technical sequence, the camera sits watchfully on a stairway. Cinematographer Dick Pope attests that this apparent simplicity was incredibly difficult to achieve; there was nowhere for him and the equipment to 'hide' in the confined space, and the lighting, predominantly a pale, dead of night, blue wash in these scenes, was immensely tricky. Johnny goes backwards and forwards from kitchen to sitting room, where Louise is passively watching television, and Sophie tries to convince him to let her go with him. He snaps, and he's off and away, pursued by music and his own demons. He dives into the maelstrom of Soho and, in the midst of the rushing scene around the Lina Store in Brewer Street, in the middle of the night, comes across a ginger Scottish boy yelling 'Maggie!' at the top of his voice. Their colloquial rap is shot through with violence and sarcasm. 'Are you takin' the piss?' asks Archie, who has come south after hitting his dad on the head with a poker. 'You're fucking giving it way, aren't yer?' sneers back Johnny, as adept at exploiting Archie's dullness for his own bullying ascendancy as he is at trampling on women.

An interesting sidelight is cast on the Mike Leigh 'method' by the fact that Archie's character is not just based on someone the actor knew, but also derived from someone Leigh himself had met, and remembered, on his travels many years previously; this is quite a frequent way of arriving at characters. The monosyllabic, difficult, aggressive creature called Archie therefore comes down two creative routes, but flares individually in the performance of the actor. The shouting scene with Thewlis was rehearsed on the steps of a church in Marylebone one early evening, in broad daylight. Suddenly a police car screeched to a halt, attracted by the shouting and swearing, and Leigh had to intervene and tell his actors to 'come out of character'. The policemen did not understand, or accept, what was going on, and the scene shifted back to the nearby rehearsal room where Leigh could verify his actors' identities and their engagement on a film created in real locations.

The episode concludes when the vagrant Maggie is finally

found wandering in a beautifully photographed waste ground of sludge, brick walls and arches (obviously unrelated to Soho; 'poetic licence' says Leigh, who filmed this sequence in the East End of London). But nothing hangs around for very long at a merely realistic level; the heightened quality of expression, though rooted in everyday speech, is a deliberate poetic tactic, just as the choice of location matches the debate. Archie has already been treated to one of Johnny's take-it-away specials on Nostradamus and the Apocalypse. In the nocturnal brick tundra, Maggie asks Johnny if he has ever seen a dead body. 'Only me own' is his enigmatic, Hamlet-style response. The mood is quite theatrical, the action set flatly against the evocative brick arches, the two young Scottish vagrants circling each other and literally wheeling out of Johnny's life, and our sights, leaving Thewlis in the foreground, head bowed in the grip of a nocturnal isolation that became the most familiar image of the film in the posters and publicity.

Johnny is now assuming the iconic status of spokesman not so much for the homeless, as for the lost and drifting, the disaffected, the rebellious, the pissed-off, the ignored. So he fights back. He keeps talking and he keeps moving. The philosophical texture of the film deepens in his next encounter, with a sad security guard, Brian (dolefully and perceptively played by Peter Wight), whom Johnny marks down as indeed possessing the most tedious job in the world. Brian guards acres of empty space and checks a few switches as light relief from just sitting and reading. He allows Johnny inside for a bit of shelter and much-needed company. His wife has long left him to live in Bangkok. Under Johnny's direct questioning, he admits to not having had a fuck for as long as he can remember.

This location was an empty new office-block on the same side of Charlotte Street as the old Channel 4 headquarters ('The ground floor is still empty, and the plants are still there; we could go and shoot the same scene tomorrow!' declares Leigh), transformed by lighting and cunning use of silhouette into a bleak 'post-Modernist gas chamber'. In this naked, neon-lit limbo, stripped of all signs of modern habitation and material consolation, apart from the rubber plants, Johnny develops his apocalyptic rant, noting that 'Humanity is a cracked egg, and the omelette stinks,' and pointing out that 'wormwood' in the Book of Revelation translates into Russian as 'Chernobyl'. The game is up, he insists to his chop-fallen auditor: 'The end of the world is nigh, Bri.' Leigh says that the sequence was much influenced by his own brief spell working as a security guard in the 1960s, an experience he first touched upon in both *Waste-Paper Guards* and *Hard Labour*, where we see old Jim Thornley night-watching in a warehouse full of hideous plastic dolls and ducks and visited by a younger, superior officer, who charges him, as a 'custodian', with looking smart and alert at all times.

In this extended philosophical exchange Leigh admits that he is subconsciously referring to a passage in Jean-Luc Godard's *Vivre sa vie* (1962) in which the actress Anna Karina, playing a Parisian prostitute, has a long conversation with the philosopher Brice Parain. Leigh likes the film very much, but finds that that particular scene becomes boring, so he tries not to be in his version. David Thewlis considers that while *Naked* is really about the death of love, 'The film is made from a love of life and an anxiety about the future. Johnny is not complacent. He's an existentialist whose own lack of compassion adds to the hostility.' Leigh adds that the backlog of film culture unavoidably 'casts a subtle shadow over what you do', and attributes the faintly film noir-ish feel of what now happens to the influence of Orson Welles's *Touch of Evil* (1958).

From an upper floor in the office block, Brian shows Johnny his regular view of a woman across the way, dancing provocatively, no curtains on the windows, drinking vodka. Johnny asks his host if he has ever seen her totally naked; Brian replies, 'Once.' Johnny promptly wheedles his way into the woman's apartment on the pretence of being the security man's ('insecurity man's') brother, and their few minutes together reinforce another *Hamlet* analogy: this is the equivalent to the closet scene where Hamlet begs his mother not to sleep again with her murderous stepfather. Johnny treats the woman, beautifully and tenderly played by Deborah Maclaren, with piteous contempt: 'From over there, you look a lot younger,' he cruelly remarks as he breaks into her dress and underclothes. But he pulls back from an invitation to bite her when he spots her skull and crossbones tattoo, freaks out, and adds insult to injury by declaring that he can't have sex with her because she reminds him of his mother. Johnny considers his mother a whore, and later in the film implies that she regularly adorned the pages of pornographic magazines; whether or not he is telling the truth remains a conundrum. This is the second key tattoo in the film; the first we see is that of Sophie, a swallow on her right upper arm, the tattooed sign of a prostitute. Incongruously, the woman has revealed that her favourite book is Jane Austen's *Emma*; as Johnny leaves, he steals it, along with her other paperbacks.

As the film progresses, the places in which Johnny finds himself define what he says and how he behaves. The character is not so much changing or developing as revealing different aspects of the same fixed personality. This coincides with how we see ourselves and each other in real life: we are not given to the fictive emotional upheavals and plummetings of traditional tragedy, we don't change very much in our lives. Leigh's work embodies this essential truth while creating a narrative and aesthetic structure around it. In *Naked* in particular, this contributes towards the picaresque style pungently reminiscent of Voltaire's *Candide*, a book Thewlis acknowledges as part of his background reading for the film. He also delved into the teachings of Buddha and James Gleick's *Chaos* (this latter was an inspirational source, too, for Tom Stoppard's 1993 play *Arcadia*, in which academic research and lost love lines ingeniously overlapped in a country house Byronic thriller).

So, after stealing the books and having breakfast with Brian – 'Don't waste your life,' is Brian's sadly ironic (coming from him) farewell line – he simply tags along with the oval-faced girl who has served them in the café. The girl is house-minding for a couple of classicists away in America: not only the house, but the set-dressing itself, is transformed into more fuel for Johnny's engine. He revs up by greeting a small brass model of a Greek discus thrower with 'It's a pizza delivery-man,' and, deducing that the house-owners are both men, declares that he is not Homer-phobic:

'I've read the *Iliad* and the *Odyssey*.' He's also seen a few films. The girl offers him the bathroom to take a shower, and he scathingly retorts, 'You're not going to creep up on me with a big knife dressed as your mother, are you?', a reference to Hitchcock's *Psycho*, bolstered in a later night-time exterior 'gothic' shot of the house. Johnny doesn't use his intellect to engage with other people; he uses it as a buffer to his own near-psychotic condition and as a weapon of subordination, just as Hamlet uses his own wit as a stalking horse under whose cover he shoots at others (that's everyone) less witty than himself.

There are moments of tenderness in all Johnny's dealings with women, but his baser instincts are likely to get the better of him. Just as he kicks his way unpleasantly out of the vodka-sodden woman's sad life, so he turns on the café girl and curses her future children, a grim echo of the womb-curse in *King Lear*. On his way, he tells her of a dream in which two skeletons are having a fuck: 'It were a right bloody racket; woke me up.' Johnny stands briefly silhouetted in a helium ornamental monstrance; is this loser the son of God? The film, gathering inexorably to its climax, has already intercut with Jeremy's descent on the Dalston flat: he has compelled Sophie to dress up in Sandra's nursing uniform, to whip him with her long hair and then to submit to an act of bestial sex in which he takes her from behind. A rape, in fact. Johnny's skeleton gag has the dual function of commenting on that scene and of reminding us again of Sandra: we saw her biological posters of skeletons on the walls of the flat when Johnny first arrived there. We are right down to the basics.

The build-up is nasty and relentless as Jeremy taunts Sophie that he hopes he hasn't given her AIDS. Only kidding, he says, but AIDS is a good thing, as the world's population needs pruning. Cut to the pub, where Sophie and Louise talk about abortion; Sophie had one when she was fifteen. What is a proper relationship, she asks Louise. 'Living with someone who talks to you after they've bonked you.' Meanwhile, on the streets, Johnny assails a man fly-posting and is in turn assaulted by him; he starts shouting at the traffic, and is then, quite arbitrarily, kicked almost to a pulp by a passing gang of thugs in an alley, an event as realistic and unsettling, and as darkly photographed, as the opening back alley shots in Manchester. Johnny arrives back at the Dalston flat for the last time, battered and bruised.

Most of Leigh's best films and plays have an almost classical structure and a powerful, cathartic climax from which the action slowly, often plaintively, subsides to a conclusion: in *Nuts in May*, Keith Pratt finally goes berserk and attacks Finger; in *Abigail's Party*, everything becomes too much for Tim Stern as Laurence who puts on Beethoven's Fifth and promptly suffers a fatal heart attack; in *Grown-Ups*, the neighbouring households and the importunate, unwanted central character, Gloria, are transfixed in noisy, farcical mayhem on a staircase. With the temporary immobilisation of Johnny, Leigh springs one of his biggest surprises as Johnny and Louise, thrown together once more, define their alienation in London by singing a sentimental song the director himself remembered from his childhood:

> *Take me back to Manchester when it's raining.*
> *I want to wet my feet in Albert Square.*
> *I'm all agog*
> *For a good thick fog.*
> *I don't like the sun,*
> *I like it raining cats and dogs!*
> *I want to smell the odours of the Irwell.*
> *I want to feel the soot get in me 'air.*
> *Oh, I don't want to roam,*
> *I want to get back 'ome*
> *To rainy Manchester . . .*

Leigh used to sing this song with his friends in Habonim ('The Builders'), the international socialist Jewish youth movement he joined as a schoolboy. In making the film, no one could trace any copyright, but after it was released, Leigh heard from a retired schoolmaster at Stand Grammar (the novelist Howard Jacobson's *alma mater*) in Prestwich, who had written the song for a school revue in 1950. Thin Man Films were happy to bung the old boy a cheque, and he was delighted to have his song memorialised, though Thewlis and Lesley Sharp sing only the chorus of the long narrative song about a girl following her chap down to Birmingham.

As if to ensure against tenderness taking hold, Johnny instantly says, 'I've got an 'ard-on.' Into the general scene of emotional carnage and depredation comes Sandra (Claire Skinner), not very fresh from a disastrous holiday and a debilitating journey. This lot is all she needs. Sandra's whirring arms and jarring inability to finish a sentence led some reviewers to detect a false note, an inappropriately 'theatrical' style of acting. But Leigh's films never work as becalmed stylistic entities where tone and narrative dictate the temperature of the acting; that is the conventional manner in fictive art. Instead, his pieces are entirely character-driven, so that, as in life, contrasting moods and exaggerations jostle up against each other regardless of an audience's preferred sense of stylistic conformity. My own view is that Claire Skinner gives a brilliant performance of deranged, end-of-the-tetherness, just as Greg Cruttwell as Jeremy conveys perfectly the grating awfulness of a man who doesn't even know how awful he sounds, and actually makes you want to kick him off the screen.

Jeremy is finally confronted by Louise, who invites him to unzip his fly as she takes up a kitchen knife. The tingling apprehension we feel is part of the sense that anything could now happen. Johnny could die. Jeremy could have his penis chopped off and thrown out the window, prefiguring the famous Bobbitt case in America which followed the film's completion. Johnny could seduce Sandra (he certainly thinks about it). Jeremy could attack Johnny and indeed kill him. Why not? None of these things happens. Jeremy leaves in his Porsche, a sneering, surviving threat to the next company he pimps off. He has thrown £380 at Sophie.

The mood of tender reconciliation is picked up again in one of the film's most memorable scenes. Johnny and Louise snuggle up to each other on the toilet floor. She asks him where he has been. 'Down the Via Dolorosa. Don't be nosy.' He rubs her bottom with his bare foot and claims to be putting the fun back in 'fundament'. They seem to be coming out the other side of the whole experience. Sophie herself is too devastated to carry on here. She picks up her things, including, oddly, a large letter 'S', a pathetic

ID substitute, that the character had accidentally come across (the aluminium memento had fallen off the frontage of an old café), and totters off to her next joint, her next round of heartless sex, her next bout of terminal loneliness.

And as Sandra luxuriates despondently in her bath, having considerately bandaged Johnny's suppurating foot, Johnny pockets Jeremy's money. Reneging on his promise to continue the patching-up process with Louise, and to return with her to Manchester when she comes home from work that night, having given in her notice, he limps out of the house and hobbles down the street. The last words in the film are between Sandra and Johnny:

> SANDRA: Enough. I've had enough. It comes at me from all
> angles. You all of you, just . . . it's the tin lid. When . . .
> how . . . will the world ever . . .
> JOHNNY: End?
> SANDRA: Yes.

This final tracking shot of Johnny coming towards us, as Andrew Dickson's marvellous serial music swells on the soundtrack, is one of the most affecting, and effective, endings in British cinema. Johnny is approaching like a beast on the loose, straight up the middle of the road, straddling the broken white line, as we back away, surely but apprehensively. Where is he going? Where will he end up? Who else will he devour and destroy? We hate him, we pity him, we love him, he's a pain, he's a phenomenon, he's a repulsive bastard, he's a prophetic saint, he's vermin, he's the life force. The film has ended, as it began, with a theft, and while we may imagine anything at all happening to Johnny, Leigh is surely correct in saying that these last three days of peculiar odyssey have not been all that exceptional in the life of this character.

Leigh himself knew what he had done and was no doubt bracing himself for the film's reception in the publicity material: 'My feelings about *Naked* are as ambivalent as my feelings about our chaotic late-twentieth-century world and probably as ambivalent as the film itself which is, I hope, as funny as it is sad, as beautiful as it is ugly, as compassionate as it is loathsome, and as responsible as it is anarchic.' But he had also created a classic statement of idiosyncratic, character-driven film-making. There was a precedent. One of Leigh's favourite film-makers is Jean Renoir, and one of his favourite films is Renoir's delightful, satirical comedy *Boudu sauvé des eaux* (1932). Leigh hadn't realised the similarities with this film until he had finished work on *Naked*. Both movies explore the tension between the domesticated and the anarchic (this is a central theme, probably *the* theme running through Leigh's work), and focus this tension in the tragi-comedy of a central character. It is a very large statement even to mention David Thewlis's Johnny in the same breath as Michel Simon's Boudu. But there it is. They are comparable soulmates.

Renoir described making his film as 'a kind of free exercise around an actor'. 'Well,' said Leigh in a television tribute to *Boudu* on Barry Norman's weekly film review programme, 'what an actor!' He counted Simon brilliant, real, funny, sad, grotesque, sympathetic; an animal, and stylish, and a slob. He noted in particular a fascinating collection of tics and mannerisms, such as the way in which he rolls his eyes in pleasure as he eats. Boudu is a pathetic suicide rescued from the Seine by a well-meaning bibliophile, whose wife and daughter Boudu promptly seduces after he's been taken in. He behaves abominably at the table, picks his nose, leaps acrobatically between doorways, and, on marrying the household's maid, jumps boat during the tipsy matrimonial party and swims off down the river. He reverts happily to hopeless, vagrant type and is last seen communing with a goat on the towpath. His future is as unresolved, and as potentially futile, as Johnny's.

One of many reasons Leigh reveres Renoir is that he always hated post-synching, that is, replacing the original performed dialogue with a dead studio recording. Renoir, like Leigh, loved the living spontaneity of performance, revelled in location shooting and the immediacy of real sound effects. He conducted free and improvisatory rehearsals with his actors, and always responded to what they gave him.

In an interview with the *New Musical Express* in November 1993, David Thewlis said that Johnny is very demonic. 'He doesn't really perform any good in the film. He compares himself to Buddha, to Christ, to any kind of prophetic figure. He says he's been down the Via Dolorosa, but he's a "turning up the tables in the temple of the money lenders" kind of Christ rather than the compassionate, forgiving, healing Christ . . . He is crying out against the fatal indifference of modern man but he's not doing anything about it. He's just trying to get people to see what's going on, which is what the film will hopefully do.'

Not according to Julie Burchill, it didn't. Shortly after that *NME* interview, Burchill attacked the film in the *Sunday Times*, saying that Leigh's characters talked like lobotomised Muppets (unconsciously invoking an insult lobbed by Phil Daniels at Tim Roth in *Meantime*); they talked, she said, sub-wittily, the way Diane Arbus's subjects look. She said Leigh films were like the *Carry On* oeuvre, insensitive even to the acuity lurking behind her own denigratory remark. She unwisely widened her attack to accuse Leigh of denying his Jewish roots, changing his name and affecting a working-class background to which he was unentitled. Leigh smote her down in a dignified, unanswerable riposte, but the idea of Mike Leigh's 'long career of sourness' (Anthony Lane's phrase in the *New Yorker*) took root alongside what Saul Bellow would undoubtedly call the mistaken feminist reading of guilt by association with character. Suzanne Moore in the *Guardian* (November 1993), under the trite headline 'Reel men don't eat quiche', commented on Johnny's energy, that drives the film dramatically, in vivid contrast to the lethargic females whose lives he routinely ruins: 'What sort of realism is this? To show a misogynist and surround him with such walking doormats has the effect, intentional or not, of justifying this behaviour.'

Does it? Who says so? How is Macbeth's behaviour justified by the mere performance of the role? Is Ian McKellen or Derek Jacobi endorsing regicide, child murder, sexual cruelty and treachery by acting in Shakespeare's play and hogging all the opportunities for soliloquy? The 'doormat' motif was taken up a week later by Helen Birch in the *Independent*, accusing Leigh of collaborating in the myth that women who lie back and have nasty things done to them wouldn't know rape from a bit of rough, consenting sex.

She reports that a group of women (an organised, or an improvised, group?) marched out of the cinema chanting 'Five pounds
for five rapes.' What did they, would they, do at *The Trojan
Women*, or *The Decameron*, or *The Taming of the Shrew*? Is there
no room for irony, for truth, for the idea that in depicting horrors
in the sex war an artist is exposing them, not endorsing them?
And who says that Sophie is an unwilling doormat in *Naked*, or
that Louise is a doormat at all? It is clear that the latter is taking
serious stock of her relationship with Johnny, whom she once
loved deeply. She exhibits both patience and tenderness in her
dealings with him, whereas she finally pulls a knife on Jeremy.

Contemporary commentators, in Britain at least, seem to have
lost touch with the purpose of narrative art, which is to describe
and challenge moral and ethical behaviour, not endorse it. And,
as a film-maker, Leigh says, 'Here is how people are, this is how
a certain character behaves, it's terrible, it's appalling, it's funny,
it's desperate, and here is a film about it all.' The actors who
played the so-called victims of Johnny's depredations did not see
it through *Guardian* Women eyes at all. Katrin Cartlidge, who
played the hopeless Goth, Sophie, was amazed that anyone could
ask a question about defending the character you have played,
'any more than you would say to van Gogh, how dare you paint
a naked prostitute, who is living in your house, and call it "Sor-
row" and ask us to look at it and feel depressed'. Sophie is twenty-
seven, looking for love, misguided, pathetic and terminally stupid.
That's who the character is. 'There are a lot of people like that
going around who have invented a way of projecting themselves;
it's a cultural thing, a sort of armour-plating.' And Lesley Sharp
(Louise), who was born in Manchester and raised in Liverpool,
was angered by the political censoriousness of some reactions:
'There are a lot of people who don't go to art house cinemas who
do have deeply troubled lives and are at risk. It's very easy if you
wear Doc Martens and black leggings, and read a lot of papers,
to say, well, it's not like that, the film is too misogynistic. That's
missing the point. We do actually live in a misogynistic, violent
society and there are a lot of women in abusive relationships who
find it very difficult to get out of them. And a lot of men, too.'

One of Leigh's oldest and firmest friends is David Canter, Professor of Psychology at Liverpool University. They met when both were members of Habonim, and Canter used to come over from Liverpool, where he lived, and stay with Leigh's family. Canter is an expert in psychological profiling, and has outlined his work with the police on tracking down serial killers in a fascinating book, *Criminal Shadows* (1994). One of his main themes is the debate about 'inner narrative', the way in which we develop accounts of ourselves and the way in which criminals develop heroic versions of themselves that implicate their relationships with other people. In Johnny, Canter sees an absolutely classic example of a criminal prevented only from killing and raping by his own fierce articulacy: 'If Johnny was only slightly less intelligent, slightly less able to verbalise his inner conflicts, then he would be a very dangerous man. The way in which his abuse of women grows out of his existing relationships with women and spills over into women who are casual acquaintances; that makes a tremendous amount of sense . . . I've always been impressed by the way Mike gets to grips with the inner lives of the characters being what drives the drama forward.'

Johnny is the new anti-hero in a tradition that includes Shakespeare's Hamlet, Dostoevsky's Raskolnikov, Renoir's Boudu. But there is another, more recent, example of the type in Leigh's own career. At drama school, Leigh became friends with a fellow student called David Halliwell. On leaving RADA, Leigh directed a play Halliwell had written in which the hero, Malcolm Scrawdyke, was an art student and rebel who formed a political party of Dynamic Erection and declared war on all teachers, puritans and dullards. He, too, behaved badly towards girls. Leigh's participation in this project was a crucial rite of passage, and we should trace a few biographical details towards discovering how little Michael left Salford and joined *Little Malcolm and his Struggle Against the Eunuchs*.

THREE

Childhood in Salford and Plans for Escape

Mike Leigh was born on 20 February 1943. The birthdate, though not the year, is shared with the American director Robert Altman, the footballer Jimmy Greaves, the singer Nancy Wilson and the actor Sidney Poitier, all of whom easily qualify in Kenneth Tynan's High Definition Performance category, artists exhibiting grace under pressure at a supreme level of skill. Leigh is in good company, and is not embarrassed by it. His place of birth was Brocket Hall in Welwyn, Hertfordshire, where his wife Alison Steadman was to be found fifty-one years later filming a ballroom scene in a BBC Television adaptation of Jane Austen's *Pride and Prejudice*.

I apologise for the apparent confusion: Leigh, a proud Lancastrian, forever proclaiming his Salford origins, was in fact born in Hertfordshire, a county in the soft south; how come? Leigh's father, who had qualified as a doctor and had taken a job at Salford Royal Hospital in 1939, the year war broke out, was serving in 1942 with the army in East Africa. He returned home on leave to visit his wife, Phyllis, and left her pregnant. In her confinement, she returned, for comfort and support, to Letchworth in Hertfordshire, where her parents, previously based in London, now resided. Most conveniently, the City of London Maternity Hospital, where Phyllis had earlier trained as a health visitor and midwife, had been evacuated to the nearby Hertfordshire stately home of Brocket Hall.

And that was how little Leigh came to be born in luxurious surroundings without a silver spoon in his mouth. When all was well, Phyllis Leigh and her new baby, a fine-looking creature with chubby cheeks and a good head of blond hair, returned to 10 Park Lane, in the Broughton Park area of Salford. Salford is next door to central Manchester, on the north-west side of the River Irwell, and is not an overspill, or a suburb, of the city, but, since medieval times, a separate borough. Even in the Domesday Book, Pevsner tells us, Salford was a separate manor. By the late nineteenth century it was a city in its own right, with a Roman Catholic cathedral and a population of almost a quarter of a million. Broughton Park is one of several villa estates in South Lancashire laid out in the middle of the nineteenth century.

Peripateticism ran in the family. Jews, of necessity, moved around incessantly during the first half of this century. Leigh's paternal grandfather, Mayer Liebermann, came to England from Russia in 1902 in order to avoid forcible enlistment in the Russian army for the stock period of twelve years. His fore-bears worked for a German firm of timber merchants, which explains the non-Russian surname: like many people, the family had no surname until a Csarist edict compelled them to adopt one, and they simply adopted that of their employers. Mayer was born a Liebermann. He had been to art school near Moscow and was due to travel on to New York, but he missed his railway connection from Hull to Liverpool and stayed in Manchester.

In Manchester, Mayer Liebermann opened up half a shop (the other half belonged to a tailor) on Cheetham Hill Road, one of the city's defining main thoroughfares, near the corner of Caernarvon Street. Progress Limited was a small factory built around his own work as a portrait miniaturist, colouring in people in family photographs and framing them. It continued to thrive, run by his son-in-law, Fred Markson, until the late 1960s, when the rapid expansion of home photography finally killed off the demand for pictures of loved ones titivated with air-brush and pencil techniques and framed in coloured enamel settings. Leigh remembers going in to Progress as a small boy and messing around with paints: 'There was always an attractively bohemian air about the place, people chain-smoking and working expertly with paints and those things called French curves which could produce all sorts of shapes. I loved going in there.'

Mayer Liebermann married Leah Blain, whose family had also emigrated from Russia, but earlier, towards the end of the nineteenth century, and had settled in nearby Blackburn, where there was a small Jewish community (her father, David Blain, had been a famous early Zionist and had run a Hebrew-language newspaper). Leah was one of five children; her youngest brother, Israel, 'Uncle Izzy', a bachelor and a surgeon, became Mike's favourite relative. From this side of the family, too, hails Evelyn Rose (née Blain), the distinguished cookery writer, Leah's niece and therefore Mike's second cousin.

Mayer (d. 1955) and Leah (d. 1956) had four children, of whom Mike's father, Abe (1914–85), was the second son. Two sons were doctors, one worked for Progress, and the fourth child, Doreen, an aunt who later used to send copies of *Plays and Players* and *Punch* magazines to Mike on a regular basis ('For years, I assumed that I would draw for *Punch*,' says Leigh), married the aforementioned Fred Markson, a Scotsman, who eventually took over at Progress. The family grew up around Cheetham Hill Road, near St Luke's Church, a handsome Gilbert Scott building, now an attractive ruin, where Mendelssohn played the organ on one of the earliest of his ten visits to England. Abe's elder brother, Eli, who worked for Progress, died of a heart attack aged thirty-eight; and Abe outlived both his sister Doreen and his younger brother Maurice, like him a general practitioner, who both died of heart attacks in the 1970s. Abe, too, was susceptible to cardiac disease, and died in 1985 after a long illness.

The brothers had changed their name from Liebermann to Leigh in 1939, for obvious reasons. The director's name could just as easily have been 'Libby'; indeed, if he ever has need of a pseudonym, he favours 'Dave Libby'. Leigh's full, original name was Michael David Leigh, and about fifteen years ago, finally becoming fed up with having that name on his passport and 'Mike Leigh' on his credit cards – the crunch came one day on a visit to a branch of the Crédit Lyonnais when a clerical bureaucrat hassled him over having the two names – he officially changed his name to 'Mike Leigh'.

Leigh says that his father's initial resistance to the idea of his son working in the arts – 'the moonings of a stage-struck girlie' was his response on learning that he wanted to go to drama school – was informed by the fact that Mayer's photo-portrait business had done very badly during the slump, and that they often did not know where the next meal was coming from. 'But they did very well in the Second World War, because if your little Johnny had been killed and all you had was a picture of him in an open-necked shirt with some unidentified female on his arm and the Blackpool Tower in the background, he could remove all that, put the lad in a collar and tie, colour it up and stick it in a frame. I grew up in a house chokka with pictures of everyone in these ruddy frames. But he was a very good, competent artist, with an incredible eye for detail.'

On his mother's side, grandfather Morris Cousin came to London from Lithuania at the turn of the century, while grandmother Annie (née Myers) hailed originally from Germany and grew up, from the age of six, in the East End of London. The old boy pushed a barrow around the East End every day (where, presumably, he met his future wife), and finished up as a master butcher at 52 Blackstock Road in Finsbury Park. Phyllis, Leigh's mother, is the middle one of three sisters; the other two are living in Israel, while Phyllis still lives in the comfortable, convenient apartment in a leafy, residential Salford lane into which she and Abe moved in 1971. She remembers meeting Abe at a summer holiday camp in 1935, at either Deal or Herne Bay, she's not sure which south coast resort. They were both members of Habonim, which had been established in Britain in 1929. Zionism is now a term implying an unpleasant degree of fanaticism, but a Zionist in those days was, as the playwright Arnold Wesker, himself an enthusiastic member of Habonim in the late 1940s, explains in his autobiography, simply someone who believed the Jews should have a land of their own.

Habonim was a social movement as well as a socialist one, and the general air of camaraderie and camping out was wedded to a committed, creative atmosphere of writing, acting, producing newspapers and plays, travelling and debating; when young Leigh eventually joined, he took off like a rocket. Phyllis and Abe, whose Habonim days were much less 'artistic' than their son's, kept in touch after that first meeting; she used to come up from London on 'the ten-bob train', and Abe and his pals would meet her on the platform of London Road (now Piccadilly) Station in Manchester. Phyllis had completed her training and was working as a health visitor in Westminster when the war broke out; she promptly moved north to Accrington, Lancashire, and took a bus each weekend to Salford to stay with Abe's parents. The couple married on 24 August 1941 at the now-demolished Manchester Great Synagogue.

Leigh's father missed his son's birth, just as, forty-two years later, the son would be abroad when his father died. Not too much can be made of this, but there is undoubtedly a persistent sense of the 'missing father' in Leigh's life and work. And Leigh has been conspicuous by his presence at the birth of both of his and Alison's sons, in 1978 and 1981. As he said of his father in a BBC TV programme, *The Long Goodbye*, in May 1995: 'If we had not been separated by being father and son, we would have really been natural buddies.' He described Abe to journalist Bel Mooney as someone who prided himself on being a man of few words, and admitted that he and his father had never really communicated with each other until towards the end of Abe's life, when he was incapacitated by a stroke, following the three heart attacks he had endured since the age of sixty.

Mooney asked Leigh to imagine what his father would be like, were he still here now. The reply indicated that Abe, who was bald from an early age, would be scrutinising his companions though thick spectacles: 'He had a way of raising an eyebrow and giving you a quizzical look that was critical, compassionate, sympathetic, sarcastic; a look that was a little bit at odds with the later memories of him where he was confused, a little lost boy who seems to have shrunk, and that makes me very sad.' In Leigh's first major film after Abe's death, *High Hopes*, the elderly mother played by Edna Doré is a portrait of loneliness and bereavement incorporating elements of his attempt to redefine his even more difficult relationship with his own mother.

Abe was not allowed home on leave from East Africa, where he was serving as a captain in the Royal Army Medical Corps, until twenty months after his son's birth. Phyllis kept a detailed 'baby book' during this period, with information about her son's development, and many photographs of a remarkably attractive little baby. When Abe did come home for ten months, Phyllis conceived her second child, and Abe went off again, this time to India. Ruth was born in his absence, but he missed only the first six weeks of her life: the war was at last over, and the young doctor returned for a post-graduate course and the start of his career as a general practitioner in Higher Broughton, a working-class district of Salford, the epicentre of Leigh's youngest years and the area memorialised in *Hard Labour*. His grandparents, Mayer and Leah, had owned 125 Cavendish Road, just round the corner from Park Lane, since 1936. When they died in the mid 1950s, the house was taken over by Abe and Phyllis, who lived there until 1971.

Abe came home from the army in 1946, and for the next ten years the family lived above the surgery at 398 Great Cheetham Street, where Phyllis also ran a baby clinic for over twenty years. Leigh's father was the fourth doctor in this corner-house residential surgery; the first incumbent was Dr Joseph Cantley (who died in 1926), father of Sir Joseph, the famous High Court judge. Abe was, Leigh remembers, always totally committed to the National Health Service: 'You were not appointed to a practice in those days, you bought one, so you inherited the patients. But he always cursed his private patients and couldn't wait to get rid of them. When the day came when he had no more private patients, that day was one of celebration as far as he was concerned. He also worked as a visiting factory doctor, mostly around Oldham. He was a Labour voter all his life.'

There was a surgery and a dispensary, which later became a changing room as, with the introduction of the National Health Service, doctors no longer had to dispense their own prescriptions, which people now took along to the chemist's. And there was a back yard. A back alley still runs behind the house, now divided into flats, which stands on a noisy corner of what was, in pre-motorway days, the main Leeds to Liverpool route taking a short cut through north Manchester. Leigh's childhood memories are vivid and various: of his friends; of the church opposite, St James, Higher Broughton (which he has never entered, though he is nowadays an assiduous and enthusiastic church tourist in general), whose bells were melted down as a contribution to the war effort and replaced by a sticky recording; of his wild, neutered mongrel dog, Snuggly, who, he says, 'made William's Jumble in the *Just William* books look like the Queen's corgis', and with whom he roamed the streets and went for the Sunday morning bagels before cleaning out his budgerigar's cage; of the Catholic processions on high days and holidays; of the traffic noise but low incidence of cars in the surrounding streets; of his father's Morris Eight and his mother's Ford Popular.

The infant director's first review appeared in a report from Cliffe Grange Nursery School, one month before his fourth birthday: this 'very interesting child' was always eager to recite, spoke clearly and was very intelligent. He was, however, 'not fond of movement' (a condition that still applies), but 'likes to be a leader' (ditto). At the age of five, he graduated to North Grecian Street County Primary School. When he received an honorary degree at Salford University in 1991, Leigh reminisced in his address about the Number One bus journey he took for a penny along Great Cheetham Street down to the primary school in Lower Broughton. On racing days, the bus was diverted around the houses because of the congestion near the Manchester Race Course, and crossed over the River Irwell. In summer, it was a short walk, about a mile, home. The carefree Edwardian river life, which Leigh remembers one very old teacher, Miss Dawson, describing, had long since disappeared as the Irwell became increasingly polluted and indeed life-threatening if you fell in (as several children of his day actually did).

Similarly, Leigh nostalgically recalled the cinemas, now gone, which he had patronised in his schooldays – the Cromwell, which laid claim to being the oldest cinema in Britain; the Rialto (which closed as a cinema in 1973 with two James Bond films, became a bingo hall, and is now the 'Rialto Pool and Bar'), immediately next door to the Higher Broughton Assembly Rooms on Great Cheetham Street, where adolescent Michael's bar-mitzvah 'function' was held, very close to Strangeways Prison; the Devonshire; the Green Bank; the Temple; and one or two Odeons. His love for the cinema was born, he said, in those haunts, and the health of the British cinema has declined, through government negligence, as surely as those fun palaces of his youth have disappeared from the face of the earth. In Salford alone, thirty-two cinemas have been closed or demolished in the past forty years. Leigh's cinematic diet consisted of the newsreels, cartoons, the Three Stooges, Charlie Chaplin, Mickey Mouse, Flash Gordon, and everything from Hollywood and the British studios. The only European films he remembers seeing before coming to London in 1960 were Albert Lamorrise's *Le Balon rouge* (1956), a saccharine short piece about a boy's pursuit of a red balloon through the Paris streets, which was shown at school, and Jules Dassin's *Rififi* (1955), which was shown in the cinema, and in which nobody spoke for twenty minutes during the famous robbery sequence.

The headmaster of Grecian Street, Leigh recalls, was 'a very tall man called Mr Small. I have happy memories of nice teachers who, if you did something marginally naughty, would say "Come out" and whack you across the hand with a cane. You'd think nothing of it. I remember one summer day, Mr Small was making a speech about obedience, and he said "Hands up everybody who would lick the sole of my shoe if I told them to." I was only half listening, so I put my hand up and I looked around to see that I was the only kid who had done so, the unlikeliest candidate, in fact, for this act of self-abasement. So I had to go and see him in his office and he sat back and lifted up his shoe and I got down on the floor . . . and he interrupted and said "Don't be silly; now you know not to say yes if you don't mean it. And try not to drift off when I'm talking to you." It was a good place, very enlightened in its own way. We were encouraged to write and paint. I edited a newspaper in my third year, aged about ten, and

I insisted on every article being written out again in black so it looked like a proper newspaper.'

These were the happiest days of his school career. The sky darkened at secondary school. Abe and his brothers had all attended Manchester Grammar School, then, as now, one of the outstanding secondary schools in the country. It was assumed that young Michael would follow them there. He scrambled through the eleven-plus, with extra tuition for his abominable maths, and sat the Manchester Grammar's examination, passing Part One but failing Part Two, chiefly because, he insists, he did not know the difference between stalactites and stalagmites. So he was assigned to Salford Grammar, 'at best a second-rate affair, if not a third-rate, and there is no doubt that there was some serious disappointment on my old man's part that I hadn't made the grade. Nonetheless, Grecian Street was a working-class school, and so was Salford Grammar, which Manchester Grammar wouldn't have been, and it became part of the making process. I was pretty badly unmotivated at secondary school. But I'm not remotely academic and I might have fared even worse at Manchester Grammar.' At least he would have been an exact contemporary there of his fellow Salfordian, the actor Ben Kingsley.

Salford Grammar was further on from Grecian Street, in the Pendleton area where Albert Finney's father (also called Albert Finney) kept his betting shop on Whit Lane. Finney's association with the school was sealed with the naming of the house drama competition trophy as the Albert Finney Cup, and young Leigh was the very first recipient, with a victory secured for Gloucester House (the other houses were York, Lancaster and Warwick) with his production of a play called *God's Jailer* which he found in the library and about which he now remembers absolutely nothing. 'That's when I thought directing a play meant getting a prompt copy and putting in moves and all the accompanying paraphernalia. I think the school was all right now I think about it. I think it was me that wasn't all right.'

(The neighbouring Pendleton High School, the sister school, produced Shelagh Delaney, author of *A Taste of Honey* (1958), a wonderful first play which led most significantly to her scripting the delightful film *Charlie Bubbles* (1968) for Albert Finney's Memorial Films company just two years before Finney gave a big break to another fellow Salfordian, Leigh, by financing *Bleak Moments*.)

Shortly after Leigh started at Salford Grammar, now known as Buile Hill High School, the family moved from above Abe's surgery into 125 Cavendish Street, Salford 7. From that moment, his mother says, Leigh became 'more of a misfit', though he himself considers his growing cussedness to be no more than a natural adolescent development, admittedly exacerbated by his dislike of middle-class pretensions at home. His parents referred him to a child psychiatrist. His gloom was fleetingly assuaged by his house drama cup triumph and his participation in school productions of Gogol's *The Government Inspector* (he played the lead, Khlestakhov) and Shaw's *Androcles and the Lion* (he played the lion). There was a strong tradition of drama in the all-boys school, and an English master called Mr Nutter furnished the shelves of the library with new plays the minute they were published; Les Blair, Leigh's friend and fellow pupil, and the producer of his first feature film, *Bleak Moments*, remembers finding John Osborne's *Look Back in Anger* within a few weeks of reading Tynan's review in the *Observer* ('I doubt if I could love anyone who did not wish to see *Look Back in Anger*. It is the best young play of its decade'). Blair saw Albert Finney as Sweeney Todd in his first or second year, and competed with Leigh at an audition for the role of Jim Hawkins in *Treasure Island*. Blair got the part. He also played a princess to Leigh's romantic hero in a Hans Christian Andersen story.

Leigh did not pine at all for the more amenable rough and tumble of Higher Broughton around his father's surgery, for it was barely a mile away; he kept the same friends, who were scattered all over north Manchester. But he harboured mixed feelings about the new ambience of suburban gentility. His friend David Canter says that whenever you went to the house, you were worried about using the wrong fork or spoon at the table. The atmosphere at mealtimes could be tense, fraught with arguments and vain appeals to standards of etiquette, as meals invariably are in such films as *Home Sweet Home*, *Meantime* and

Life is Sweet. Leigh and his friends played Scrabble, at which the young host was virtually invincible, but they favoured the 'rude words' version and frequently had to tip over the board when Phyllis put her head round the door of the bedroom.

Over the next few years, in his school reports, Michael's biology teacher remarked on his offensive 'individuality', his housemaster recommended 'less jest, more zest', one teacher acidly pointed out that 'Life is not all a cartoonist's paradise,' and his headmaster summed up one term's endeavours with a sad shake of his head: 'This is a sorry business.' Leigh scraped three O-Levels and started a miserable sojourn in the lower sixth on Art, History and English A-Levels while supposedly catching up with a few more O-Levels. He played truant for a few weeks, the first his parents knew of it being a telephone call from the school asking if Michael was going to be ill for much longer. Michael was skiving off in Manchester, and explained to his parents that he was doing some work in the Central Reference Library; in fact, he was slumped in adolescent melancholia over what to do with his life, no less. An almost surreal notion of applying for drama school took hold while he studied the advertisements in copies of *Plays and Players* supplied by Auntie Doreen.

Phyllis Leigh now says that her son 'really belonged to the area where we lived first, over the surgery', but Leigh disputes this maternal diagnosis. The one indisputable fact is that, after the move to Cavendish Road, but not necessarily because of it, Mike's artistic inclinations were increasingly apparent. He had avidly read such comics as the *Eagle*, the *Beano* and the *Hotspur* since the age of seven. He was now completing some extraordinary cartoons and complex drawings, heavily influenced by the 'St Trinian's' style of Ronald Searle. In 1955, aged twelve and preparing for his bar-mitzvah, he produced a synagogue scene, 'The Blowing of the Shophar', which is a teeming little masterpiece of detailed line drawing; the synagogue interior is almost bursting with character and humour. This sense of sarcastic fun found another outlet in the pages of the monthly *Young Elizabethan*, initially *Collins Magazine*, which paid him good pocket money for an endless stream of jokes, poems, stories and drawings.

A typical *Young Elizabethan* article was headed 'How to make two old orange boxes from an old desk, written and illustrated by Michael Leigh (14)'. This catalogue of subversive carpentry tips was a recipe for havoc in a style worthy of Jerome K. Jerome: the destruction of an old desk, the probable mutilation of exposed limbs in tipping it on its side ('Turn this magazine 90 degrees to the right and look again at fig. I'), the precarious stacking of the extracted drawers, the recycling, or even burning, of the desk's top-board ('this part of the desk makes a very fine "flushed" contemporary door. Alternatively, walnut wood, you will find, burns well'). After hammering out the footrest and the cross bars, 'you are left with two fine old orange boxes – with a difference; these are orange boxes of which you can say, "Ah! I made them myself!" (fig. III)'.

Outside of school, Leigh was now thriving in the Manchester branch of Habonim at 88 Bury Old Road. He attended summer camps and winter activities over the Christmas break all round the country in the last few years of the 1950s. Several firm lifelong friendships were made. Ruth Lesirge, whose family lived in north London and who now works in community care after years of teaching in secondary schools and adult education, was particularly struck, when they first met, by Leigh's drawing skills. 'We were staying one Christmas at a women's teacher-training institute in Ambleside, and Mike made these huge, witty cartoons and stuck them inside all the frames of the portraits on the walls of the great and the good. And he wrote hilarious comments underneath. There was a striking mixture of extreme cleverness and huge crudity, and he was always perceptive about people. In that respect, he was potentially lethal.' She also noted that his sometimes terrifying exterior – his conversation, then as now, was littered with cruel put-downs, quips and insults – masked a considerable capacity for kindness and gentleness.

Like Leigh, David Canter only passed a few O-Levels, but he persevered at school in Liverpool, taking some more and eventually going on to the city's university. Canter extended his interest in psychology into some experimental hypnosis; one of the other camp leaders – Leigh, like most of his friends, was a leader –

was injured and Canter jokingly said that he would practise some hypnosis on her and make her feel better. Afterwards, he congratulated her on acting up the pretence so well; she replied that she hadn't been acting at all, and that had she not been 'under' she would not have been able to keep a straight face. Habonim was also crucial in that boys mixed with girls at a time when they had less opportunity to do so while attending single-sex schools. There was a relaxation that may not have been so easily found between girls and boys outside such gatherings, though Canter is doubtful whether much serious shagging went on: 'Sexual freedom was more talked about than anything else. Boys and girls were certainly together at night in their tents, but I remember hearing shouts coming out like, "Stop getting so excited over my elbow!"' Leigh demurs at this, admitting that while full-scale promiscuity was obviously not the order of the day, there was a little more serious sexual activity going on in those tents than Canter suggests.

David Canter initially found young Leigh both charismatic and distressing: he effortlessly commanded any group he was in, and there was the edginess and verbal cruelty which still occasionally flashes to the surface today. But these were happy days, and talents were treasured. Canter remembers some spoof competitions Leigh devised, much in the spirit of his mock carpentry lesson. He once suggested that they take the chunks of pineapple out of a tin and rebuild the pineapple. They used to ask each other what they would choose as an epitaph, and Leigh suggested: 'Here lies Mike Leigh; or is it here; or is it here; or is it over there?'

(There's a neat little exchange in *Naked* between Brian, the security guard, and Johnny. 'What're you doin' 'ere?' asks Brian, the morning after their long philosophical discussion. 'Well . . . you see . . .' replies Johnny, 'I was over 'ere, like this (*Takes one pace to his right*), but that didn't work for me, so I thought I'd try it over 'ere (*Back to his first position*), but I don't think there's much future in this one either. Fuckin' 'ell! 'Ave you got any suggestions?')

Another lifelong friendship was forged with Colin Cina, later a distinguished painter and currently Head of Fine Art at Chelsea

School of Art. He hailed from the Gorbals in Glasgow, where his father was an engineer and his elder brother (with whom he was packed off to camp) a brilliant scientist. He recalls meeting Leigh in a field in Staffordshire wielding this amazing pen, a Rapidograph, a bulky object with a stylus nib. 'I was absolutely fascinated by this little chap, who not only drew wonderful cartoons, but had already – at the age of about eleven – learned to write in that curious mock-cursive script he still uses. I suppose we became the court jesters in the group. Mike was one of those kids who seemed to be able to understand the world before he had actually experienced it. There was a sort of wisdom in him that we all just took for granted.'

By this time, when he was seventeen, Leigh knew that he wanted to leave school, leave home and go to London. His appetite for the performing arts had been awakened not just by the cinema and the end-of-camp revues with Habonim (he invariably wrote half the sketches and directed the performance), but also his joyous discovery of Picasso, Surrealism and *The Goon Show* (with Peter Sellers, Spike Milligan and Harry Secombe) on BBC Radio. He was even diverted, if not smitten, by compulsory family visits to the Hallé Orchestra and the D'Oyly Carte. Leigh sheepishly describes himself today as 'a closet Gilbert and Sullivan freak'; after suffering a few hernias in middle age he acquired a rowing machine and climbed aboard to the accompaniment of his Gilbert and Sullivan tapes and Ravel's *Bolero*. He also visited the Library Theatre in Manchester, and was reluctantly dragged to the ballet. 'I saw a touring Old Vic production of *Macbeth* in which the set comprised merely tartan drapes, but what I remember most vividly, and affectionately, is that, near the end, a sword flew off its handle and knocked a woman's specs off in the stalls, and this woman promptly stood up and harangued the actors. I loved that bit!' But the most important part of his artistic consumption was the cinema, by several million reels.

Mike Leigh's Salford is as important to his artistic evolution as the same landscape was to L.S. Lowry earlier in the century. The great permanent exhibition of Lowrys in Salford Art Gallery indicates the extent to which the painter absorbed the atmosphere of the area, not just in his well-known industrial scenes of scurrying mill workers, but in the representations of houses, parks, outdoor social events, churches and river scenes. There is a superb painting of an overcrowded outpatients' hall in Ancoats Hospital which has the same feel of institutional stagnation you get in the labour exchange scene in Leigh's *Meantime*. Lowry used to wander round nearby Pendlebury (where he lived) and Salford in his baggy suit and battered hat and just sketch away, leaning against the red-brick terraced houses while children played on the pavement and adults scurried to work or the shops. Leigh remains similarly immersed in this terrain, though his objectivity within it is far more grimly satirical than Lowry's. He laments the passing of the cinemas, the gradual disappearance of the familiar landscape, and recalls that when his pet budgie, Pip, died, he and David Canter retrieved the corpse from the dustbin where Abe had instructed him to throw it, and solemnly reburied the bird in a shoebox, with lit candles, on a building site in Singleton Road. They extinguished the candles by urinating over them, and the ex-budgie.

Visiting the area with Leigh, it becomes clear that everything in his work that involves net curtains, bleak moments, dead afternoons, peculiar relatives and the daily, grinding sadness of people's ordinary lives, comes from this suburban patch of Salford, with its quiet streets of Edwardian villas, 1930s estates, leafy lanes and bland (or suffocating?) respectability. Upwardly mobile Jews moved on to adjacent Prestwich, where Auntie Doreen's house contained the first television set that Leigh ever saw, perhaps in 1949 or 1950; Sunday afternoon tea was a ritual here, the short journey made *en famille* in Abe's Morris Eight. Another young resident of Cavendish Road was Elaine Bookbinder, a.k.a. Elkie Brooks, the singer.

His favourite Uncle Izzy, Leigh's father's uncle, who lived with his bachelor brother, the other Abe, in Park Road, great-grandma Blain's house, was another advocate of 'the world elsewhere', and Mike stayed with him whenever his parents went away; Izzy made Mike laugh, he was a bit of a character. He was also the only relative with any real money, some of which he fortuitously left to his responsive nephew when he died in 1973; Mike used this minor windfall as a deposit on the house in Wood Green which he and Alison bought a couple of years later.

Uncle Izzy appealed to young Mike because he was a sort of anarchist, he chain-smoked, and had a brusque style and a great sense of humour. And he swore at everyone; so much so that he was known around the hospital where he worked as 'Bloody Hell Blain'. He was qualified as both a doctor and a dentist (he had been round the world as a ship's doctor in the 1920s), and was actively involved as a general surgeon at the Jewish hospital in Manchester. During the Blitz, when the sirens went off, he refused to stop operating. Leigh remembers that he would come round to the house for a meal and not use his napkin. And in a house where Leigh was obliged to answer the telephone with the words, 'Doctor Leigh's house,' he loved seeing Uncle Izzy, when he was there, pick up the phone and quizzically yell, 'Hello?'

Uncle Izzy built a house at the end of the 1920s, where he lived with his mother and his bachelor brother Abie, a furrier and travelling salesman. His mother died a few weeks before Leigh was born; he would have been her first great-grandchild. Uncle Izzy, Leigh learned, had had an affair with a non-Jewish doctor in Manchester but did not marry her for as long as his mother was alive; by the time his mother died, the woman had married somebody else. Leigh remembers: 'I really loved him. He had become a part-owner of the Metropole Hotel in Whitby, and we used to go there for holidays on a deal he arranged. He kept a room in the hotel and used to drive over there at weekends in a big Ford V8 Pilot, at incredible speed. He had the first car radio I can remember, and he used to come back from Whitby with boxes of herrings and kippers – he'd go out on the trawlers – and give them, as an unwanted favour, to my Mum. In those pre-freezer days, she was therefore lumbered, and had to go down the street, chatting up neighbours and trying to get rid of them before they went off.

'He had a Catholic housekeeper called Theresa who henna-ed her hair every week and was an appalling cook. He bought pork pies and ham in York – an unforgivable thing for a Jew to do – and

I loved him even more for that, too. He was an expert philatelist, a compulsive card player and a collector of antique silver. In short, quite a character!'

More windows were opened on the world by a strange and beguiling relation, Harold Rottesman, whose mother was a cousin of Mayer Liebermann. Harold was therefore a distant cousin of Mike's, though he lived very nearby with his parents in Huntley Road. His father was a sculptor with a hump back ('Very unpleasant man,' says Leigh) who restored artefacts in Catholic churches, and his mother a stalwart of the Manchester branch of the Gilbert and Sullivan Society. Harold was a few years older than Mike, very bright, and went to Manchester Grammar and Oriel College, Oxford, where he read English and pioneered taped drama. He introduced Mike to the work of Saul Steinberg, the brilliant *New Yorker* cartoonist, and to James Thurber; he later adapted Thurber's *The Thirteen Clocks* for BBC Radio. He also had an 8mm camera, with which he compiled short little bits of film. And he was gay.

Mike remembers sitting in Harold's cluttered front room in Huntley Road with another friend when he was about fifteen years old, and his (Mike's) father coming round to bang on the door angrily at one o'clock in the morning, shouting 'Where's my son?' The first time Leigh ever met an actor he was with Rottesman, who took him along to BBC Radio in Manchester, where he was working as a supporting actor, and introduced him as 'my nephew'. Leigh remembers the camp actor (though not his name) shaking him by the hand and exclaiming, 'Ooh, he's very *padded*, isn't he?'

In later life their relationship was bedevilled by professional complications: at the Midlands Arts Centre, Mike would have to read unsolicited scripts, and one day he received a play for children written by 'Harold E. Rottesman' full of homoerotic *double entendres* and obscenities. He got someone else to write back. And when he was rehearsing *The Knack* at the Royal Shakespeare Company, Harold turned up, gushingly, with a whole crowd of school-boys, causing an embarrassing fracas backstage. Leigh later heard of strange tea parties in south London, where Harold would hold court with young boys in pinafores serving food and ministering to showbiz guests he'd inveigled along. The tragic conclusion to a crucial friendship that gradually petered out came when Harold finally stuck his head in the oven and committed suicide circa 1970. Leigh found this news deeply upsetting.

Elements of autobiography are buried in all Leigh's films and plays, but only *Hard Labour* is set in Salford. In 1971, when Abe and Phyllis Leigh had just moved from Cavendish Road to the flat where Mrs Leigh still lives, in Upper Park Road, their son paid his first visit. He found another guest there, an Irish woman called Bridie Williams, who had known the family since the 1940s, was closely involved with them all, and did the house-cleaning. Bridie was always known by that name, though she always referred to Phyllis as 'Mrs Leigh'. That relationship is clearly the basis for Mrs Stone and the working-class Mrs Thornley (played by Liz Smith in her first major role) in *Hard Labour*. 'Mrs Thornley' was the name of Abe's caretaker at his branch surgery. Of the four Jewish characters – Mr and Mrs Stone, the rather noisy woman who comes to collect old clothes and toys for charity and clears out the children's bedroom, and the tallyman – it is the latter through whom Leigh expresses most directly an idea of the working-class Jewish experience. In the film, the tallyman is selling boots to Mr Thornley. Such characters went around the neighbourhood, indeed still do, selling anything you might want – clothes, shoes, ornaments, household appliances – on tick. As it happens, Mike's sister's father-in-law was a tallyman. More instant research.

The scenes in the Stones' house were shot in a house (on the brink of demolition) just two doors along from where the Leighs had lived in Cavendish Road, which leads off Singleton Road. In *Who's Who* (1980), one of the toffs suddenly says: 'D'you know who I saw? Janey Singleton-Cavendish!' The other internal reference is to Leigh's father's Aunt Janey, who used to come round to the house wearing thick spectacles and look through the windows; there is something of Auntie Janey at the core of Brenda Blethyn's desperately funny performance as a persistent and not always welcome visitor, shouting her raucous 'cooees' through the double glazing in *Grown-Ups*. Shortly after *Hard Labour*, Leigh created a powerful play, *Babies Grow Old* (1974), about old age and doctors for the Royal Shakespeare Company, and that, too, drew on his immediate experience of his father's surgery, and the people who came to be treated, not to mention the high incidence of doctors on both sides of the family. And the old lady in *Babies Grow Old*, Mrs Wenlock, has the first name 'Phyllis'.

As a teenager, Mike went his own way with his own friends and never had all that much to do with his sister Ruth. Her development was much more conventional than his, and she eventually married an accountant with whom she had a daughter, Barbara, and a son, Paul, who has become deeply Orthodox and is currently reading mathematics at Trinity College, Cambridge. Leigh himself always regarded himself as Jewish, rather than a Jew; like Jonathan Miller in *Beyond the Fringe*, he did not go the whole hog. While his parents remained stalwart members of their Jewish community, religiously and socially, Leigh himself claims that religion has played no part in his life: 'I walked away from all that as early as I can remember and certainly, by the time of my bar-mitzvah, I did not believe in God. And I still don't.' He is quick to point out, however, that he is 'a deeply spiritual person', which is obvious, he reckons, from his work.

Further, he has no wish to be identified with any sort of Jewish mafia or community, and consistently refuses interviews, for example, with the *Jewish Chronicle*. 'Having said that, I remain in constant struggle with my roots. One of the best gags in Woody Allen's *Annie Hall* occurs when he is asked if he's Jewish, and you see Woody for one split second in Jewish licks and all that. Isaac Bashevis Singer is very important to me. Otherwise, Groucho Marx is as Jewish as I get. I couldn't wait to eat bacon and pork, and religiously did, and do, so!'

His sister Ruth did not follow his rebellious example. Phyllis says that whenever Mike rings up today he always asks after Ruth. But they are hardly in touch; their lives have simply diverged, as happens in most families. This separation of Leigh from the suburban, domesticated (not so much the religious) side of his family life has been a source of creative tension throughout his

career. Some dictatorial male figures – Keith Pratt in *Nuts in May*;
Laurence in *Abigail's Party* (who suffers a fatal heart attack); the
teacher, Mr Butcher, in *Grown-Ups*; the two contrasting husbands
played by Alfred Molina and Jeff Robert in *Meantime* – take some
elements from teachers and his immediate family. Pratt exclaiming
to the Birmingham biker, Finger, 'Be told!' is actually reworking
a phrase Leigh associates with his father. Phyllis herself is philosophical about spotting the direct references, though she rather
blanched at Mrs Stone's exaggerated display of silverware in *Hard
Labour*: 'I mean, who's got it?' As for the rest, she smiles patiently.
'I don't mind. It's got Mike where he needs to be.'

Coming towards the end of his school career, there had been
desultory chats at home about whether Michael would be going
on to study architecture, or art, or English, perhaps even drama
at the new department opening at Manchester University. Abe
had long given up hopes of his son following his own footsteps
into medicine. There was no discussion about drama school in
London. Meanwhile, young Leigh's ambitions were intensifying.
The spirit of working together in a collaborative spirit in Habonim
undoubtedly informs the method of work he so painfully and
painstakingly developed over the coming years. By the time he
was fifteen, he was a group leader.

In 1959, at a Habonim camp in Brittany, France, he appeared
in a production of Arnold Wesker's *Roots* in a marquee. The play,
which had just appeared at the Royal Court, recounted the escape
from her background by the heroine, Beatie Bryant, into the
deluding intellectual life of the metropolis. Its author was riding
the crest of the new wave of British theatre at the Royal Court,
and was an Aldermaston veteran himself. When Wesker's Beatie
returns home to Norfolk, she spouts patronising jargon picked
up from her boyfriend. But she battles through to find her own
voice in a moving tribute to the virtues of widening your horizons,
striking out and discovering new worlds. The play was a rallying
cry to Leigh and his friends, as influential as Osborne's *Look Back
in Anger*, and he took instant action.

The following year, 1960, was a real watershed. Over Easter,
Leigh and a group of Habonim friends – including Cynthia Anson

from Leeds, his 'first proper girlfriend' (she went on to study at Manchester University) – joined the Aldermaston march to ban the bomb. And in the summer of the same year, Leigh's life as a young Zionist came to an end. Habonim was ultimately a propaganda machine whose object was to persuade young left-wing Jews to embrace the socialist way of life by settling in a kibbutz. (There were, and still are, several kibbutzim founded by British members of Habonim.) To this end, the movement ran an annual 'Israel Camp', heavily subsidised by the Jewish Agency, and in 1960 Leigh and many of his friends (including Colin Cina and his future wife, Gill Nicholas, Cynthia Anson and David Canter) embarked on this enlightening expedition. They sailed the Mediterranean on an ancient, rusting ship, the *Artzah*, which had been famous after the war for running the British gauntlet with its cargoes of illegal immigrants to Palestine, like the *Exodus*. Leigh's gang slept on the deck in their sleeping bags, gazing up at the stars. When they landed, they visited all the Holy sights, had a great deal of fun, sex and cheap Israeli wine, and picked olives and figs in a kibbutz. At another kibbutz, Leigh and Cina participated as dissidents in a debate over whether or not it was possible for artists to live in a kibbutz.

(Leigh quickly became disaffected with Israel and its policies, and for over thirty years refused to visit the country. But he relented in 1991 when, with some hesitation and a little coaxing from Alison Steadman, he accepted an invitation to attend the Jerusalem Film Festival with *Life is Sweet*. He found the experience, though mostly enjoyable, also deeply traumatic.)

The group of Habonim friends returned to England. Leigh had now realised that movies meant more to him than anything. But how to get involved? He had applied to drama schools in London because part of the fantasy was in escaping from Manchester – which city, as he said years later, 'was not the exciting mecca of anarchy and culture that it is today' – and he'd been reading about London theatre in magazines. He knew he wanted to work in films, and he knew he wanted to get away from home. He felt bullied and repressed at home and that he had done a lot less well at school than he should have because of all the strictures imposed upon him with regard to staying in during the week, going to his room to work, and so on.

'I had directed a show at Habonim,' he remembers, 'and a party was going off in a hired coach to perform it in Liverpool. They came to the house and waited for me to come out, but my father wouldn't let me go because it was a weekday.' Everyone in the family had a bad temper ('I was smacked around the head an awful lot in moments of anger'), and that fraught domestic atmosphere not only turned Leigh against wishing to stay around and add some more of his own – he does not deny that his own temper was and is as short as everyone else's – but also later suffused his films and plays. There was real *angst*. And real creative pay-off.

To his utter astonishment, and the initial dismay of his parents, he won a scholarship to RADA – 'The most wonderful and also the most mystifying thing that had ever happened to me' – which paid for his tuition fees but not for his board and lodging in London. His parents accepted the inevitable and wished him well. As so often in his life, and work, Leigh found out what he really wanted to do by reacting against his experience. RADA was a step in the right direction, but he instantly became a critical dissi- dent. 'The experience of going there was wonderful, and seminal, and stood me in stead for the rest of time. And it was a total disaster.'

FOUR

On the Fringe with Friends
in the Sixties

Leigh's first professionally produced stage play, *Bleak Moments* (1970) at the Open Space (Charles Marowitz's Tottenham Court Road fringe powerhouse), which was later translated into his first feature film, was his tenth 'improvised play'. Each play thus far had been improvised not in performance, but in rehearsals. Actors have never wandered around making up their lines in a Mike Leigh piece. And still the word 'improvise' is both inadequate and misleading; it suggests actors pretending to be trees, or mumbling instant responses to what they have just heard. It reeks of ramshackle self-indulgence.

By the time he discovered how he really wanted to work, Leigh's method was rigorous, controlled and painstaking. Arriving in London at the start of that quest in 1960, Leigh found a world in cultural transition from post-war austerity to the 'Swinging Sixties'. He could see foreign films any day of the week. He could (and did) stay up all night at the National Film Theatre. The Royal Shakespeare Company was formed in 1960 by Peter Hall and opened for business at the Aldwych.

Leigh is not exactly a lady-killer but he does have reservoirs of charm when required, he is a caring and considerate friend, and he is always funny to be around. His ambience and atmospheres were exclusively heterosexual, communal, white and basic. As they are, for the most part, in his films and plays, which fact sometimes offends the new critical proselytisers anxious to even things up on behalf of sexual or racial minorities. All of his friends testify that Leigh was at the centre of any group, dominating it

58

with his irrepressible vocal energy, proposing the cultural and social agenda. A great deal of cooking from modest resources went on, and Leigh owns up to one special dish with no name that he regularly improvised using calves' tongues, milk, marmalade and onions. Sounds like tsimmes from hell, or something Aubrey might have put on the menu at the Regret Rien in *Life is Sweet*, and not a recipe you'd find in one of his cousin Evelyn Rose's cookbooks.

Young people talked incessantly about the future of the universe and related cultural matters. The Sharpeville massacre, followed in 1961 by the Cuban missile crisis and the erection of the Berlin Wall, created a wave of uncertainty about that future universe. These concerns, and the explosion of the new rock and roll music, initiated a new transatlantic fraternity of the young which was sealed by two momentous events in 1963: the assassination of President Kennedy on 22 November and, a few months earlier, Martin Luther King's famous speech at the Lincoln Memorial in Washington: 'I have a dream that one day sons of former slaves and the sons of former slave-owners will be able to sit down together at the table of brotherhood.' Those youngsters and students became an identifiable social group, 'teenagers', politicised and rebellious, with icons and role models like James Dean and Elvis Presley. The developing Vietnam War would be another rallying point for the teenagers who matured into the peace and protest generation, outraged by the My Lai massacre and the assassination of Luther King on a motel balcony in 1968, and unified once more in music and soft drugs at the Woodstock Festival in the summer of love. In 1969, men walked on the moon.

It is impossible to contemplate Leigh's emergence and work in a limbo, separate from, or uninformed by, these happenings. The 'happening' itself became a random artistic collision between the visual arts and the drop-out, hippie phenomenon. Leigh never had anything to do with all that, but his work was in some pure sense a democratic response to what was going on around him. In addition, his antennae were finely tuned to traditional grievances like the generation gap, the stand-off between the sexes (sexual intercourse was not invented until 1963, according to

Philip Larkin) and the class war. He absorbed the consequences of global upheavals while considering the intimacies of bedroom, bathroom and sitting room stasis. When he came to London, one of the first films he saw was *Shadows* (1959), an 'improvised' film by John Cassavetes in which an unknown cast was observed living, loving and bickering on the streets of New York. For the first time, he felt it might be possible to create complete plays from scratch with a group of actors.

Leigh needed a lot of convincing, however, and he used his time creatively in the 1960s discovering how best to proceed by eliminating the obvious alternatives. In the first five years of the decade he not only studied at RADA, but worked as an assistant stage manager in repertory, acted in films and on television, took a foundation-year course at Camberwell Art School while attending evening classes at the London School of Film Technique (now the London International Film School), where Arnold Wesker had also been a student, and spent a year in the theatre design department of the Central School of Art and Design. In 1965 he formed a company, Dramagraph, with the actor/playwright David Halliwell, and directed and designed the first production of Halliwell's *Little Malcolm and his Struggle Against the Eunuchs* at the Unity Theatre in King's Cross, London.

Halliwell, a blunt, bearded fellow from Brighouse in Yorkshire, had arrived at RADA the year before Leigh. He was seven years older, having completed both his secondary education and a spell at Huddersfield College of Art. He knew of Leigh first as 'the boy who plays the boy', on account of Leigh's appearance in a production of Pirandello's *Six Characters in Search of an Author* which also featured Sarah Miles in the cast. He met him at a party soon afterwards and found 'this cheeky little man' who immediately and spiritedly engaged him in a slanging match. Each responded to the other's forthright, sarcastic mode of address.

Leigh was as much of a square peg in the round hole of RADA as was Halliwell. RADA had not yet adapted to the new liberated sixties mood, although the Royal Court revolution had changed the 'voice' and concerns of the modern actor, and Karel Reisz's classic slice of Nottingham life, *Saturday Night and Sunday Morning*

(1960), starring Leigh's Salford example Albert Finney, was the talk of the town. Leigh felt that John Fernald, the principal, had his heart in the right place ('he was interested in Brecht'), but 'most of what we got was a load of old nonsense, really.' The mime course was run by a lady who wore a hat. Peter Barkworth's acting technique classes instructed students in how to 'think, move, speak', in that order, as a solution to all challenges on stage. And while Leigh himself was floundering towards some sense of verisimilitude, he found himself being taught how to 'laugh, cry and snog' for weekly rep purposes, and how to handle a matchbox. Matchbox-wise, students learned how to detach a match by pre-setting it; Leigh was more interested in examining how you might extract a match in a real and convincing way, not as a suave trick of business.

Two aspects of his training did make an impression, however. He became fascinated by some exercises with the director James Roose-Evans, who employed a method derived from a visit to Lee Strasberg's Actors Studio in New York. This was to do with expressing the inexpressible through the movement, and touching, of hands (Leigh has subsequently used this technique to allow actors to progress beyond the parameters of naturalistic improvisations). And he was touched, too, by one particular improvisation conducted by Peter Barkworth in which two talented students – Sheila Gish and Ian McShane – were separately briefed with incompatible information and then thrown together. It remains a fundamental rule in Leigh's way of working that each actor in any improvisation, or rehearsal, knows only as much about any other character as his or her own character would know at that point in the story. In other words, the films and plays are developed in such a way that the actors (and indeed the director) do not know what will happen until they have explored and discussed the possibilities in the situation where Leigh has placed the characters.

Otherwise, Leigh responded negatively to RADA's agenda. He became a sullen and disruptive student, his reports were bad (Fernald sent him a 'buck-up' letter at the end of his fourth term, deploring his 'impertinent attitude'), he was threatened with the withdrawal of his scholarship and, although he completed the course, he was denied his diploma. Fernald later relented and sent him one in the post when Leigh subsequently needed it to explain his academic position before joining the foundation year at Camberwell Art School.

James Roose-Evans had directed Harold Pinter's *The Dumb Waiter* (on a double-bill with *The Room*, directed by the author) at the Hampstead Theatre Club, which he ran, in early 1960. A few months later, Pinter's *The Caretaker* opened at the Arts Theatre and soon transferred to the Duchess. Leigh was mesmerised by the play and that production ('It just seemed so *real*'), and directed it himself at RADA in his second year, with a student cast including Richard Kane (who appeared in *Who's Who*), Roger Hammond (who also appeared, very briefly, in the same film) and Terence (now Terry) Taplin, who later joined the RSC. The experience had a profound effect on Leigh, and he has been a devotee of Pinter ever since.

Over the next few years, Leigh would supplement his discovery of Pinter with that of Beckett, whose novels he read avidly; he shared this enthusiasm for Beckett's novels with David Halliwell and, much later on, David Thewlis. Another big influence on Leigh was the surreal writing of Flann O'Brien, who, like Beckett and Pinter, seemed to express a kind of tragi-comedy that Leigh found particularly appealing. In *Nuts in May*, Keith Pratt says, 'Oh, we went to a quarry today. There was a man chipping away at a wall.' Leigh says the line is his, and it's also a Beckettian concept. The quarry scene in that film obviously has Beckettian overtones, as does the extraordinary sight of the skinhead Coxy rolling around in his barrel in *Meantime*. (Leigh says that, during a Beckett season at the Royal Court many years later, in the mid-1970s, he once stood in the gents and peed next to Beckett, but lost all courage to say anything.) And it is an important clue to the nature and texture of Leigh's work to realise that, alongside this modernist influence, he has always relished the visual worlds of George Grosz, Picasso and Hogarth. Dickens is obviously a crucial point of comparison and, perhaps more surprisingly, he greatly admires the novels of E.M. Forster, 'because he deals with his characters both passionately and dispassionately; the character is always at the centre, but there's always a high degree of objectivity, too.'

His very first employer after RADA was Carmen Silvera (renowned for her performance in BBC TV's World War Two sitcom series *Allo, Allo*), who hired him as an assistant stage manager at the Leatherhead Rep. On a fit-up for a revival of *The Amorous Prawn*, someone on the stage asked Leigh to catch a plug, he looked down from the flies, and took it right in the eye. He fetched up in University College Hospital eye annexe and therefore failed to fulfil the second half of his job description, 'ASM and parts'. He did not very much mind missing the pantomime, and was already determined anyway to be a director. His role in the final-year show at RADA had been the clown Costard in *Love's Labour's Lost*, and the agent James Sharkey (then working for Al Parker), who told Leigh he had 'a marvellous face', despatched him to Shepperton Studios (after Leatherhead) to see about the leading role in a film called *Two Left Feet*, a title which might have been construed as an insult to counteract the facial compliment. The part, as it happened, turned out to be small, one of three teddy boys who appear endlessly but do little. Nonetheless, Leigh attended the whole shoot at Shepperton – the film was directed by Roy Ward Baker and starred Nyree Dawn Porter, Julia Foster, Michael Crawford and David Hemmings – whether he was called or not, watching and learning. He loved every minute.

He was recruited for another small film part in *West Eleven*, directed by Michael Winner, starring Alfred Lynch, Diana Dors and Eric Portman. Winner wanted to be reminded of 'that thing' in which he had seen Leigh at RADA. '*Six Characters*,' said Leigh. 'Of course it was,' burbled Winner, '*Six Characters in Search of an Author*. Pinero! Pinero! It's not often I remember the name of a playwright!' Leigh was cast as a student who had to be filmed eating, and a tray of doughnuts was duly provided. Leigh quietly demurred, saying that he did not have a sweet tooth. 'They said, "How about bacon and eggs?" and I said, "Fine." Winner was showing off all over the place while they were lining up the shot, and a props man came by announcing "One bacon and eggs!"

Winner yelped, "Oh, bacon and eggs!" and took the lot and wolfed them down. The props man said, "That's all very well, but what are we going to give *him*?" And Winner shouted, "Doughnuts, give him the doughnuts." So I had to spend several days sitting there eating the fucking doughnuts.' He looked slightly dejected, too, as a young deaf-mute in an episode of *Maigret*, the successful BBC TV series of the early 1960s, interrogated by the pipe-smoking tec of Rupert Davies. At the end, Leigh, clean-shaven and confused, is shown the door. A comment there, you feel, on his acting career.

Domestically, he became a north Londoner, living with friends in Euston, Gospel Oak and in Parkway, Camden Town. Some time in 1962, Leigh moved, aberrantly, south of the river to a flat on the Old Kent Road, where he struck up an important friendship with Paul Rowley, a student at Camberwell School of Art. Leigh met Rowley through one of his Manchester friends, David 'Crock' (as in Davy Crockett) Plagerson, who had begun studying at Camberwell (today he makes and sells attractive model Noah's Arks). Encouraged by Rowley and Plagerson, Leigh embarked on the foundation-year course at Camberwell in 1963, drawing and painting with energy and flexibility. His portfolio is particularly impressive in the life-class department.

And it was in the life class that Leigh suddenly realised where his future as an artist lay. As a drama student, the process of learning somehow had been one of regurgitation. The students never went out on the street to work, let alone to look. And yet, surely this was the whole point of one's work in drawing or theatre or movies? The material was all around – as obvious and evident as the nude body of the model whom he was drawing – and it was the artist's duty to get out there and experience it, and then absorb it into the creative process. That blinding, obvious revelation has informed Leigh's entire outlook ever since.

He enrolled on the night course at the London School of Film Technique in Charlotte Street for £36, and the place became his second home. By night, he attended the film school while Rowley took an evening job as an usher at the Aldwych Theatre. Leigh was a beneficiary of the system whereby the Aldwych ushers smuggled their friends in to see shows, sitting on the stairs or in vacant seats at the back of the stalls. 'I think I saw Beckett's *Endgame* fourteen times. It was fantastic. And I went to the first ever first night of Peter Daubeny's World Theatre Seasons, a stilted production of Molière's *Tartuffe* performed by the Comédie Française.' This was the first time the simultaneous translation system had been tried out, and the audience tuned in to it on little grey contraptions that resembled hand-held parking meters: 'The radio wavelengths had not been negotiated properly, so that the ponderous Anglicisations of a not very funny performance were interrupted every five minutes by radio cab signals – "Anyone free for Charing Cross?"; "There's a customer at Muswell Hill roundabout" – which of course created waves of laughter in the audience and utter confusion on the stage. The actors could not understand why they were going down so well when what they were doing was so deadly.' But Leigh treasured this exposure to European theatre, and was just as impressed by the RSC work of Peter Brook: *King Lear* with Paul Scofield (Beckettian, bleak, savage and nihilistic) and his stunning production of Peter Weiss's *Marat/Sade* which had arisen out of Brook's Theatre of Cruelty experiments at LAMDA, all of which Leigh saw, inspired by the visionary French director Antonin Artaud. Leigh saw *Marat/Sade* in 1965 with David Canter, who looked at the actors playing paranoid schizophrenics sitting around the walls (the death of Marat was 'performed' by the inmates of an asylum) and said: 'They've got those people dead right. That's what they do, sit very still.' Leigh knew that this production had been developed through improvisations – he saw a television documentary on it which demonstrated how the actors had based their characteris-ations on people they had visited in a mental hospital – and he wondered why such work could not be channelled into creating an original piece rather than interpreting a received text. In other words, why not go further with the process?

Leigh moved with Rowley into rooms in Tottenham Street, just around the corner from the film school. One remarkable con-temporary there was Biltin Toker, a rich Turkish student who had graduated as an architect in Oxford with another friend of

Leigh's, Richard Rambaut (who had studied architecture and film and later became an art director in films, including Leigh's *Bleak Moments*; he died of a heart attack, aged thirty-six, in 1974). Toker had founded, and funded, *meanwhile*, a magazine printed on triangular, folded paper which you read upside down. He also inaugurated a series of talks and invited whichever celebrity was in town to come and address the students, take questions, and receive a diploma. Toker's powers of persuasion were legendary, and Leigh therefore met and listened to Alfred Hitchcock, Jean Renoir, Fritz Lang, John Huston, Richard Brooks, François Truffaut, Alexander Mackendrick, Dmitri Tiomkin, Jean Simmons and many others. This period of apprenticeship was completed, after a year at Camberwell, with a year at the Central School of Art and Design, which Leigh found disappointing because of having to design plays to no particular brief, though his costume drawings for a putative production of *Richard III* look much more than promising.

During this year, 1964, Leigh teamed up again with Halliwell, who had been trying to write a play for Peter Cheeseman, director of the in-the-round repertory theatre at Stoke-on Trent, while employed there as an actor and resident dramatist. Halliwell, always touchy and argumentative, had fallen out with Cheeseman and been fired. Leigh, who said he would direct the play if it was ever finished, and formed a company called Dramagraph with Halliwell in order to do so, embarked on a campaign of encouragement so as to squeeze it out of his temperamental friend, who was living in a flat in Islington with his two RADA contemporaries Philip Martin and Richard Wright (now Richard Kane), whom the landlady always called 'Mr White'; in fact, says Halliwell, she called all three of them 'Mr White'. Halliwell's first choice of title was 'One Long Wank', but it was decided something less obvious and self-descriptive might be in order, as well as something newspapers would be prepared to print, so *Little Malcolm and his Struggle Against the Eunuchs*, long-winded but memorable, was preferred.

The play itself was inordinately long, too (the initial running time was over four hours), and was rejected as 'unperformable' by James Roose-Evans at the Hampstead Theatre Club. Halliwell and Leigh hired the Unity Theatre for a fortnight in the freezing cold March of 1965. Leigh says that Halliwell, who played the leading role while zealously guarding every word of his text, was impossible to direct; Halliwell says that Leigh directed the play very badly; and Philip Martin, also in the cast, fell out irreconcilably with his flatmate and author. Another actor contracted appendicitis during rehearsals and had to be replaced (by Michael Cadman). They had trouble casting the girl because Northern working-class actresses were put off by the obscenity. The actress finally cast, the only one they could find, was an upper-class girl who was, according to Halliwell, completely wrong: 'She was very tall, taller than me and Philip and, needless to say, the director. She was called Julian Burberry. Her father had dreamt of having a boy but got a girl and called her "Julian" anyway. We tried to persuade her to drop the "n" and make life easier for herself, but she wouldn't, and one of the reviewers referred to her as "Julian Burberry (a girl)" so she couldn't be mistaken for a bloke in drag. But a bloke in drag would probably have been a better idea. I'm not attacking Julian Burberry as an actress. But she was huge. And she wasn't right. So she was very unhappy, too.'

Although audiences were poor and the production doomed, the show was a watershed. It convinced Leigh that he should really only direct his own work. But the play has a rawness, rebelliousness and crude vitality that later became characteristics of Leigh's own stuff. Malcolm Scrawdyke is clearly a precursor of Johnny in *Naked*. And the action, performed in a series of vengeful fantasies about conspiracy, rejection, sexual timidity (and violence) and peer group pressure, surely reflected elements of the perpetrators' own existence, especially Halliwell's. Scrawdyke (in America, the play was retitled *Hail, Scrawdyke!*) was a loutish art student and absurd ideologue from Huddersfield who had trouble with girls and a hatred for his teachers. Jeremy Kingston, writing a perceptive and encouraging notice in *Punch*, noted that the play shared a deeply felt schoolboy coarseness with Alfred Jarry's *Ubu Roi* (1896), a piece originally written as a vicious attack on a loathed mathematics master. There was also a rave review by Alan Brien in the *Sunday Telegraph*, and these cuttings were promptly despatched to the producer Michael Codron.

Codron telephoned, but the Islington landlady, who was deaf, never passed on his message to any of the three 'Mr Whites'. Luckily, Codron then sent a telegram and invited Halliwell to his office in Regent Street for tea. A special performance was arranged for him on the set of another production (a comedy starring Harry H. Corbett, *Travelling Light*, in the Prince of Wales). The producer told Halliwell that *Little Malcolm* was the best first play he had ever seen, that Halliwell himself should not appear in the leading role, that the new director, David Calderisi (Leigh had had enough), should not be entrusted with the professional presentation, and that he intensely disliked Leigh's model of the proposed new design (Halliwell had begged Leigh to provide one, and the reluctant Leigh had badly injured his left thumb in the process; he still bears the scars to prove it): 'That's one career we must nip in the bud,' Codron is reported to have said. Leigh was getting the thumbs down all round.

Codron presented *Little Malcolm*, directed by Patrick Dromgoole and starring John Hurt, at the 1965 Dublin Theatre Festival, in the Gaiety, and then at the Garrick Theatre in London. Good reviews were no insurance against poor houses, and the theatre owners instructed Codron to withdraw the play after a fortnight. I saw the last Saturday matinée of an electrifying, unprecedented sort of modern play, something I identified with, and was horrified by, as a student on the brink of university. I suppose it was my *Look Back in Anger*. John Hurt's Malcolm Scrawdyke shares the same plinth in my pantheon as David Warner's disaffected Hamlet, directed by Peter Hall for the RSC in the same year. By the time the play came off, everyone, including the Beatles and Laurence Olivier, was rushing to catch it. Halliwell's name was made, although he has never fully consolidated that early reputation, despite having written some good plays since. In the early 1970s he ran a lively fringe outfit, Quipu, with David Calderisi, and developed for a time a quirky, and I always thought over-obvious, theory of 'multi-viewpoint drama'. Leigh remains a loyal and supportive friend, and they keep in regular touch.

The whole *Little Malcolm* experience was formative, but negative. Leigh was left feeling that he couldn't direct, though he knew deep down that he could. He took solace in the wisdom of Peter Brook, who said that each new task of directing was like starting out blind on an unknown journey. This idea gnawed away over the next few months. Leigh's London base by the middle of this maelstrom decade – after his sojourns in Camden, the Old Kent Road and Tottenham Street – was Richard Rambaut's house in Wyndham Street, Marylebone. Harold Wilson's Labour Party was in power, Winston Churchill died, and Leigh's girlfriend at the time was Sandra Haill, whose sister, Lynn, is currently the publications and programmes editor at the Royal National Theatre.

Colin Cina – already married, enjoying his first flush of success as a painter and living in Primrose Gardens, Hampstead – remembers this time as one of hectic book buying (and selling, when the money ran out), the acquisition of 16mm movie cameras, and a constant stream of friends of both sexes. 'I've never been able to talk as freely about work as I could with Mike. We were entirely supportive of each other. The critical debates about what we were doing came a few years later, when everything became more focused for everybody. We were unburdened with theory in those pre-Derrida days; there was no idea that you had to grasp a whole lot of philosophical and psychoanalytical concepts in order to be an artist, which is a big problem for kids today. There hadn't been feminism, but there was a sense of egalitarianism and we certainly saw ourselves as opposed to the right. Our heroes included Brecht and George Grosz, but it was all jumbled up in a sense of fun and cartoon.' The summer of 1965 marked the end of Leigh's first phase in London.

Between 1965 and 1970, Leigh's activity was both hectic and wildly various. He produced (as we shall see) nine plays of his own, and wrote the only full script he ever completed before a rehearsal process, *Waste-Paper Guards*, directed in Birmingham by Les Blair, who also acted in the cast of three. David Canter considers this play, in its depiction of someone performing a really useless task, that of keeping an eye on discarded waste paper rubbish, a premonition of the comic banality of the security guard in *Naked*, employed in unoccupied and unfurnished offices (the bareness is another application of the title). Leigh wrote *Waste-Paper Guards* for Halliwell's Quipu, but Halliwell refused to produce it and the text is now lost, though Blair says that most of the waste paper comprised letters from the Lord Chamberlain – the official censor, who was not done away with until 1968 – indicating which words could not be used in public performance. Each sheet was headed with the legend '*Honi soit qui mal y pense.*'

Before *Little Malcolm*, Leigh had been approached by the television journalist Richard Lindley, who was a friend of a neighbour, about appearing on a religious programme, *Sunday Break*, as 'a typical, articulate young person' talking about sin. Soon afterwards, Lindley (later a familiar face on various current affairs programmes, including *Panorama*) was involved in another series of *Sunday Break* in Birmingham, and invited Leigh to appear as an interviewer. The programme was recorded at the new Midlands Arts Centre for Young People in Cannon Hill, and Leigh interviewed the director John English. Once *Little Malcolm* was over, he wrote to English, was invited to Birmingham and given *carte blanche* as a resident assistant director.

Leigh had applied for the ITV television directors' scheme, which awarded young directors attachments to regional theatres. Although at his interview he expressed a desire to direct Beckett's *Endgame* – a choice of text he remembers the judging panel found incomprehensible – he had been placed on the shortlist of six when John English invited him to the Midlands Arts Centre. He took the job and renounced the possibility of the ITV award. At the Arts Centre he directed *Endgame*, a play he loved, and the only play, he soon realised, he really wanted to direct. After the disaster of *Little Malcolm*, it was important to prove to himself that he *could* direct a play.

This was an important break for Leigh, but he found the Arts Centre pretentious and stuffy. The place was officially opened by Princess Margaret while he was there, and Leigh was instructed by John English to be in a room 'improvising' with some kids while she went around, so that she could see the sort of thing that was going on. Leigh, who was by this time completely serious about his improvisatory work, refused point plank to cooperate in this PR exercise, much to John English's irritation.

Leigh had started improvising *The Box Play* in the evenings with a group of teenagers and some young adults, one of whom was Les Blair, recruited to the company to play a father figure at the ripe old age of twenty-five. Since Salford Grammar, Blair had graduated from Liverpool University with a poor degree in economics and done a series of odd jobs, including driving a van for a company called Perry's Peeled Potatoes. He joined Leigh in Birmingham and took a job writing copy for an advertising agency. They found a flat near the Arts Centre which Blair says had more light fittings than any place he has ever known; when they left, the owner billed them for all the light bulbs they had blown.

The Box Play was a family scenario staged in a cage-like box, a structure suggested to Leigh by a small house his sister Ruth had bought on the eve of her marriage. Leigh dictated to each actor what his or her part should be, and improvisations proceeded from there; the difference in the finally evolved Leigh technique was, and is, that he discusses with each actor a list of people they know, or have known, and selects from that discussion the real person who then forms the basis of the fictional character they work on during the rehearsal and writing period. Paul Clements, a colleague of Leigh's during this period in Birmingham, recalls in *The Improvised Play*, his admirable 1983 handbook, that *The Box Play* was a very funny absurdist cartoon, at a time when 'dotty families who lived in boxes seemed in no way unusual'. Leigh has never since worked in any abstract, formalist style; this piece was influenced not just by the absurdist drama of Ionesco and N.F. Simpson, but perhaps more directly by the work of his own artist friend Colin Cina. 'The play represented a completed congruence between our work,' recalls Cina. 'In creating this transparent box, Mike absorbed all sorts of contemporary ideas in art such as the space frames (which contained objects) of Roland

Pichet and the confined environments of Francis Bacon's screaming popes. He was attempting to translate all that back into the
social-realist Brechtian theatre of pre-war Germany; in the play,
the teenagers lived out their experiences of adolescence by creating
this symbolised reality. It was visually very exciting and cleverly
lit.' Cina is convinced that, after *Little Malcolm*, *The Box Play*
was cathartic for Leigh and proved to him that he could instigate
something 'really interesting'.

He quickly followed up with two more 'improvised' pieces
with the youngsters in the Midlands Arts Centre. *My Parents Have
Gone to Carlisle* was a kind of early inversion of *Abigail's Party*
from the offstage and unseen Abigail's (Jane's, in this play) party-
throwing point of view, decked out with fantasies. Soliloquies
were a feature of all these early improvised plays, a theatrical
device renounced by Leigh as his work, paradoxically, became
more convincingly theatrical. The third Cannon Hill play was *The
Last Crusade of the Five Little Nuns*, subtitled 'a facetious absurdity
in two acts', in which five comic nuns loaded a rowing boat in
the first act and fell in with a monkey and an old man on a desert
island in the second.

The month of July 1966 began with the anti-Vietnam War dem-
onstration in Grosvenor Square and ended with England beating
Germany 4–2 in the final of the football World Cup at Wembley.
The nation sat glued to its radios and television screens while
Geoff Hurst scored a famous hat-trick, Bobby Moore at last lifted
the golden Jules Rimet trophy and Bobby Charlton cried openly
and unashamedly on the shoulders of his team-mates. Leigh and
Colin Cina, however, were incarcerated in the latter's new Renault
4 – 'I was terribly proud of it because I'd bought it from sales of
my paintings' – en route to Bristol. Cina had been invited to
prepare a one-man show for the Arnolfini Gallery, and Leigh had
volunteered to check out the premises with him. 'We stopped
halfway for a sandwich in a pub and looked in a Rediffusion
shop window opposite Wells Cathedral where we noticed all the
pre-match ballyhoo going on. We weren't really interested. And
of course when we got to Bristol, the Arnolfini was all shut up;
they'd all gone off to watch the bloody football! So we stared at

Leigh's paternal grandfather Mayer Liebermann (right), in Mogilev, near Moscow, c.1900, before emigrating to England.

LEFT: Abe and Phyllis Leigh at their wedding reception in the Grand Hotel, Manchester, in August 1941.

BELOW: Abe and Phyllis with young Michael, aged twenty months, in Salford.

LEFT: Michael, aged six, pretending to be a statue – or directing traffic? – at Blackpool, on holiday in 1949.

BELOW: Family group drawn by Leigh in 1955, showing the influence of Ronald Searle.

BELOW: Michael aged eleven, nearest camera, at North Grecian Street County Primary School, Salford, in 1954. The murals of a train and footprints on Everest are Leigh's own work.

Family group in 1956:
Abe and Phyllis,
flanked by Ruth and
Michael, behind two
grandmothers, Annie
Cousin (left) and Leah
Liebermann.

Leigh borne aloft by his Habonim friends on a portable
lavatory, Wirral peninsula, 1959.

Leigh as Costard the clown in *Love's Labour's Lost* at RADA, 1962, with fellow students (from left) Terence Taplin, George Layton and John Davies.

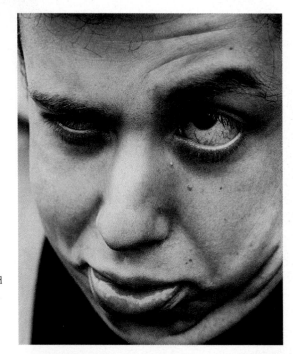

OPPOSITE AND RIGHT: Two pictures taken around the time Leigh left RADA in 1962. The one opposite was used as his *Spotlight* photograph.

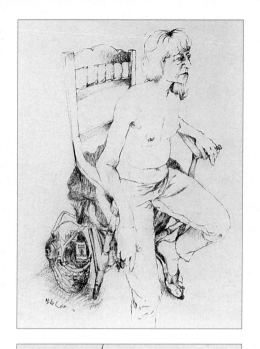

ABOVE: The future film director in Birmingham in 1966, en route to the Royal Shakespeare Company and a decisive move back to London.

OPPOSITE: From Leigh's sketchbook: in the Camberwell School of Art life-drawing class in 1964, where he glimpsed his creative destiny in observation, not regurgitation . . .
. . . and in the theatre design department of the Central School of Art and Design in 1965.

ABOVE: Anne Raitt as the repressed and lonely Sylvia in the film of *Bleak Moments* (1971).

RIGHT: Leigh's original poster design for the stage play *Bleak Moments* in 1970, showing its working title and the names of two actors, George Coulouris and Derrick O'Connor, who did not figure in the eventual production.

the place for a few minutes, then drove back to London, chatting away non-stop.'

After the Birmingham interlude, Leigh finally decided to 'stop buggering around' and managed to find a flat of his own in Cranleigh Street, Euston, on a corner with Eversholt Street, where he lived for the next ten years, hatching there his crucial assault on the British theatre and cinema as a writer/director, as well as wooing his future wife, Alison Steadman.

In the autumn of 1966, Leigh took his last acting job with Peter Cheeseman's company at Stoke-on-Trent, playing Fabian in *Twelfth Night*, the anonymous and unrewarding foil to Sir Toby Belch and Andrew Aguecheek in the gulling of Malvolio. The cast also included Anne Raitt (soon to grace the stage and film versions of *Bleak Moments*), Ron Daniels, later a director with the RSC and, in Leigh's view, 'undoubtedly the unfunniest Malvolio ever seen in the history of the British theatre', and Ken Campbell as Valentine, whose rasping one-line account of Olivia's mourning state ('And watered all her chamber round with eye-offending brine') he counts the most memorable Shakespearean delivery of his fast-fading youth. Leigh also co-directed a schools production of *Julius Caesar*, playing the title role so he could get off the stage quickly and direct the rest of the action.

The playwright and novelist Shane Connaughton, himself starting out as an actor at Stoke a couple of seasons after Leigh, suggests that both Cheeseman and Ken Campbell, like Leigh, preferred rigour and discipline, however much those qualities might masquerade as anarchy and theatrical lunacy. Cheeseman, he says, always started work each morning with a 'limbering up' session, and ran his theatre in a primitive, Methodist style; and Campbell, who went on to run his Road Show (with Bob Hoskins and Sylvester McCoy), to write his own plays and finally to emerge in the 1990s as a solo performer *sans pareil*, was a complete original with a strict way of working – he would not, for instance, allow the actors to mime properties in rehearsal. Connaughton, who eventually worked as an actor with Leigh in *Four Days in July*, sees much of both Cheeseman and Campbell in Leigh: 'I always think that Ken is a serious person pretending to be mad;

that Mike is a mad person pretending to be serious; and that Cheeseman is a serious person *being* serious!'

Towards the end of the year, Leigh auditioned for the last time as an actor. His target was Gillian Diamond, casting director of the RSC. She was not impressed. But within a few weeks he was coincidentally offered a post as an assistant director with the company. He was browsing soon afterwards in the Aldwych files when he came across his own card, written by Diamond: 'Very wooden. Does not really think what he is saying when acting. Really wants to direct. Told him that's what he should do.' And what he did. 1967 was Peter Hall's last year in charge of the company he had founded, and Leigh's recruitment was unexpected because he did not have a degree, though he had written to Hall earlier, and had initiated a friendly relationship with David Jones, one of Hall's most trusted associates, a civilised and crucial influence on the company over many years.

At Stratford-upon-Avon, Leigh assisted Peter Hall on a disastrous *Macbeth* (Paul Scofield and Vivien Merchant), John Barton on his exciting *Coriolanus* (Ian Richardson in a blond wig), and Trevor Nunn on a knockabout *The Taming of the Shrew* which featured Janet Suzman and Michael Williams as Katherina and Petruchio, with the late Roy Kinnear, Frances de la Tour and Patrick Stewart in memorable support; one of the huntsmen was played by Ben Kingsley, whom Leigh now met for the first time. At Nunn's insistence, Leigh took charge of the improvisatory rehearsals to establish the 'play-within-a-play' set-up. He also took understudy rehearsals. And he persuaded the powers that be to allow him to work with some of the under-employed actors on an improvised play to be staged in the old conference hall, now the Swan Theatre.

The play was *NENAA*, an acronym for North East New Arts Association, which explored the fantasies of a Tynesider called Gerald (played by Gerald McNally), working in an Italian café in King's Cross with ideas of founding an arts association back home. His daydreams are counterpointed with those of the café's regular customers. The chief liberation for Leigh, at last working on an improvised play with professional actors (after the Birmingham

74

amateurs), was the realisation that 'if an improvised play was really to be a totally organic entity, genuinely evolved from characters and relationships, then I had been wrong in starting rehearsals on these by stating plot or theme, and then "filling it in".' This admission was made in his fascinating document submitted to the George Devine Award committee of 1970 (he won the George Devine Award, but not on this occasion – three years later). He continued: 'I saw that we must start off with a collection of totally unrelated characters (each one the specific creation of its actor), and then go through a process in which I must cause them to meet each other, and build a network of real relationships; the play would be drawn from the results.'

Elsewhere in his RSC year, Leigh counted his experience, though negative, invaluable. He learned how not to do things and he was entrusted with a production of Ann Jellicoe's *The Knack* for the touring Theatregoround wing of the company run by Terry Hands. Leigh's cast comprised Lynn Farleigh, John Shrapnel, Peter Geddes and Derrick O'Connor. Just before the opening at a school in Leamington Spa, the RSC associate director John Barton turned up for a run-through and ordered a postponement. He suggested canvassing the actors, and all but one of them agreed to cancel. The show was then re-rehearsed with Hands and Trevor Nunn chipping in.

'The whole thing was excruciating and humiliating because of course I had to sit there all the time for technical reasons. There was nothing wrong with my production, which was downbeat, and dry. John Barton had an idea of what a comedy should be like that did not correspond to the work I had done. So this was the nail in the coffin, the final straw.' Leigh's contract was terminated, along with the idea that he might take over Theatregoround. The senior directors all knew he really wanted to do his own thing, and David Jones took him for lunch in the Dirty Duck and suggested he apply for the television directors' course at the BBC. He did, and was subsequently turned down three times.

Terry Hands now admits that the RSC failed to spot 'this new Ben Jonson' in the making: 'It is true that nobody really trusted Mike to run Theatregoround. Trevor [Nunn] and I didn't have the vision to see that Mike should have been given a corner to do his thing on his own terms. In our defence, there was a strain of charlatanism in the RSC at that time centred around people like Michael Kustow and Charles Marowitz. Young directors were not yet fashionable, and Trevor and I had decided to build a directors' theatre in which we would take wild, strange personality actors and give them technique. Hence the casting, for instance, of a neurotic, Alan Howard, as Henry V. Mike suffered because we could not at first tell whether or not he would be another Kustow.' But, to their credit, the RSC never fully gave up on him: they knew there was *something* special going on, and Leigh would return in the next decade to work there twice, once very successfully, on *Babies Grow Old* (1974) in Stratford, and a second time, with no luck at all, on the aborted Aldwych Theatre project in late 1978. Not least among the pluses of his first stint in Stratford was the friendship he forged with another young assistant director, Buzz Goodbody.

But for the moment, kicking the Stratford dust from his heels, Leigh directed a couple of London drama school productions, a *Romeo and Juliet* (with Sharon Duce) at Webber Douglas, and Thomas Dekker's *The Honest Whore* at E15 Acting School. At the latter venue, sometimes mistakenly associated with Joan Littlewood's old Theatre Royal, Stratford, but in fact situated in Loughton, east London, he also filled a gap in the schedule with an improvised play, *Individual Fruit Pies*, whose cast included Gwen Taylor, Sarah Stephenson (later in *Bleak Moments*) and Robert Putt, the stroppy chauffeur in that delightful little scene in *Naked* where Johnny gets into a parked car, which is presumably waiting for some similar-looking media lout or pop singer whom the chauffeur has never met before, and is summarily ejected when his false claims on cars and chauffeurdom are quickly exposed. As in *NENAA*, there were strong fantasy elements in a realistic setting of seven characters in a London rooming house over a period of five winter Sundays. Dreams and squabbles climax in the fight over a baby and the death of a bedridden old woman.

Even more significantly, Leigh met Alison Steadman for the first time. Alison was in the year behind Gwen Taylor and Robert

Putt, and not involved in the play. But she recalls the buzz of excitement over Leigh's working methods that spread through the school: 'I was having a chat with him in the bar and I was called away to rehearsal, and I can remember him saying we must carry on this conversation. I didn't want to let it go. The improvisations we were doing at the school were like what you see on *Whose Line is it Anyway?*, where you felt impelled to be funny, rather than encouraged to investigate characters and emotions. Talking with Mike made more sense.'

Another fortuitous coincidence drew the couple a little closer together: Colin Cina came to the first night of *Individual Fruit Pies* with his wife, Gill. When they turned up at the school, Mike was temporarily tied up in an appointment and Alison instantly recognised Gill as one of the prefects, a bit older than herself, at her old school in Liverpool, Childwall Valley High. (Gill was obviously a natural authority figure; she is now a magistrate in the courts at Horseferry Road, Victoria.) But Mike was approaching a crisis point in his career, and his personal life was virtually on hold. He devised a short tragi-comedy for the Royal Court's Theatre Upstairs, *Down Here and Up There*, which dealt with the lack of faith of a divinity teacher, his mounting problems and suicidal depressions. The cast included Gerald McNally as a 'Gerald' similar to that in *NENAA*, and Gwen Taylor and Robert Putt.

'The conflict for me during this whole period was brought about by my lingering conviction that I should take time out, sit down, and write something. I went through one of my wobbly patches, of which there have been several. It was now (in 1968) eight years since I had left Manchester and I had a strong urge to return. Subsequently, I realised I had really wanted to go and stay with my parents for a while. There was something I wanted to plug back into, but I couldn't discover what it was until many years later, after my father died (in 1985) and I had spent a little time in therapy. The possibility of staying at home was never discussed at this stage. I sub-let my flat in London and took a very cheap place in Levenshulme [a suburb to the south-east of Manchester city centre] and resolved to find a way of surviving.'

He stumbled across a part-time lectureship in a Catholic women teachers' training college, Sedgley Park, which ran a joint drama course with the all-boy De la Salle College at Middleton. Between the autumn of 1968 and the summer of 1969, Leigh devised and directed *Epilogue* with this drama course, and also two big-cast projects with the Manchester Youth Theatre, whose director, Geoffrey Sykes, had responded to Leigh's getting in touch with him. He also wrote a play called *Monsters* (whose cast list included a character called Candice-Marie, unforgettably resurrected in another guise by Alison Steadman in *Nuts in May*) which he threw away.

Epilogue reiterated some themes of loss of faith and caused a bit of a rumpus, as it focused on a priest with doubts, in an institution of Catholic education; it also prefigured some episodes in *Hard Labour*, notably the scene in the confessional at the end of the film where Mrs Thornley 'confesses' that she does not love her husband. The performance took place in the new studio theatre at Sedgley Park, now a police training college, in Prestwich. In *Big Basil*, the first of the Manchester Youth Theatre plays, the central character is a small, misanthropic fifth-former who gradually accepts that the world is tolerable if you are philosophical. The cast of thirty-four characters included a schoolmaster played ('brilliantly', says Leigh) by the future RSC and opera director Steven Pimlott – 'We used to quiz each other on Gilbert and Sullivan' – the actress Julie North, and the theatrical administrator Robert Cogo-Fawcett. The second Youth Theatre production, with another huge cast, was *Glum Victoria and the Lad with Specs* – yet another exercise in alienation and not feeling wanted that somehow reflected Mike Leigh's own cumulative sense of professional frustration, even as he discovered the way in which he preferred to work.

He knew he wanted to make films. But he knew he could only work, for the moment, in the theatre. In the spring of 1969, he drafted the policy statement of 'The Working Theatre Company', an informal alliance of personnel including Buzz Goodbody, Gerald McNally and the playwright Mike Stott. Their aim was to found and run a small community theatre with a permanent professional company in any town or city which wanted them.

Talks were held in Rochdale, Durham, Burnley, York and Leeds – none of which then had a professional repertory theatre – but nothing transpired. When the directorship of the Hull Arts Theatre, newly founded in Spring Street by Alan Plater (the home, these days, of John Godber's Hull Truck), came up, Leigh and co. put in a joint application which was confidently spurned. The collective collapsed. Returning to London from Manchester, Leigh would renew his now obsessive quest to put on improvised plays and make films.

In late 1969, he was approached by three black ex-RSC actors – Louis Mahoney, Alton Kumalo and Oscar James – about running an actors' workshop in a basement in Westbourne Grove. He joined them. One of the other regulars was Joolia Cappleman, a gifted character actress with whom Leigh formed a long-lasting personal and professional relationship (*Bleak Moments*, *Dick Whittington and his Cat*, *Who's Who*). One day, Kumalo brought along the Bermudian actor Earl Cameron. Six months later, after Leigh's first major London production, *Bleak Moments*, had opened at the Open Space, Cameron approached Leigh and offered him a one-off directing job in Bermuda. He was looking for a director to replace Robin Midgley, who had been sacked from a production of *Othello*, and indeed a play to replace *Othello*, which had been scrapped. Cameron was to star in a huge cast of amateur actors on his native island. One of the points at issue was the casting of white actors. Leigh first suggested *Macbeth*, then, getting nowhere with that idea, Brecht's *The Caucasian Chalk Circle*, but Cameron could not see that Azdak, the judge, was a great part (he doesn't appear until quite late on in the proceedings).

Leigh then suggested Brecht's *Galileo*: 'This was, without question, the biggest mistake I have ever made. I did my best, but the play is immensely difficult and Earl Cameron's insecurity made the whole experience deeply depressing. It was totally bizarre, because all of this was happening miles from anywhere – the nearest place to Bermuda is Florida, 900 miles away – and I found that Bermuda was a very strange, claustrophobic and indeed rather alcoholic place.' Leigh walked off the production, was persuaded back, and the cast and crew thanked him for his pains and contribution with a present of a return ticket to New York and a flat in which to stay there once the show was over. They did not, Leigh pointedly remarks, give any sort of present to Earl Cameron.

'The lesson of it all was that I had done the production merely because I had said that I was available to direct plays. I thought: this is stupid. From now on, I'm just going to do my own thing. It was the worst production of anything *ever*. It made the *Little Malcolm* experience seem like *Naked*. I decided this was *it*: I was never, ever, going to direct anything again except my own work. I had already wangled my way into the Open Space, directed a new piece to general indifference and immediately got together again with Les Blair and formed Autumn Productions in order to make a film of that piece.' *Bleak Moments* was the result.

The manner of working was at last fixed. There would be discussions and rehearsals. Plays or films would develop organically with actors fully liberated into the creative process. After an exploratory improvisation period, Leigh would write a structure, indicating the order in which scenes happened, usually with a single bare sentence: 'Johnny and Sophie meet'; 'Stan and Gordon in the parcel van'; 'Betty does Joy's hair'; 'Jim's stag party'; 'Wendy confronts Nicola'; 'Cyril, Shirley and Wayne look for Wayne's sister'; 'Lorraine and Billy go to bed'. It was simple, and unalterable. And it was rehearsed and rehearsed until it achieved the required quality of 'finish'. There was, Leigh now knew, no such thing as an 'aimless direction'. It was always a question of the end product, the final fiction, the story, the lives and the characters. And the supply of material was both unquantifiable and endless.

Mike Bradwell, the founder of Hull Truck in 1970, who had been a student at E15 when Leigh went to teach there, was an early disciple. 'You have to remember that Mike was completely unknown. He couldn't get his work put on. People did think he was a wanker. He never went to San Francisco and put flowers in his hair; he sort of hung around Camden Town looking miserable. He used to spend a lot of time with failed poets, people around Unity Theatre, odd antique dealers trying to write a

William Burroughs novel.' Bradwell moved into the Cranleigh Street flat for a short time and recalls a popular late-night game of cartoon consequences in which one of four or five people sitting around (including, say, Bradwell and the actors John Shrapnel and Derrick O'Connor) would utter a line and Leigh, hunched over his drawing pad, would sketch a strip cartoon, frame by frame, instantly, on the spot. 'We invented this character called Chopper the Copper whose penis and truncheon were always at the same expectant angle, and at one stage we had the idea of trying to sell a cartoon book called "The Further Adventures of Chopper the Copper and the Men from the Eisteddfod".'

This tumultuous, formative decade still left Leigh stranded on the margins of British theatre and film, but you would be hard pressed to find anyone of contemporary distinction who worked harder, or in more various situations, over the same period. And for so little recognition. A key to it all is Leigh's curiosity about human behaviour. Critics sometimes complain that he patronises working-class characters, when they really mean that he celebrates grotesquerie and fallibility in his fictional creations and, by implication, all of us. Ruth Lesirge, his friend from Habonim days, crucially remarks: 'If you listen to Mike talking, he doesn't patronise anyone. He talks to a five-year-old in the same way he talks to a ninety-five-year-old. And he also asks as searching a set of questions of a teenager as he would of any actor he is working with. He makes no compromises in that sense. He instinctively recognises people's worth, whoever they are. How can you call that patronising?'

One thing had emerged for sure. This guy was a director. He had hung up his masks as an actor. And he knew exactly how he should now proceed: 'There are some very good people who can't direct. There are some not very good people who get away with something that might be called directing. For myself, as someone palpably keen on the ensemble ideal, as an actor I was hopeless at taking part in an ensemble, partly because I don't suffer fools gladly or easily; also because – and this is the ordinary stuff of paranoid schizophrenic dictators, including benevolent despots such as myself – as long as I am in control, a position of power,

I can then relax. But it only works because I am incredibly tough about the discipline surrounding the circumstances. All directing is a lonely business. Directing in the theatre is infinitely more lonely. In a film you share much more with the cameraman and the sound man, and so on. Some people are temperamentally suited to the loneliness of the long-distance director. By their chemistry. I don't *think* I am. I *know*.'

FIVE

Bleak Moments and
Television Times

After that higgledy-piggledy decade of activity, Leigh had not exactly arrived, except at the way in which he wanted to work. His campaign was still confined to the theatre, but in the first few years of the 1970s he managed to convert two stage plays (*Bleak Moments* and *Wholesome Glory*) into films – the first, the feature film of the same name, the second, *Nuts in May* for BBC Television, where he had breached the citadel with *Hard Labour* thanks to the support of the innovative and radical producer Tony Garnett. He had to scrub around to get going. Charles Marowitz allowed him to take a late-night slot in his Open Space venue, and the result, opening in March 1970, was *Bleak Moments*, seventy-five minutes of tortured, semi-articulated anguish in suburban South Norwood between Sylvia (Anne Raitt) and her retarded sister (Sarah Stephenson); Sylvia's friend at work (Joolia Cappleman); a teacher (Eric Allan), Sylvia's prospective boyfriend, barely capable of looking her in the eye; and Norman (Mike Bradwell), a gormless hippie from Scunthorpe who admits only to hailing from Doncaster and who is renting garage space to produce a student newspaper.

Marowitz watched a first-draft run-through and was appalled. Leigh says he saw it simply as a boulevard piece of sit-com; it did not conform to Marowitz's view of what constituted experimental, improvisational theatre. The characters were speaking quietly and sipping sherry. They were not shouting abuse at each other and tearing their clothes off. 'The first night,' recalls Leigh, however, 'was absolutely charged, very precise, highly modulated, absolutely organic and impeccably acted.' That opinion was not shared by Irving Wardle in *The Times*, who mistakenly thought that the stuttering and stumbling was a consequence of Leigh's improvisational methods. Indeed, he mistakenly thought that the actors were making it up as they went along. He interpreted the halting atmosphere as one derived from actors' embarrassment, though he did credit the playing with 'a constant sense of dread, as though these people are making small talk in a town stricken with the plague. Their fingers writhe ceaselessly, their smiles switch on briefly over grimly fixed masks, every action they make is rigid with some unspoken obsession.' And although he concluded that he mistrusted Leigh's methods, Wardle thought *Bleak Moments* was 'worth seeing as an honest and clear-headed piece of research: unlike most "experimental theatre" it would satisfy laboratory requirements'. A few days later, Benedict Nightingale was more unequivocally positive in the *New Statesman*, pronouncing the production 'amusing, touching, unpretentious and good'. After a fortnight of performances, *Bleak Moments* made way for round-the-clock showings of Paul Morrissey's film *Flesh* (1969), produced by Andy Warhol, in which Joe Dallesandro pounded the Manhattan mean streets hustling for sex and drugs.

Leigh and Les Blair, who had formed their own company, Autumn Productions, were meanwhile pounding the London pavements composing letters to Elizabeth Taylor, the British Film Institute, Albert Finney . . . anyone they could think of who might be interested in helping them make a film of *Bleak Moments*. Their cinematographer was to be Bahram Manocheri from the film school, with Roger Pratt as his assistant. Pratt produced a newspaper, *Sinic*, at the film school for which Leigh drew the emblem of a rotting pear and provided a cartoon strip called 'Little Sergei', which featured childish, bizarre action such as perambulators going up and down stairs, as in a pre-pubescent Sergei Eisenstein epic. (Pratt would remain a regular Leigh collaborator right through to *High Hopes*, when he was lost to bigger money-spinning movies such as *Brazil*, *Batman*, *The Fisher King*, *Shadowlands* and *Mary Shelley's Frankenstein*.)

Leigh also got on to Tony Garnett at the BBC; he would soon

prove an ally in his early television breakthrough. Garnett much admired the stage performance, and was impressed with the sub-sequent film. The BFI production board, run at that time by Bruce Beresford, who had also seen *Bleak Moments* at the Open Space, and was just about to return home to Australia and begin making his own movies, came up with a minimal contribution of £100 – the minimum amount which allowed for an experimental film agreement with the unions. But Albert Finney and Michael Medwin's Memorial Films, who had recently made Lindsay Anderson's *If . . .* and Finney's *Charlie Bubbles*, and were about to produce Stephen Frears's first movie, *Gumshoe*, delivered the main financial backing, as well as a lot of *Gumshoe*'s short ends, i.e. unused spare bits of film rolls.

In October 1970, Leigh felt he could at last proclaim his artistic status. He wrote to his parents in Salford: 'Just to let you know that at last it's signed and sealed, and Albert Finney has put up the whole £14,000 for *Bleak Moments*. We start 4 January, rehearse for four weeks, and shoot for six weeks until 14 March. So . . . I'm a film director, etc.' Once the film was in the can, they were fractionally over budget. The project wobbled slightly, but Tony Garnett stepped in and interceded on Leigh's behalf once more with Albert Finney. Leigh finally telegrammed his parents: 'Euston 8 September 71 STOP Albert Finney has given us the three grand STOP all is therefore well STOP Mike.'

Even though the sound quality is poor and the pace a little on the leisurely side – Leigh came on stage after a screening at the NFT's 'Long Weekend with Mike Leigh' retrospective in May 1993 and punctuated the appreciative silence with the remark, 'That's the slowest film ever made with jokes in; it's like watching paint dry' – there is a tonal assurance and technical finesse in the presentation of the marvellous performances that proclaims both originality and talent. Sylvia is heard playing Chopin's E-flat Noc-turne over the opening credits. The general inability to express inner feelings reinforces a mood of bleak, Slavic despair. Indeed, the retarded sister's hopeless infatuation with the hippie Norman, a risible, moth-eaten equivalent of Vershinin in *Three Sisters*, and the sense of the grinding continuity of unfulfilled lives at the end, creates an ineffably sad, Chekhovian atmosphere, unrelieved by the sort of cathartic climax that characterises most of Leigh's subsequent work.

The bubble never bursts. It just expands. Even the exterior shots have a plaintive, insistent quality, with beautifully composed views of pebbledash houses and garages, of clear roads and tall trees, around West Norwood and Tulse Hill. Here is certainly an extension of Leigh's feelings about Salford, a poetic sensitivity to what G.K. Chesterton called 'the significance of the unexamined life'. Leigh did not use a musical soundtrack until *The Kiss of Death* in 1977, but Sylvia's stumbling Chopin is beautifully contrasted in performance with Norman's version of 'Freight Train' and his similarly inept version – 'same three chords' says the actor Mike Bradwell, who certainly plays the guitar better than Norman – of another blues standard, 'Cocaine Blues'. A fragile tenderness imbues the non-action, too, with Anne Raitt's Sylvia, who works as a typist in an accountant's office, achieving moments of astonishing serenity, green eyes steady with boredom and disappointment, hair swept back in a Brontë bun (Peter the teacher, the nearest she gets to Heathcliff, picks up her copy of *Wuthering Heights*).

There is one scene where the camera merely scans each tense and furtive face in the sitting room, and you ache for someone to scream. But this is a world of stifled cries and whispers. Sylvia and Peter go to a disturbingly miserable Chinese restaurant where the only other customer singly and aggressively scoffs his food and sups a pint in the corner. The tension is unbearable, and when they leave, the solitary man is just starting to scowl into his dessert of tinned peaches and thinly diluted cream. Things only become tougher back home, where Sylvia invites Peter for coffee and sherry. Peter asks her if she prefers to watch television or radio and she fussily exploits his solecism before he ploughs on to mention Marshall McLuhan (a reference that predates Woody Allen's McLuhan gag in *Annie Hall* by six years) and ingenuously remarks on the conflict between content and the means of communication. What is so gruelling here is Leigh's refusal to play by the usual rules of comic embarrassment, let alone stock cinematic formulas of seduction. Sylvia fills and refills the sherry glasses, puts her legs up on the sofa and shockingly says that, in her head, she was inviting Peter to take off his trousers. She lives briefly with this tactical mistake as a joke, then recants, saying it wasn't a joke. Peter can hardly think straight, declines more coffee and goes out the front door, *pulling on his gloves*. The gloves somehow say it all. You never notice people in other films wearing gloves.

The reviews were ecstatic. John Coleman in the *New Statesman* hailed 'the most remarkable début by a British director, working on an absurdly low budget and with unknown actors, that I have ever seen', and within the year the beginning of Leigh's transatlantic reputation was made by reviews such as Roger Ebert's in the *Chicago Sun Times*: '*Bleak Moments* is a masterpiece, plain and simple . . . its greatness is not just in the direction or subject, but in the complete singularity of the performances. There have never been performances just like this before in the movies; Anne Raitt and Eric Allan have scenes together that are so good, and so painful, that you find yourself afraid to breathe for fear they will step wrong. They never do.'

That last Ebert remark conveys the success with which Leigh created the theatrical tension of the best acting in new-minted screen terms. Sometimes his stage plays – notably *Ecstasy* and *Goose-Pimples* – have bristled with a genuine unease and sense that something might go seriously wrong which is the hallmark of all the most truthful and dangerous acting. It may have been the rareness of that which partly, and perhaps understandably, baffled Irving Wardle at the Open Space. To capture that particular form of performance excitement on film is even rarer, and Leigh's best films, from *Bleak Moments* on, always have that edginess and raw, unsettling vitality. 'The danger of theatre is fantastic,' says Leigh, 'and film should aspire to that theatrical element of danger wherever possible. While it is true that you do have much more control over a film in this respect, I am not a Hitchcock or a Greenaway, for each of whom the whole film is only about rigid control.' That flexibility, as opposed to laxity, derives from the nature of the performances; for Leigh, it's all to do with the tension between control and fluidity.

Eric Allan, who has worked seven times with Leigh – as much as anyone, including Alison Steadman – points out that most directors, especially in the theatre, are concerned with *effects*. 'I was standing around in rehearsals of Edward Bond's *Lear* [1971, immediately after *Bleak Moments*], and I said to the director, William Gaskill, that I didn't know what to do. He said, "Express frustration for me," and went back to directing the scene. The problem was always standing on the stage expressing something when you weren't involved in the text being spoken. And even on the line, it's often a concern with the laugh line, with the effect of what's coming out. It's never like that with Mike. Refreshingly, he's always concerned with *causes*. Uniquely, he leaves you alone as an actor to get on with the job and not worry about the effects, or what the production is saying.' In the 1982 BBC TV *Arena* programme about Leigh's work, Allan developed a fine metaphor to explain this: underneath whatever you were doing with text, he said, you created an escalator on which you travel, and the only person who worries about when you come off is Mike Leigh.

Blair both produced and edited *Bleak Moments*, and it was the last time he ever worked with Leigh. He wanted to be a director himself, and the curious thing is that he adopted exactly the same sort of approach as Leigh, though using a much looser system of improvisation and character development. Garnett was providing several films a year for the BBC on his own producing contract, unimpaired by either the head of plays or the BBC controller. 'Nowadays,' he says, 'you have to ask the controller if you can use the bathroom. I just told Gerald Savory, the head of plays, what I was up to and he left me alone to get on with it. Which is exactly how it should be.' (A point eloquently reiterated, incidentally, by the television and film writer Andrew Davies in his 1995 Huw Wheldon Lecture to the Royal Television Society; it was Huw Wheldon, a legendary BBC controller and managing director, to whom Garnett had written about Leigh when he had been turned down yet again for a trainee directorship.)

Garnett had an informal stable of colleagues – Ken Loach, the producer Kenith Trodd, the writer Jim Allen (who had been filched from the long-running Granada soap opera *Coronation*

Street) – to whom he added, whenever he could, new talent. He spotted Leigh's potential immediately. 'I could see that this lad, Mike, was never going to be able to do what he wants to do in the cinema. His conditions were expensive, not for the scale of the thing – there were never going to be Cossacks coming over the hill – but for the time required. I knew nothing would happen for him until he got established. So I decided that I would give him one of my last available slots.'

Leigh's *Hard Labour* used up most of Garnett's remaining budget for that year's television films. The seventy-five-minute stage play of *Bleak Moments* had been expanded into 110 minutes on film, with the addition of such scenes as the restaurant outing, the exterior sequences, the schoolroom where Peter is humourlessly resisting the idea of a humour project with the third form, and the diversionary visit of Sylvia's friend, the Malteser-munching Pat, to Pat's mother with Sylvia's severely withdrawn sister Hilda in tow. Pat's mother is in bed and has left her teeth on the side table, much to her daughter's fury and embarrassment. The old woman is played by Liz Smith, whom Leigh would cast as the central figure, Mrs Thornley, the Catholic house-cleaner, in *Hard Labour*. As he started work on this film, boosted by Garnett's faith in him and revelling in the idea of working on location in Salford, Leigh headed north and interviewed actors in Manchester, lodging there with his sister.

One night he drove over to Liverpool to see *The Foursome* at the Everyman Theatre. Ted Whitehead's wonderful, scatological beach play had been premiered in the Royal Court's Theatre Upstairs in 1971; it was one of the few unsolicited plays to be produced at the Court, and the first Upstairs play to end up in the West End. The Liverpool Everyman quartet comprised Jonathan Pryce, Michael Angelis, Polly Hemingway . . . and Alison Steadman. Leigh booked a ticket and announced his presence, inviting Alison for a drink in the downstairs bistro bar after the show. Over their bottles of Newcastle Brown (everyone drank 'Newkies' in the Everyman in those days), Leigh told her about *Hard Labour* and asked her to be in it. She had been at the Everyman for a year – the company, which also included Antony Sher, was one of the finest in the country at the time, and was enjoying great local and national success in plays by John McGrath and, soon after Alison left, Willy Russell – but the idea of a holiday at the end of this season, a chance to work with Leigh, and television wages, was a strong temptation. She accepted on the spot (Leigh also cast Polly Hemingway in *Hard Labour*, but not that night).

Liverpool was Alison's home town. She was the youngest of three sisters, with a ten-year gap from the second, who is a hairdresser and wizard cake-maker in Swindon; the eldest, a housewife, lives in Liverpool. Their father was a production controller at Plessey, the electronics firm. Alison, brought up almost as an only child, certainly from the age of eleven when the older girls had left home, had started acting with the Liverpool Youth Theatre while training at a secretarial and commercial college ('Which I hated. I used not to go for weeks and then turn up and this teacher used to say, "Oh, you're back, I thought we'd seen the last of you!"'). On the advice of a helpful young assistant director at the Liverpool Playhouse, Tony Colegate, she applied to the E15 Acting School – 'He advised against RADA' – and secured a place to go there in the autumn of 1966. (Colegate subsequently died, too young, while running the Library Theatre in Manchester.) Since then, and her first meeting with Leigh during her second year, she had worked in various regional repertory theatres, starting at Lincoln, where her first role was that of Sandy, the seductive schoolgirl in *The Prime of Miss Jean Brodie*. A local journalist was expelled from the theatre after sneaking into the flies to watch her nude scene (it was only 1969, but Alison eschewed the proffered body stocking), a freakish premonition, perhaps, of the steamy sequence in Dennis Potter's TV series *The Singing Detective* (1986) where Alison's character in the famous *al fresco* sex scene is spied on by her own son concealed in a tree.

During the preparation of the film, Mike and Alison, as they both say, 'got together'. After a week of the initial rehearsals, with Leigh organising everyone, Alison recalls him turning to her and saying, 'Now you want to get away by seven o'clock, your boyfriend's coming over . . .' and she heard herself saying, 'No, no, it's not a boyfriend, he's just a friend.' And she thought,

'That's a bit embarrassing, why did I say that?' And 'I suddenly realised that I was making it clear to him that I was not committed in any way. So it went from there.' Alison moved into Cranleigh Street for three years before the couple bought the house in Wood Green. They took a flat together in Manchester during the filming of *Hard Labour*.

Alison met Leigh's parents. Leigh says that his love life between 1960 and 1972 had been a complete enigma to his parents. 'They were resistant to the point of hurtful rudeness about not wanting to meet any girlfriends unless they were Jewish. The result was that two serious girlfriends of the 1960s were not allowed to meet my parents, and both complained of being treated as if they were whores.' But by the time Abe and Phyllis heard about Alison, who is not Jewish, they seemed to buckle in a mood of reconciliation, and said they would be very happy to meet her. 'So, one night during the shoot of *Hard Labour*, we all went out for a meal together, and of course they thought she was great. They obviously woke up to the fact that they had been unreasonably outmoded on this issue and, in deciding to reform their attitude, I respected them.'

Hard Labour was just seventy minutes long, not perfect, but the film most clearly drawn in all Leigh's work from the background in Higher and Lower Broughton where he grew up. The polarity between the worlds of Mrs Stone and the lady who cleans her house is icily delineated. In the middle, as it were, is the new housing estate, where Mrs Thornley's son, a car mechanic played by Bernard Hill, lives with his wife Veronica, an auspicious first glimpse of Alison Steadman in her nagging and retentive mode, setting out her coleslaws and mayonnaises and pieces of fruit cake for a Sunday tea while singing the praises of her environment: 'What I like,' she says of the uniformly dreary residential estate, 'is that every house is just that little bit different.'

Alison had made a fleeting television appearance as a lady fencer in Maupassant's *Bel-Ami*, but this was her first sustained role in front of the camera, and she felt nervous: 'Rehearsals had been fine. You have to learn to see the camera as a friend, not an enemy, and I had not managed to embrace the camera, bring it in to the situation.' Hill, later immortalised as Yosser ('Gi' us a job') in Alan Bleasdale's TV series *The Boys from the Black Stuff* (1982) was making his professional début. Leigh had seen him act in 1968 with the Salford Players while he was working at the De la Salle College, where Hill was training to be a teacher – 'He was brilliant.' Together with Gerald McNally, who was lecturing at what had just become Manchester Polytechnic Theatre School, he managed to have Hill's grant switched to the Poly, from which he had just graduated when Leigh came to cast *Hard Labour*. After the film, Hill joined the Everyman company and played John Lennon in Willy Russell's first big hit, *John, Paul, Ringo, George . . . and Bert* (1973), alongside Trevor Eve as Paul, Antony Sher as Ringo, Phillip Joseph as George, and George Costigan as Bert, with a bespectacled Barbara Dickson providing piano and vocal support.

Hard Labour sags and wanders a little, but there are memorable, distinctive qualities: the opening high-angle shot over the Salford back-to-backs, where Mr Thornley is returning home from the night shift, foul-tempered and bawling for food, just like D.H. Lawrence's miner Lambert in *A Collier's Friday Night*; the poetic but never sentimental photography of the red-brick terrace houses and pubs, and St Boniface's church; Mrs Thornley rubbing Ellman's liniment very hard into her husband's hairy, arthritic shoulder; Ben Kingsley as a vowel-elongating, nasally melodious Asian taxi driver (with a market stall) who arranges the abortion for Mrs Thornley's daughter, beautifully played by Polly Hemingway; the visit of the tallyman, memorably characterised by Louis Raynes; and the final, superb confessional scene, followed by Mrs Thornley blankly polishing Mrs Stone's windows while the credits roll and a dog barks.

As Mr Thornley, Leigh cast an Oldham market stall-holder, Clifford Kershaw, who had been an extra in *Coronation Street*, and while there is a bovine, innocent integrity to the performance, it does rather jar against the fine quality and detail of the rest of the acting. Especially that of Liz Smith, who made her name in the film and went on to become one of our outstanding middle-aged character actresses. The guilty submissiveness of Mrs Thornley – she tells her daughter that 'You have to suffer to bring children into the world,' and the priest that she doesn't love people enough – is almost transformed by her confession that she doesn't love the husband with whom she sleeps once a week, on Saturday nights. The poignancy of that climactic moment is humorously reinforced by the priest who, having granted Mrs Thornley absolution from her sins and given her a penance of 'Five Hail Marys, one Our Father and a Glory Be', asks her to go in peace and pray for him while he casually resumes the study of his *Manchester Evening News* on the other side of the grille. When shooting the film in the church, Leigh and the cast had come across a pile of football pinks (the final-score editions) with doodles all over them in one of the confessionals.

The most substantial theatre piece Leigh produced after *Bleak Moments* was *Babies Grow Old* in 1974, which marked his return to the RSC in Stratford-upon-Avon. He kept his fringe theatre commitments bubbling with some interesting, though much slighter, projects. When shooting on *Bleak Moments* was over, he and two of the actors (Joolia Cappleman and Reg Stewart, the solitary diner in the Chinese restaurant) took a lunchtime spot in the Basement Theatre, underneath L'Escargot in Greek Street, for *A Rancid Pong*. The couple squabbled in a large bed. He had been out on some illicit job; and there was a smell. 'The joke was extremely grotty,' says Leigh. 'I got a potty and a plastic turd from the joke shop in Tottenham Court Road and made some urine with yellow ink and put some red in it, and this of course was the first thing the lunchtime audience saw as they came in. With their sandwiches.' *Wholesome Glory* (which became *Nuts in May*) was followed at the Theatre Upstairs with what would be termed nowadays an alternative Christmas show, Leigh's own *Dick Whittington and his Cat*, of which I have decidedly mixed memories. A Yorkshire boy (Paul Copley) comes to London to seek his fortune in a fantastical, lightweight preview of the Everyman element in *Naked*. Adult actors played children, the cats were cockney wideboys, and Philip Jackson quick-changed as Dick's father and a racist airline pilot who was dead against cats. Leigh was pleased with the show when he discovered what it was: a comic morality tale in a storybook style, with a choric

Father Christmas, and he reckons some of its spirit carried through to *It's a Great Big Shame!* at Stratford East twenty years later. He also took up an invitation from Mike Ockrent at the Traverse in Edinburgh to fill a late-night spot during the 1973 Festival: *The Jaws of Death* was a *jeu d'esprit* for a seriously under-employed private detective (played by Richard Ireson), his dozy secretary in a ponytail and platform shoes (Alison Steadman) – 'the very antithesis of chic', said one reviewer – and a guy with a parcel who kept turning up like a bad penny (Adrian Shergold). The main joke in this little half-hour spoof detective thriller was that the characters kept falling asleep; the show's starting time was 1.20 a.m., but it still played to totally alert, packed houses.

The return to Stratford-upon-Avon was effected by the opening of The Other Place as an official performance venue further along Waterside from the main theatre, on the way to Trinity Church and Shakespeare's tomb. Buzz Goodbody had been at the RSC as an assistant director since 1967 and, in Leigh's time with Theatregoround, had collaborated with him and Terry Hands, on a teachers' course. Goodbody opened the season with her own shortened *King Lear* in April. The programme also included Keith Hack's production of *The Tempest* (with Richard Griffiths and Ian McDiarmid joining the RSC for the first time), a revival of David Rudkin's *Afore Night Come*, and Nicol Williamson's production of *Uncle Vanya* (Williamson was playing Macbeth and Malvolio on the main stage over the road).

Babies Grow Old opened at the end of August at a cost of £142, eight pounds under budget, and played a short season at the Institute of Contemporary Arts in London the following spring. The chief character was Mrs Wenlock, an elderly woman crippled with rheumatoid arthritis and living alone in the suburbs of Birmingham. Her daughter Elaine, six months pregnant, visits from Rhyl, with her doctor husband, Geoff, in order to try and convince her mother to adopt the forthcoming baby. Elaine's cousin, Barry, has been invalided out of the British Army in Northern Ireland where he's had his leg shot off. The group is completed by Geoff's friend Charles (played by Matthew Guinness, Alec's son), another doctor on the point of giving up his job because he can't cope.

The doctors do not recognise, or want to know, how ill and destitute the old lady is; there's an avalanche of dirty dishes in the kitchen sink.

Sheila Kelley, who played Elaine, recalls a great interest within the RSC. A common response was that this kind of acting hadn't been seen before, and that the actors looked as though they were just chatting to each other. Like Irving Wardle at *Bleak Moments*, people assumed, wrongly, that the script was being improvised on the spot. 'I do remember thinking that what opens up inside is that reason of why you wanted to be an actor in the first place,' says Kelley. 'It's a creative art, and you are creating a character. This isn't anything unusual. This should be the norm in our profession. But it's not the norm. What Mike does is what it should *all* be about. Which is why actors respond to it. He is not teaching us anything. He is taking from the way we work, and he is working with, rather than against, that.'

Michael Billington in the *Guardian* hailed 'a genuine work of art'. The resonating figure of the tragically abandoned old woman, a figure who runs through Leigh's work from *Individual Fruit Pies* and the Liz Smith performances to Edna Doré's old mum in *High Hopes*, took Terry Hands by surprise. 'It really was a shock. Ours was an empire-building time with grand projects – the Peter Brook productions, *The Wars of the Roses*. We were still young when Mike returned to us, and so was the company, really. Our view of the world was guided by the classics. Mike made us look at the old, the poor, the ordinary. And he made it hurt. He still does, though with the dying or despairing asleep on our streets every night, the shock is less. In the RSC, we were ignoring these issues, even though we often did *King Lear*. But every *Lear* the RSC did after the Brook/Scofield version was dreadful. The play is always directed by people who are much too young. The show is never about the old.'

It was now nearly three years since Leigh had made a film, and he was deep into one of his periodic bouts of angry frustration. He was cross that no one from the nearby BBC Birmingham studios of Pebble Mill came across to Stratford to see *Babies*. The producer of Pebble Mill's Second City Firsts, the new TV plays slot, was Barry Hanson, who was not keen on Leigh's work. Leigh filled a sudden gap in the Bush theatre's schedule by throwing together, in just six days, the short *Silent Majority*, in which the actor Stephen Bill (married to Sheila Kelley) was attempting to console and seduce his own wife, played by Julie North, in a bedsit, while the pair of them were being harassed by their landlady, played by Yvonne Gilan.

While Kelley was rehearsing *Babies* in London, Bill was appearing with Jim Broadbent in Shakespeare in Regent's Park. In *Two Noble Kinsmen*. As the two noble kinsmen? 'No, the two noble pratters-about at the back.' They would meet up with Kelley and Leigh and Alison in the evening for a drink, which is how Leigh's deep and abiding friendship with the couple, and indeed Broadbent, was hatched. These days, Mike and Alison usually spend New Year's Eve, and their son Leo part of the summer holidays, with Sheila Kelley and Stephen Bill, who have lived in Leamington Spa for the past dozen or so years. Both still act, though not all that much, and both, intriguingly, have forged considerable reputations as writers.

Stephen Bill was initially encouraged to start writing by Pedr James (director of BBC TV's *Martin Chuzzlewit*), but claims Leigh as undoubtedly the biggest influence on him in attempting 'to put ordinary people together and to see what emerges'. And Kelley, an actress of deep, spiritual density, found she was spoilt by working in what should be 'the normal way' and removed her name from *Spotlight*, the actors' directory, six or seven years ago (she has since put it back in). She now writes fiction, and plays the Irish fiddle. She was one of the winners of the 1993 Ian St James Awards, with her short story collected in an omnibus edition with the other winners, *Flying High*. She has a very good answer to the most common accusation levelled at Leigh, that he knows what he wants and gets the actors to make it all up for him: 'He no doubt thinks that he might deal with this or that theme. And of course what happens is to a large extent dictated by the actors he assembles. But he *must* keep his mind open, and he can't have too much preordained detail in his head because he couldn't then work with the actors and respond to what they are giving him.

The whole process would fall apart. So, to protect his own creative spark, he cannot know what the film or play is going to be before he starts. He couldn't possibly.'

Barry Hanson finally relented and invited Leigh up to Birmingham for a chat the Monday after Mike and Alison were married, in St Pancras register office, in September 1973. Hanson said that his colleague Tara Prem had written a script about an Asian family, and that perhaps Leigh might like to direct it. Leigh turned on his heel, walked straight out of Hanson's office and took the train back to London in a huff. In later years, when his children were small, Leigh used to threaten them at mealtimes with 'Eat your supper, or Barry Hanson will come and get you.' There was, however, a happy sequel to Leigh's wasted journey. Hanson moved on to another job, Tara Prem took over, and gave Leigh *carte blanche* for two short studio productions (the only time Leigh has worked in a studio, apart from the recording of *Abigail's Party* in 1977).

The second of these items, *Knock for Knock*, has disgracefully been wiped: Sam Kelly, an actor with experience of variety, pantomime and television sitcom, played an insurance salesman in a Manchester office trying very hard for half an hour not to sell any insurance to a little Mr Purvis, played by Anthony O'Donnell. 'It was,' says Kelly, 'completely mad, especially my character, Bernard Bowes. He was the sort of frantic man who sat behind his desk offering his client a cigar and slamming the box shut before his client could get one out.' *Time Out* magazine hailed 'the funniest thing on the box for months' and suggested that Sam Kelly, 'with his double-handed face scratch, suggestive laugh and all-over-the-set delivery, gives the performance of the decade'. O'Donnell recalls that the performance was completed in two uninterrupted takes – 'uniquely for its time; it was like going back to live television' – with cutaways completed afterwards. Mr Purvis referred to his insurance broker, one 'Reg Dixon of Blackpool Tower Insurance'; Tara Prem subsequently received a charming letter from the real-life Reginald Dixon, the Blackpool Tower organist, saying how much he enjoyed the play and thanking her for the 'plug': 'It reminded me that my car insurance premium falls due on 1 January 1977 – which took the edge off the giggle somewhat.'

In sharp, downbeat contrast, *The Permissive Society*, the first studio piece, cunningly belies its own title in the shifting, tentative relationship of a ukulele-strumming boy (Bob Mason) and his first girlfriend (Veronica Roberts) on a Friday night in a seventh-floor Lancashire flat. The boy's blowsy, divorced sister (Rachel Davies) is preparing for a night on the town. But as the young couple depart for the pub, nervous hostilities on hold, the sister returns home, jilted. She stands alone in the kitchen in long shot. There is a clever stylistic contrast between the crude banter of the siblings and the shy probing of the young couple. Their exchanges are increasingly coloured by the domestic bossiness of the girl, an only child, who triumphantly drags words like 'peristalsis' from her school biology lessons onto the tea table.

Leigh had also been kept going at the BBC by Tony Garnett on an unusual commission of 'five-minute films' to be slotted in immediately before the 9 O'Clock News on BBC 1, or dotted around the schedules like currants in a cake. The head of plays, Christopher Morahan, was keen on the idea, which originated with Leigh, and Brian Wenham, the controller of BBC 1, ordered a sample few as a pilot project. Five were completed. Leigh's plan was to make thirty or forty of them – 'a great mosaic of material, like Robert Altman's [much later] *Short Cuts*' – but Morahan started dithering, suggesting other participants like Harold Pinter and Jack Gold. Leigh said no way: 'The whole point was my authorship and a consistent, teeming social picture.' Morahan accepted this, but the idea faded as he thought further on Leigh's suggestions. 'It was a great tragedy,' says Leigh, 'because it felt dead right for the time, and it could have been a wonderful, original piece of programming.' The quirky quintet of items was not broadcast until the 1982 season of Leigh's work on television.

Three of the five are gems. *Afternoon* is a spikily written little bad-mood piece for three female afternoon drinkers: the hostess, played by Rachel Davies, Pauline Moran as her teacher friend, and Julie North as a newlywed with the bloom still on, impervious to such exchanges as 'All men are bastards'; 'As a species, I think you're right.' Outside on the estate, children are running home from school. The debate over whether or not to have children, a classic Mike Leigh preoccupation, informs *The Birth of the 2001 FA Cup Final Goalie*, in which an amateur goalkeeper loses a match 5–0 and goes to the hospital, where his wife is about to give birth, in his kit; six years later – the longest time-jump in any Leigh film, and ironically in the shortest of them – we see the glum goalie kicking a ball about with a little boy (a girl had been expected) in a desolate landscape of grass and council flats. And in *Old Chums*, Tim Stern (who had played the cat in *Dick Whittington* and would soon feature in *Abigail's Party*) and Robert Putt play old school-friends meeting by chance as the first is driving off in an invalid car to see a film called *The Blazing Inferno*. 'What happens if you want to get your leg over?' asks the tall friend as he tries to arrange his limbs around the gear stick, proceeding to a grim litany of sexual boasting. The tone is both light and seriously off-colour, the technical touch delightful: Tim Stern drives off and Robert Putt walks away, leaving the camera behind. The less successful five-minute films are *A Light Snack*, in which Richard Griffiths as a window cleaner gazes wistfully at a sausage roll on a kitchen table while two workmen in a sausage roll factory chatter at cross purposes; and *Probation*, set in the bare, functional waiting room of an East End probationary office, and at least notable for a frisson of racial tension as an officer preparing a report for a black boy's court appearance leaves him to make a cup of tea with the jovially sarcastic admonition, 'Don't nick anything!'

Both Tony Garnett and David Rose, who was head of drama at BBC Pebble Mill and responsible for Barry Hanson and Tara Prem joining him in Birmingham, consider the narrative line in Leigh's work to be sometimes sacrificed on the altar of characterisation. The tension between story and character is fundamental to all drama, and Leigh sets about tackling the problem in a highly individualistic manner. That problem is only partially resolved in films like *Hard Labour* and *Who's Who*, whereas *Abigail's Party* and *Grown-Ups* ring with the satisfying clamour of perfect plotting driven by rich character revelation. As Rose says, 'His characters are so rich and so deep. You can take risks as they are so thoroughly understood by his actors. It seems to me that when an editor makes his cuts with Mike, he allows the shots to linger a little longer than is normal, because the characters are so engaging and there is so much going on. In most films, the actor is delivering everything, or 80 per cent of everything, and you daren't hang on because there won't be any more.'

While working on *Wholesome Glory* in the Theatre Upstairs, Leigh and his actors – Alison Steadman as Candice-Marie Pratt, Roger Sloman as Keith Pratt and Geoffrey Hutchings as Keith's brother, Dennis – often talked of how interesting it would be to see these characters enjoying the countryside, on location. The play as it stood was confined to bedsit-land, and when Leigh raised the subject with David Rose, Rose suggested making a film entirely on location around Corfe Castle in Dorset, for the simple reason that he came from Purbeck and no one ever made a film about it! 'I told him about the quarries in the district and asked him to film everything out of doors, under the skies; he reneged only slightly on this condition – there is one sequence of about one minute twenty seconds, in the Greyhound pub near Corfe Castle, and one short scene in a toilet. Apart from that, the only interiors are those of some very small tents.'

The work produced, *Nuts in May*, marked Leigh's major breakthrough with the British public as an original comic artist, and the film today has achieved a cult status only exceeded, perhaps, by *Abigail's Party* and *Meantime*. Leigh's own view is that the piece is really an urban film which just happens to be shot in the countryside. In parts it is, as the Americans would say, 'fall-over funny', and surely indicated that its writer and director would become an idiosyncratic fixture on the British cultural scene for some time to come. While filming in Dorset, however, Leigh was distressed to learn of the death by suicide of his old friend and associate Buzz Goodbody. She died in April 1975, aged twenty-eight, on the eve of her production of *Hamlet* (Ben Kingsley in the lead) opening the second season in The Other Place in Stratford.

'We heard it on the news,' Leigh recalls, 'as we drove back to Swanage from a rehearsal around Corfe Castle.' The cast included three of the *Babies Grow Old* company who had known Goodbody very well in Stratford – Sheila Kelley, Matthew Guinness and Eric Allan. 'It was terrible. Very sad. I rather think she didn't intend to do it, but was making some sort of gesture. She should have got out of the RSC. We loved her to death, but she was potty. She always went out on a limb for me, one of the few people who did from time to time.' Trevor Nunn saw Goodbody's *Hamlet* through to its opening night, one of the most exciting in the company's history. A major talent had been lost. Mike Leigh, another child of the sixties, but one who survived, was on the brink of a little, already belated, compensatory recognition.

SIX

Nuts and Nibbles at Abigail's Party

You always know where people live and what people do for a living in Leigh's films and plays. Where they live and what they do defines who they are. Never was this truer than of Keith and Candice-Marie Pratt, the holiday-making urban misfits in *Nuts in May*, the first of Leigh's two major works for the BBC 'Play for Today' slot produced by David Rose in Birmingham. They live in Croydon, the south London suburb with faceless office-block architecture and a proud record of amateur dramatics and choral singing. Keith works in the social services and plays the banjo. Candice-Marie works in a toyshop, composes little poems and songs and goes to bed with a fluffy blue hot water bottle called Prudence. They are also rabid vegetarians, health freaks, crass conservationists and sexual frigidaires. They have no redeeming features whatsoever.

Keith, played by Roger Sloman as a bald-pated fanatic with a gleaming eye and a pinafore, wears special gloves to drive his Morris Minor convertible and lays down laws about how many times you should chew a piece of food before swallowing it (Gladstone is supposed to have chomped on each mouthful seventy-two times, an admirable example to Keith). His powers of observation extend merely to noting the sort of information you can tick off against a survey questionnaire. Striding around Corfe Castle with a map at the ready, he absorbs the scene, stops dead in his tracks, and proclaims with the inappropriate sonority of an Old Testament prophet: 'There's a car going up the B3351.' The comedy of the film lies not only in the exposure of these animated archetypes, but also in the variety of ways in which a camping holiday that is planned down to the last detail – tent-rigging procedures, dietary schedules, local excursions, and the search for unpolluted milk on a nearby farm – is subjected to critical derision not only by Keith's fellow creatures in the Great Outdoors, but by the Great Outdoors itself: the skies open with wonderful contempt and piss all over the expedition to Lulworth Cove, which is conceived by Keith as though he were Scott approaching the Antarctic, or Napoleon contemplating the siege of Moscow. Candice-Marie, whom a bespectacled Alison Steadman invests with a velveteen whine, weak 'Rs' and a daunting, incredulous vacuity, has conspired to a culpable degree in Keith's ludicrous campaigns, happily cocooned in their circumscribed world from which they presume to sally forth in risible postures of global and environmental concern. They are historically, and hysterically, poised between the weekend hippie syndrome of the late 1960s and the New Age ecological freak-out of today.

The perennial appeal of *Nuts in May* lies, too, in a theatrical structure applied to a realistic, outdoor setting. Interestingly, this is not the result of the piece's origins as a stage play (the film bears next to no relation to *Wholesome Glory*), but of Leigh's method in manipulating his characters into situations of conflict and confrontation. The Pratts' idyll is first threatened by the arrival of Ray, an amateur geologist and Physical Education student at a teachers' training college in Cardiff. Little Ray (the seraphically anonymous Anthony O'Donnell) has a little tent and a very loud radio. He is advised in no uncertain terms by Keith to keep his distance in the camping site, but closer contact ensues after the bedraggled, drenched Ray is given a lift in the Morris on the way back from Lulworth. 'Our larder isn't sticking into you, is it?' asks Keith, hopefully, as Ray cringes on the back seat. Emboldened by Ray's hangdog compatibility, Candice-Marie crawls into his tent to show him the stones she has collected on the beach; Keith explodes with jealous rage after spying on them from behind the bushes with his binoculars, like a character in a farce.

The Pratts are not yielding to the outdoor life, as they like to think they are, but imposing their own home-life priorities and demands upon it. They visit a quarry, as if they were minor royalty, where Eric Allan had researched his quarryman role for three weeks. Allan had been even closer to the site than he intended, for he had fallen into a late-night drinking altercation with the manager of the Swanage hotel in which the entire cast and crew were staying – the manager was called 'Pratt', amazingly enough – and been obliged to retire to his dormobile on the cliffs nearby. 'I joined this guy and his assistant chipping stones. We were producing Purbeck stone which was riddled with little fossils; when sawn and polished up, it gave a kind of marble effect. They were building a new post office near Corfe Castle, and our stuff was being picked up and transported over there.'

Allan became so involved in the experience that he not only learned a new trade but entered into the domestic lives of the quarrymen. He does feel guilty, though, that he did not come up with a more interesting performance: 'I've often felt, working with Mike, that the whole joy of it – in this case, a sort of Dorset quarry holiday for three weeks – means that you feel as though you haven't earned your money.' Leigh reckons that Allan under-estimates the essential plus points of extended research even in a minor role: the accent, the marination in local references, 'not to mention the fact that he does actually do the business with the hammer and the chisel without buggering his hand up'. One day, the big digger lifting the stone exposed a surface indented with mid-Jurassic dinosaur footprints. The discovery was instantly incorporated into the dialogue, a good example of how many of Leigh's most vivid moments are forged in the design or physical properties of the given location. Another instance of such seren-dipity occurs in the scene in *Grown-Ups* by the room partition, a feature of the Canterbury house unlooked for in the first place but gratefully, and amusingly, absorbed when found; yet another in the Oldham house in *The Kiss of Death* where one of the girls sits down on the toilet next to a Robert Burns plaque – which came with the house, not the production designer – and which read 'If at first you don't succeed, try, try and try again,' a misattributed legend (coined by W.E. Hickson, not Burns) that could apply to both her immediate situation and the one next door where a young boy is thwarted in his romantic intentions.

In the 1993 NFT retrospective, Leigh showed a black and white slash dupe of *Nuts in May*, the cutting copy, which runs a full forty minutes longer than the final film and which, like the four-act version of *The Importance of Being Earnest*, suggests that a fair amount of baby was thrown out with the bathwater. This version was known as 'The Plastic Tadpole' for no other reason than that the BBC insists, for accountancy and internal information purposes, on all projects having titles from the earliest stages of development. With Leigh, as there is never a script or an inkling of subject matter in advance, this once led to a series of spurious titles which, as Paul Clements remarked in a useful anthology of them, conjures up an unlikely menagerie: *Hard Labour* was 'The Electric Weasel'; *The Permissive Society*, 'The Clockwork Chipmunk'; *Knock for Knock*, 'The Elastic Peanut'; *The Kiss of Death*, 'The Concrete Mongrel'; *Who's Who*, 'The Porcelain Pig'; *Too Much of a Good Thing*, 'The Chocolate Chicken'; *Grown-Ups*, 'The Iron Frog'; *Home Sweet Home*, 'The Wooden Egg'; and *Four Days in July*, 'The Hot Potato'.

Most of the *Nuts* cuts were made in the elaborately funny erection of the Pratts' tent, with Keith trying to locate all the eyelets while laying out the pins and matching up the colours on the instruction manual; in some of the travel sections; and in little sequences such as Ray's Canadian Army exercises. But you can't have everything, and even Wilde's masterpiece is immeasurably tighter and tauter having met the cutting requirements from his producer, George Alexander. We still have the deliberately excruciating songs, including Candice-Marie's 'I want to see the zoo', a strange subject for a vegetarian who obviously hasn't thought through the moral inconsistency of gawping at caged animals while refusing to eat their carcases or wear their skins. Poor little Ray is compelled to join in the choruses of this interminable folk ditty, and just when you think the narrative is going to dwindle into thinnish satirical whimsy, the motorcyclists from hell, or rather Birmingham, roar into the camping site.

Honky and Finger are played by the married couple of Sheila Kelley, in leathers and glittering block heels, and Stephen Bill, a beanpole, beer-swilling plasterer in flares, with a laughing cackle as crude and nauseating as a game show host's. For all that, they are a likeably vulgar and fun-loving pair, in obvious contrast to the Pratts. They go to the pub, they break the rules, they drive Keith crazy. Finger farts in Ray's tent. The crunch comes when they start lighting a fire in contravention of the site rules, and Keith erupts, his rage enhanced by the use of a wobbly hand-held camera as he attacks Finger with a sawn-off shot-branch. In a curious way, Keith at last achieves an atavistic authenticity in this berserk, climactic explosion, and you feel it is doing him a lot of good, especially when he breaks down sobbing and retreats from the fray, and the camping site, with the pathetic adieu to Finger that 'I was only trying to advise you for your own good.' En route to the farm where they first went in search of unpolluted milk, the Pratts are stopped by a local bobby, who searches their boot and advises them to change one of their tyres (going as bald as Keith) as soon as possible. You can just see them back in Croydon, chopping up cheese and slicing carrots, justifying their humiliation, and outdoor expertise, to each other.

When Stephen Bill and Sheila Kelley first moved into their house in Leamington Spa, they went to a party across the road and met a designer from Peugeot Talbot, the car manufacturers, in Coventry, who started quoting the dialogue of *Nuts in May*. He said that they often held *Nuts in May* socials at the works. Bill was acting at the Belgrade Theatre in Coventry on the night of the broadcast. 'I do a lot of telly, acting and writing, and you rarely get that cross-the-board reaction when something goes out. *Nuts* was one of them.' His face was well known from the long-running motel soap *Crossroads* at the time, which caused another of those famous rehearsal mishaps when he went out, in character, with Kelley for a cup of tea. Or, as he ordered it in character, 'A coop of tay.' A waitress came up and accused him of having appeared in *Crossroads*. Bill decided to stay in character and carried on in Finger's best broad Brummie: 'You *what*? Me, in fuckin'

Crossroads? You off yaw trolley, or whaa . . . ? Fook off, yoah. Bleedin' *Crossroads*, me? You whaa . . . ? Aagh, fook off!' The waitress fled in disarray.

Kelley recalls being asked by Leigh to come down with Bill from the Midlands on her motorcycle, which she had bought during the RSC season at Stratford, and at that stage in rehearsals when she and Bill were first called to the campsite they roared up on the bike in full, noisy and vengeful character. 'The one thing we had been told was not to drive on this particular patch of grass. We were told that, however, as Stephen and Sheila. As Finger and Honky, we would undoubtedly drive on the banned patch of grass, so we revved up and did wheelies all over the place.' The woman who owned the farm adjacent to the campsite was out like a shot – it was her vegetable patch – but the actors assumed she was someone in the cast behaving in character as a spoilsport. They had not yet met the formidable Richenda Carey, who played the campsite manageress. And they redoubled their wheely exertions, adding a stream of high-decibel verbal abuse that turned the air, and very nearly the grass itself, blue. Immediately, Leigh's assistant ran over to the farm owner, consoling her with apologies and desperate explanations, at which point the mistake was realised and the tearaways at last 'came out of character'. The rural hostess, eventually assuaged, withdrew her initial insistence that the whole crew should depart, but she drew the line at allowing Sheila Kelley to use her toilet for the duration.

There is a way of looking at Mike Leigh's work in which all the characters are, to a greater or lesser degree, misfits. People are invariably at odds with their environment, their loved ones, their homes, their backgrounds. This unsettled pawkiness is something deep inside Leigh himself, and his work is often the creative expression of a restless, churning ambivalence about life, love, people, home, work and even recreation. All of this informs the character of Trevor in *The Kiss of Death*, the 1977 BBC TV film which is one of Leigh's favourites, not least because, as he has often said, Trevor contains certain autobiographical elements. It is also the occasion of a wonderful performance by David Threlfall as the sloping, smiling, shy and critical undertaker's apprentice with a book in his pocket whose moods and personality really constitute the subject of the film. There is no particular dynamic, or story, as such, but a series of sharply observed and brilliantly acted scenes conveying the texture of life and death in Oldham, Lancashire, at a particular time. 'The whole thing,' Leigh says, 'and this is very personal, is about received notions of how to be, and how to behave, both generally, and in relationships. All that upwardly mobile rubbish in *Hard Labour* with Alison's role is obviously the beginning of all kinds of stuff, and it's all about insiders and outsiders and received ideas. I'm certainly perverse. As a reflex reaction, I always opt for the dissident role in any situation.'

The shakedown of the big-city teenage rebellion is evinced in this time of flares, brown shirts with round collars, the first noisy discothèques, and snogging on sofas. Trevor and his friend Ronnie form a foursome with Kay Adshead's predatory, gum-chewing Linda and Angela Curran's Betty Boopish, stay-at-home, incipiently matriarchal Sandra. They echo, more innocently and adolescently, Ted Whitehead's lubricious quartet on the sand in *The Foursome*, and they tentatively anticipate the full-blown, foul-mouthed filthiness of Andrea Dunbar's *Rita, Sue and Bob Too* (filmed by Alan Clarke in 1986). But the brake on Trevor's *joie de vivre* is the factual premonition of everyday death. One of the girls asks him what is he reading. 'A book,' he replies with enigmatic sarcasm, echoing Hamlet's 'Words, word, words,' and, again, fast-forwarding to Johnny in *Naked*. In the opening sequence of a funeral arriving at the church, we hear an ice-cream van's jingle in the background, a typical Leigh touch, and completely true; it feels as though it just might have been playing as they shot the scene. It wasn't, as it happens. It was added in afterwards.

We see Trevor and his boss, Mr Garside, played by Clifford Kershaw from *Hard Labour*, dressing a corpse and bantering like Shakespeare's gravediggers. 'How's your wife?' Trevor asks. 'I worship the ground that's coming to 'er.' In this scene, Leigh recalls, 'Our cadaver was played by a real actor, an old extra. When he turned up, we saw to our horror that he had a twitch.

And he couldn't keep his eyes shut. He was also partially deaf. So when we were rehearsing the Queen joke [the Queen visits a hospital ward and a little head at the end of the row says, 'Sling yer 'ook,' and the Queen turns to the matron and says, 'He seems a little upset,' to which the matron replies, 'Well, *you'd* be a little upset; he's having all his teeth out tomorrow!'] this acting cadaver heard a bit of it and started to laugh. Someone else said, "Don't corpse!" and that was it . . . we all went.'

One event does affect Trevor profoundly: the central incident of a cot death. He and Garside are called to a house on a middle-class estate where a baby has died. He becomes even more introverted after wrapping the baby, who bears an eerie resemblance to a green porcelain doll ('The baby's corpse was made by the medical artists at Manchester University,' says Leigh; 'if it looks like a doll we shot it wrong. It should have looked, and did look, very real'), and sliding it on a steel tray into the mortuary fridge like a loaf of bread going into an oven. A pair of cold feet sticks out from the shelf above. Soon after, he helps Linda's elderly neighbour up the stairs after she has collapsed. 'She looks dead paarly [poorly],' exclaims Linda in her broad accent, a slight variation on her favourite phrase in which everything is 'dead baaring [boring]'. The old lady asks Trevor his name, and he hers. She's called Dolly. 'Hello, Dolly!' he returns, unforgivably. The old dear is palpably at death's door, and sinking fast. She says no to a cup of tea, but when Trevor accepts one, she revives cantankerously with 'If he's having one, I'll have one!'

This thematic binding of examples of mortality is an exposure of Leigh's technique at its most skilful, because you do not make all the connections and ironic juxtapositions as you watch the film for the first time. They just coalesce around you, so that you later remember that Trevor's tour round the area with Linda takes in the cemetery as well as the pub and the shoe store where she works. And the metaphor of a contrasting vitality suggested by Linda's non-stop, flirtatious and slightly vampiric gum-chewing is wittily extended when she waits to meet Trevor outside the Roxy cinema where the poster of the current film shows a huge shark with a gaping mouth and dangerous teeth: *Jaws*. This kind of deliberate, careful composition of a film justifies Leigh's anger whenever 'media studies' people and TV comedy buffs draw simple analogies between his work and sitcoms and soaps. 'I get angry because there is nothing, no situation, in my films that is inorganic. But if the commentators simply mean that there are populist elements in my work, I'm happy with that. I have no wish to be seen only by a few people in art houses. I want my work to be popular, mainstream, and enjoyed by the greatest possible audience. I try for that all the time.'

There had always been bits of 'indifferently played' music in Leigh's films – Norman's blues guitar in *Bleak Moments*, Les's George Formby-style ukulele in *The Permissive Society*, Keith Pratt's banjo in *Nuts in May* – always accompanying the voice. But never a full score on the soundtrack. Leigh had met the composer and conductor Carl Davis when they were working on a small commission for Barry Hanson, the film titles trailer for Thames Television's 'Plays for Britain' series in 1976. Davis was intrigued by Leigh, finding him both charming and odd. They got on well, and Leigh asked him to write music for *The Kiss of Death*. As an American, Davis had difficulty understanding both the actors' accents ('I'd never heard accents like that until I met some of my wife's aunties'; he is married to Jean Boht, the popular Liverpudlian actress) and the meandering nature of the film. 'I'm a rather literal person, and it took me time to realise that the film was about the characters' lives, not so much what happens.' But having decided that he was going to have music, Leigh involved Davis to the same extent that Karel Reisz later involved him on the film of *The French Lieutenant's Woman* (1981): 'Karel Reisz said that music is completely integral, and that you would choose music in the way you would choose costume, or prop, or dialogue. It works that way for Mike, too. Every good film director has the same approach. A director like Fred Zinnemann, with whom I had a disastrous working relationship on a film called *Five Days One Summer* (1982), said that my trouble was that I wrote music people wanted to listen to; they pulled my score and got something even worse by Elmer Bernstein!'

Davis liked the fact that if he wrote something good, Leigh

wanted the audience to hear it, and the score for *The Kiss of Death* is both jaunty and plaintive, light and melancholic, deftly played by a classical woodwind ensemble of flute, oboe, clarinet and horn. In their later collaboration, *Home Sweet Home* (1982), the postmen film, Leigh told Davis he was looking for something very odd to counterpoint the pedestrianism of these people's lives. 'In desperation, I said, "God, I've just had a letter from something called the London Double Bass Quartet; how about a quartet of basses?" And he said "Fabulous," and that's what it is.' Both Davis scores are classy pieces of work in their own right. But he denies having an interest in the independent life of such scores. 'You try and write music of a certain aptness and quality that fits each particular sequence. *Home Sweet Home* is, I think, terrific, telling you the story very well, and the score is indeed a counterpoint to the film and at the same time it adds a sort of edginess.'

The kissing part of *The Kiss of Death* is an extraordinary scene, comparable to that between Sylvia and Peter in *Bleak Moments*. Linda and Trevor are on the sofa, she chewing away, he nervously amused but not exactly apprehensive. The more predatory Linda becomes, the more laughable Trevor finds the situation. 'You can kiss me if you like,' she says. 'Put your coffee cup down.' 'I haven't finished it,' smirks Trevor. The playing is slow, nobody's rushing anything, apart from Linda who wants to complete the ritual with a snog. Trevor becomes giggly, then repelled, then confused, then he bursts out laughing. Now Linda switches, and Trevor is in control. He grabs her by the lower jaw and kisses her fiercely, savagely, on the mouth. Shaken, she nonetheless stands up and says 'Are you coming upstairs?' Trevor starts gig-gling again, and the giggles become stronger and stronger. Linda snaps. 'You'd better go, then.' Trevor pulls up his knees on the sofa, adopting a foetal position. Linda is now hard, and very beautiful. Trevor leaves. She shouts after him. The playing of Kay Adshead and David Threlfall indicates every stage of this sexual jousting match with faultless accuracy and perception. We glimpse, as if in a series of intuitive flashes, an entire catalogue of human emotions in the mating game: anxiety, cruelty, affection, wonder, contempt and playfulness. This is how love scenes are endured in life, not in the movies, but distilled and refined for *this* movie. This sequence, camera tight in on the two faces, with no long shot and no trickery, is one of the highlights in the Leigh canon, and all about the performances, which are fresh, funny, completely original, and entirely truthful.

The undertakers' car does double duty at marriage services – the film could be subtitled, with chilling accuracy, 'Four Funerals and a Wedding' – so the penultimate scene finds Trevor outside a church talking to a little bridesmaid who has refused to stay inside for the ceremony: she says she doesn't like boys and will never get married. Trevor is at ease with her, highly amused and sympathetic. As the camera pulls out from the terraces and high-rise flats, and soars above the Pennines, Ronnie and Trevor drive off, still giggling, in the wedding car. Leigh's plan was to have a final scene in which they drive to Blackpool and pick up two girls on the motorway, girls with long hair wearing jeans and duffel-coats, girls with whom they could communicate: 'That would have told the story of escape from those small-minded, rather bone-headed girls in Oldham and their middle-class aspirations.' But he ran out of time.

It is a cruel irony that the piece of work for which Mike Leigh and Alison Steadman together remain best known is a flatly photographed, crude studio recording of a fringe theatre play that never even transferred to the West End. *Abigail's Party* is not a television film, but a hastily compiled television studio play which merely replicates the Hampstead Theatre production that opened in April 1977 after the cancellation of a few previews. The show, an instant smash hit, was a fluke from the off. It all happened at short notice because another play had been cancelled, and Leigh says that Michael Rudman and David Aukin, respectively the artistic director and general manager of Hampstead, put pressure on him in a Chinese restaurant: 'Say yes or no. Now.' He said yes, even though he was busy preparing for his BBC TV film *Who's Who*. His attitude was one of doing the thing quickly and getting it out of the way; and it remains the best-known piece he has ever written and directed.

Leigh had a natural affinity with the cosy, unpretentious theatre at Swiss Cottage. His admired teacher at RADA, James Roose-Evans, had founded the Hampstead Theatre Club in 1959. And Leigh and David Halliwell had gone there (unsuccessfully) with the unwieldy first draft of *Little Malcolm and his Struggle Against the Eunuchs* a couple of years later. Leigh had received a friendly letter from Rudman when *Bleak Moments* was running at the Open Space; Rudman was at that time in charge of the Traverse in Edinburgh. They circled each other for several years, and the long-postponed cooperation which led to *Abigail's Party* yielded three more significant and highly successful stage works over the next ten years: *Goose-Pimples*, *Ecstasy*, and *Smelling a Rat* (commissioned under the subsequent regime of Michael Attenborough and Dallas Smith and produced soon after Attenborough left by his successor, Jenny Topper). Aukin, an old friend of Rudman from Oxford days, defined the appeal of Hampstead as 'a theatre without a memo, without a TIE [Theatre-in-Education] team, no "outreach", no marketing, no development officer: just one play on the stage and another in rehearsal.' He was shocked when *Abigail's Party* wasn't quite ready for the appointed opening date, but managed to hide an 'emergency' week or two away thereafter: 'One learned how to produce Mike Leigh!' Aukin continued his association when he took over from David Rose as head of drama at Channel 4 and continued that company's commitment to Leigh's work by earmarking £1 million, two thirds of the budget, for *Naked*.

Abigail's Party was so successful that it returned to Hampstead after its initial run, in the summer of 1977. In all, it played 104 performances (coincidentally, the running time was usually 104 minutes), and managements, led by Michael Codron, were queuing up to take it into the West End. By which time, Alison Steadman had become pregnant – 'In those days,' she says, 'we didn't do plays with a view to a West End transfer; nowadays people ask about that the minute you open' – and the possibility that the production might continue with another actress playing the gorgonic Beverly was out of the question. So a recording was hastily arranged at the BBC as a 'Play for Today', produced by

Margaret Matheson and transmitted in November of the same year.

This again was a makeshift arrangement: Caryl Churchill's play about the Diplock trials in Northern Ireland was suddenly cancelled by the BBC 'for legal reasons', leaving Matheson with an empty studio and no time to rehearse a replacement. 'She persuaded me to wheel in *Abigail's Party*,' says Leigh, 'despite my reservations about televising an essentially theatrical piece. This rushed tape version is really quite a mess. Look at it, and you'll see patchy, inconsistent lighting, and even the odd microphone in shot! As a location film-maker, I hate videotape studios; I swore I would never again set foot in one after *Abigail's Party*, and I haven't.' As a fringe producing company, Hampstead had no rights in the TV version, and the BBC was refusing to make any payment to the theatre. The BBC team hired the actors separately and built their own set, which was a confused imitation of Tanya McCallin's garishly gorgeous Hampstead design. 'This is where Mike was terrific,' recalls David Aukin, praising his colleague's integrity: 'He told the BBC he would not sign his contract until instructed by David Aukin. In that way, they were forced to come to terms with Hampstead and to pay us a pittance.' And to give them a credit.

Leigh's embarrassment over the technical deficiencies was lost on the nation's viewers, who have loved *Abigail's Party*, and Alison Steadman's performance in particular, ever since. On its third showing, there was an ITV strike, an unattractively highbrow programme on BBC 2 (Channel 4 had not yet been invented), and a raging storm throughout the British Isles. This was how, apart from its intrinsic merits, *Abigail's Party* attracted no less than sixteen million viewers and a permanent place in the nation's affection, on a par with Christmas highlights of Morecambe and Wise and comedy series such as Frankie Howerd's *Up Pompeii!* or Harry H. Corbett and Wilfrid Bramble in *Steptoe and Son*. But *Abigail's Party*, for all Leigh's insistence on its technical imperfections, is not a sitcom, or an extended comic sketch. In form and substance it is an extremely cunning subversion of a West End boulevard comedy, with the shape and energy of the best in the genre, and its own stark inevitability. A notably sleek structure of tension, acceleration and climax, it is more akin to Greek tragedy than to most television comedy.

Abigail is a fifteen-year-old whom we never see. She is having a party across the road while her mother, Susan, has taken temporary refuge with Beverly, a quondam beautician, and Laurence, an estate agent with 'Wibley Webb', who have lived in Richmond Road for three years. Beverly has also invited a couple who moved into the road just two weeks ago, the bespectacled, girlish nurse Angela and her computer operator husband, the taciturn Tony, an ex-footballer with Crystal Palace. (The actor in question, John Salthouse, did in fact play professional football for Crystal Palace until an injury halted his career and he took to the boards.) Susan has been divorced for three years. The neighbours exchange small talk, with Beverly taking the ascendant at every opportunity as she fills up the glasses, doles out her cheese and pineapple nibbles on sticks ('Take another one, Sue . . . save me coming back!') and shimmies provocatively around the leather sofa and onyx coffee table, playing Donna Summer and José Feliciano records while further belittling her already quite small spouse, who likes classical music.

The action is really an experiment in different levels of control, domination and dramatic tension, with Susan rushing to the lavatory to be sick after one too many gin and tonics at the end of the first act ('That's it. Bring it all up. That's it. Better out than in,' we hear Angela advising Susan off stage). Laurence, taunted for preferring James Galway to Elvis Presley, is goaded beyond endurance by Beverly's explicit close dancing with Tony, and the temperature rises to boiling point in a ridiculous argument over the comparative merits of a reproduction of van Gogh's yellow chair at Arles and a cheap erotic painting Beverly likes but Laurence derides. She tells him to drop dead. Laurence explodes with rage, slams Beethoven's Fifth onto the record player, and does as he's told: he drops dead of a heart attack. The women are petrified in panic: Angela, giving Laurence a superfluous kiss of life, is stricken with an appalling cramp, Beverly tells Susan to go home in no uncertain terms, and the distraught mother cannot hear her daughter over the telephone for the rising din of rock music, gatecrashers and general mayhem.

This is not light comedy. It is heavy hysteria, and audiences in the theatre are clambering aboard an unstoppable rollercoaster. On television, the effect was necessarily muted, but the level of the wonderful performances undimmed. Leigh had to replace nearly all the music with artists recorded on British labels, for copyright reasons, in case the BBC sold the play to the United States (it never did). Thus José Feliciano became Demis Roussos and, most outrageously in Leigh's book, Elvis gave way to Tom Jones. There are also a few cuts in the television version, notably the first page of Act 2 dialogue between Beverly and Angela.

Leigh describes the exact location of the play as 'theoretical Romford', which disappoints me as I thought I had sleuthed 'Richmond Road' to the real Richmond Road behind the town hall in Ilford, Essex. The houses are exactly the sort of decent, ordinary 1930s houses Angela and Tony would inhabit – though there is a tinge more Chigwell and Woodford about Beverly and Susan in their different ways. Susan's former husband, an architect, has already remarried, which only compounds her dilapidated brand of middle-class gloom, while Beverly has no intention, she kids herself, of languishing in the purlieus of the lower-middle class for too long. And as Beverly says, 'Mind you, Ang, your house is smaller than this one, yeah, because I know they are smaller on your side, yeah.' The London side of Essex, anyway, is definitely our terrain, where important distinctions are made between leather and 'leather look', and where the class and ethnic composition of the area is on the turn.

Laurence is trying to safeguard a heritage of which he barely has a nodding acquaintance, chatting up Susan about 'culture' and Paris for tourists, and clinging to the fact that L.S. Lowry's father was an estate agent, as though that entitled him to boast about the bound and gold-embossed complete works of Dickens and Shakespeare on his fitted shelves: '*Macbeth* . . . part of our heritage . . . of course, it's not something you can actually read.' And yet Laurence does have an inkling of sensitivity, and one moment of blinding clarity: 'You know, I think musicians and artists, they're very lucky people. They're born with one great advantage in life. And d'you know what it is? Their talent. They've got something to cling to.' Most creditably, he takes a sort of train-spotting historical interest in the local area and explains to Susan that some of the houses are indeed late Victorian, while some were built before the last war. But Laurence's suppressed racism also emerges in this exchange with Susan; she clearly welcomes the increasing 'cosmopolitanism' of the area, and he certainly doesn't.

Angela, whom Beverly insists on calling 'Ang' (pronounced diphthongally, with a soft 'g', as in 'sponge', or 'Angela' without the 'ela') as a form of social appropriation, works as a nurse at the non-existent St Mary's Hospital in Walthamstow. Janine Duvitski researched Angela's career for a fortnight at the Royal Free Hospital in Hampstead. She considers herself a bad example of someone to talk about working with Leigh. 'I cheat quite a lot. I went into a supermarket in character as Angela and I hadn't had time to get any food for my dog, so I picked up this tin of Chum. And suddenly, there was Mike – you never know whether he's following you or not – leering around the corner of the dog food section, whispering cheekily, "Your character doesn't have a dog!" You do laugh a lot. In fact, I don't think I ever stopped laughing the whole time. I always think of our rehearsals in that church hall whenever I read about the play being done in Japan. I had never done parts like that before. I was doing real kitchen sink stuff, playing young, unmarried mothers.

'At the final rehearsals I suddenly saw Tim Stern do this heart attack and of course I knew that I would be expected to do something. I pretended I hadn't seen it and crouched down like a squirrel who's had too much to drink, and Alison is saying, "Come on, Ang, you're a nurse, yeah," and I ignore her and then Mike's voice booms out from the back of the stalls, "Get up!" and I got up and I did my best. And I really got that terrible cramp, so Mike said, "We'll have that!" Jonathan Miller came in for one session to show me what you do – the theatre rang up his wife Rachel, who's a GP, at home, but he answered and said he'd come in – but I never liked the ending and I still don't.' The interesting thing about Duvitski's performance is that she is indeed embarrassingly grotesque and painfully gushing and anxious to please, but she is also patently a very good nurse. This, of course, is absolutely crucial. In a 1994 revival of the play at the Theatr Clwyd, Mold, the actress playing Angela reproduced the outer symptoms of Duvitski's creation – the dank hair, the specs, the hunched torso, the nerves, the girlish, floral blue dress edged with patterned lace and the clumpy shoes – but she missed entirely the inner warmth and well-meaning centre of the character which guarantees our faith in her professional competence.

Angela had met Tony while working nights when he came in for an emergency operation. 'It was important,' says Duvitski, 'that he, an athlete, met her like that, because she was probably quite good at her job and he found that attractive.' The beauty of John Salthouse's performance is that he conveys so much with so few words, mostly grudging disappointment at the marriage into which he has mistakenly fallen. He is the very picture of a man putting up with a lot but not for much longer, which is why he is so easily diverted by Beverly's flirtatiousness and not too reluctant to go and offer assistance at the mounting riot of Abigail's party: available crumpet and flowing booze are a nostalgic pang of the past for a former soccer player.

Beverly asks Angela if he is violent. 'No, he's not violent. Just a bit nasty. Like, the other day, he said to me, he'd like to sellotape my mouth. And that's not very nice, is it?' 'It certainly isn't, Ang!' It is clear that the eruption of sadistic sexual violence in *Naked* does not herald a new subject for Leigh. Traces of it are as discernible in *Abigail's Party* as they are in *The Kiss of Death*, *Goose-Pimples*, *Smelling a Rat* and *Life is Sweet*. And those traces become heavily marked tracks in *Hard Labour*, *Ecstasy*, *Home Sweet Home* and *Meantime*.

Alan Bennett introduced another screening of *Abigail's Party* as part of his ideal night's viewing: 'A Night in with Alan Bennett', BBC 2, July 1992. His other chosen programmes were an episode of *Whatever Happened to the Likely Lads*, Malcolm Mowbray's *Days at the Beach* (starring Julie Walters), a Melvyn Bragg profile of Sir John Barbirolli, and snippets of such comedy programmes as *Dad's Army*, Jimmy Edwards in *Whack-O*, and John Cleese in *Fawlty*

Towers. Bennett admitted that he would run a mile from all of Leigh's characters, and that the only puzzle about Beverly – 'a brutal hostess with shoulders like a lifeguard and a walk to match' – was that she had managed to escape strangulation for so long. Bennett is expressing the malevolence Laurence feels towards his wife, and which Tony feels towards Angela, as a form of extreme irritation and dislike. Misogyny might be putting it too strongly. But Laurence and Tony are certainly soul brothers of Trevor and Ronnie in *The Kiss of Death* in this respect. And the misogyny, of course, belongs entirely to the characters, and not to the writer/director, whatever the feminist deconstructionists might suppose. Bennett also had something interesting to say of Leigh's style: 'Mike Leigh taps a level below dialogue as it is generally written, though the minute you hear it, it's instantly real and recognisably awful, a verbal muzak hilarious in a play but deeply dreary in life.'

The business of where Leigh stood *vis à vis* the lifestyles represented on stage became an area of heated discussion, and words like 'condescension' and 'patronising' started to appear regularly in reviews. These sentiments were always proffered by middle-class critics who may not have been best placed to know what lower-middle-class people like Beverly or Angela would think of their fictional representations, or indeed what was meant by the vocabulary of politically correct critics. But the whole debate started here, and one speech in particular became a rallying cry for commentators from Dennis Potter to Julie Burchill. When Susan arrives, she hands Beverly a 'thank you for inviting me' bottle. Beverly unwraps it: 'Oh, lovely! 'Cos Laurence likes a drop of wine, actually. Oh, it's Beaujolais. Fantastic! Won't be a sec, I'll just pop it in the fridge.' The middle-class audience response to this line was to laugh knowingly at Beverly's absurdly misguided action of chilling a bottle of red plonk. The letters page of *The Times* reacted to the fracas at the time of the first transmission on the whole vexed topic of wine bottles in fridges.

In later years, the sin of Beverly's social solecism was thrown back in Leigh's face by Julie Burchill, who galumphingly pointed out that anyone who knew about Beaujolais *would* pop it in the fridge (not in 1977 they wouldn't), and that to assume that Beverly was committing a social gaffe somehow compounded Leigh's condescension as it exposed his own naff level of vinous ignorance. But the joke *was* intended as one about the absurdity of putting a bottle of Beaujolais in the fridge. And so what if it *was* a joke at the character's expense? It is a curious idea that an audience which laughs at a preposterous character is colluding in an act of class warfare. No such objections are ever raised when pompous clerics and ignorant shysters are pilloried by Ben Jonson. It is the contemporaneity, the living reality, of the characters that deadens some critics' satirical antennae.

When *Abigail's Party* was first shown on television, the late Dennis Potter, who considered television to be the true national theatre, and could justly lay claim to being one of its leading figures, was writing a television review column in the *Sunday Times*. He went bananas. He felt that Leigh's play was 'based on nothing more edifying than rancid disdain, for it was a prolonged jeer, twitching with genuine hatred, about the dreadful suburban tastes of the dreadful lower middle classes . . . it sank under its own immense condescension. The force of the yelping derision became a single note of contempt, amplified into a relentless screech. As so often in the minefields of English class-consciousness, more was revealed of the snobbery of the observers rather than the observed.'

This broken-backed polemic was unsupported by detail or example and was palpably untrue in the body of its allegations, and especially in its final assertion. I have already indicated the amount of information available to an audience about the characters, the quiet gentility of Susan, the stoical resentment of Tony, the unfortunately manifested good nature of Angela, the short fuse and anxiety to please and impress of Laurence. Beverly is undoubtedly a monster. But she is also a deeply sad and vulnerable monster, a fact that seems to have eluded Potter while he salivated on his sofa and hallucinated other people's dastardly class-war strategies. The whole point about Beverly is that she is childless, and there is a sense in which that grotesque exterior carapace is a mask of inner desolation.

ABOVE: After the wedding ceremony, in the Cranleigh Street flat, September 1973: Mike and Alison with their respective parents, Abe and Phyllis, and Marjorie and George Steadman.

LEFT: Leigh's poster for his RSC production of *Babies Grow Old* on its transfer from Stratford-upon-Avon to the ICA in London in 1975.

Toby Leigh, aged several months, on the kitchen table in Wood Green, photographed by his father after a family holiday in France, 1978.

Alison Steadman, Roger Sloman and Geoffrey Hutchings in *Wholesome Glory* (1973) in the Theatre Upstairs at the Royal Court.

Nuts in May (1976) was the film that grew out of *Wholesome Glory,* transported to the Dorset countryside: Steadman and Sloman as Candice-Marie and Keith entertain Anthony O'Donnell as Ray, their fellow camper.

RIGHT: Angela Curran, John Wheatley, David Threlfall and Kay Adshead in the discotheque scene in *The Kiss of Death*, 1977.

BELOW: Alison Steadman as the monstrous Beverly, with Janine Duvitski as Angela and (on sofa) Harriet Reynolds as Susan, in the legendary *Abigail's Party* at Hampstead Theatre, 1977.

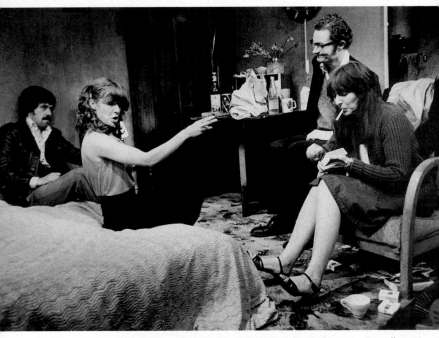

Ecstasy at Hampstead Theatre, 1979: Stephen Rea, Julie Walters, Jim Broadbent and Sheila Kelley in a baleful bedsit boozerama.

Segregated neighbours in the well-structured BBC film *Grown-Ups*, 1980: Lindsay Duncan and Sam Kelly, Philip Davis and Lesley Manville.

Goose-Pimples at Hampstead Theatre in 1981 is the only Leigh play to have transferred to the West End: Jill Baker, Jim Broadbent and Marion Bailey surround Antony Sher as the hapless Muhammad.

Timothy Spall, Eric Richard and Tim Barker as the three hopeless postmen in another notable BBC film, *Home Sweet Home*, 1982.

Tim Roth and Gary Oldman in *Meantime*, 1983, a film which widened Leigh's popularity with a younger audience.

ABOVE: Mike Leigh
on the Great Wall of
China, May Day, 1985.
An unforgettable stop
on the long march home
in traumatic times.

LEFT: Alison, Leo,
Toby and Mike.

The short film *The Short and Curlies* (1987) marked the start of Leigh's latest phase of ascendancy. David Thewlis as Clive, a rubber-purchasing customer in Joy's (Sylvestra Le Touzel) chemist's shop...

...and Joy, a rubber-wearing one at Betty's hairdressing salon, 'Cynthia's'. Betty is one of Alison Steadman's favourite roles.

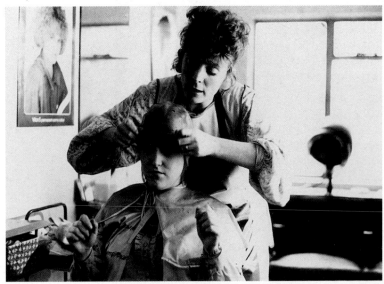

Alison Steadman told *The Face* magazine in 1983 that, 'Although it was great fun, in real terms she is probably one of the saddest characters I've ever played. There is nothing for her that's real, no love, no hope, no feeling for anything that isn't all down to baubles and shiny beads. It's the world of frozen pizzas and the neat set of fake nails.' To greet such a vapid creature, and a play like *Abigail's Party*, with cries of 'unfair' to the lower-middle classes is like accusing P.G. Wodehouse of unreasonable treatment of the landed gentry, or Shakespeare of callously tilting the balance of sympathy against rustic mechanicals and foppish courtiers. Leigh's friend David Canter recalls that they used to talk about monsters and monstrosity all the time. 'Monstrosity was always a general term of endearment for someone behaving inappropriately or insensitively. The power of what Mike does is to do with finding a way of getting actors to create monsters that are acceptable from within themselves. The improvisation and rehearsal process requires the actor to learn more about himself and to find aspects of himself that he can express. The game of starting by finding another character whom they know is really just a way of enabling the actor to be liberated into evaluating *himself* and looking inside.'

A play is only a play, a character only a character. Neither is masquerading as life, or a person, but as a fictive accompaniment to life and people, with sometimes some relation to those abstract generic terms, sometimes not. And we are surely, in the theatre, as in life, allowed to laugh *at* people as well as *with* people. Or is that privilege now to be denied us? There are no rules that all drama should conform to the same liberal consensus. Even the usually sensible Michael Billington jumped off his trolley as he hurtled by *Abigail's Party*, sermonising that in attacking other people's lifestyles, the underlying assumption was that the attacker's own lifestyle was in some way better or superior. I see no such underlying assumption whatsoever. As Alan Ayckbourn's most tirelessly eloquent apologist, Billington knows very well that the world on which Ayckbourn unleashes his most devastating comical derision is not too far removed from the world in which he happily (or unhappily) resides.

Leigh's characters come from deep inside his actors, and must therefore relate to circumstances with which they are familiar, and at the very least sympathetic. Most of his actors come from the sort of background they end up inhabiting as characters. That is usually the whole point. Leigh helps them towards a full realisation of those characters, shaping and manipulating their lines, motivations and emotions, and the overall portrait, as the work evolves. And those actors who express qualms about the 'nastiness' of a portrayal – as Jim Broadbent now does about his car salesman Vernon in *Goose-Pimples*: 'a character of no redeeming qualities whatsoever' – tend to do so because the character in the end got them down, not because they disapproved of 'having a go' at someone from the lower orders (Broadbent, incidentally, hails from middle-class Lincolnshire farming folk, but he's a true plebeian at heart). One critic, at least, was more easily pleased by *Abigail's Party*. A seventeen-year-old pupil of Gunnersbury School for Boys won a prize of £10 in an *Evening News* critic's contest for his unqualified rave and perspicacious remarks on the reversals and nature of true satire. His name was Tony Slattery, later better-known as the stand-up comedian and television star and, ironically, scourge of the critics at a 1995 Olivier Awards ceremony.

The larger Leigh controversy arises in the first place because actors in his plays and films both inhabit and 'objectify' their characters to an extent that is unusual in British acting. Costume, hairstyle, accent, physical mannerism and movement, all external aspects of the character, are as seriously weighed and considered as the spiritual essence. In *Nuts in May*, Roger Sloman as Keith Pratt has a stuttering, fussily assertive gait that suits his jaw-thrusting self-importance exactly, and Alison Steadman seems to glide in a slipstream of fancifulness, her anorak, woolly hat and lank hair perfectly in tune with someone who loves the pastoral idea of animals and the countryside to excess while working in a toy shop. Candice-Marie is a name Leigh used once before, in his discarded play *Monsters*, and he now claims that the moniker is totally wrong for Steadman's character: 'The name lodged with me when I first heard it. The baby of a cousin of a lady radiographer who was in a flat next to me when I went back to Manchester at the end of the 1960s was christened "Candice-Marie". I heard all about it because I was attempting to seduce the radiographer, and I suggested the name to Alison. I realised later, of course, that no one born when Candice-Marie was born – much earlier than that baby – would have been called Candice-Marie. Not for a split second.'

This sorry lapse apart – though not many of us, I would imagine, share Leigh's scruples on the matter – names and demeanours are inseparably just. Walks, too. Trevor and Linda in *The Kiss of Death* are good examples of ambulatory perfection: Trevor slides along the Oldham streets in a fatuous, sloping style, his mop hair and silly grin borne along in concert; Linda hobbles in a discomfort she has learned to live with after years of pushing her feet into unsuitable shoes, a complaint that is ironic enough given that she works in a shoe shop, but serious, too, in the long-term prospects for her already crumbling deportment. This detailed physical observation is unique to Leigh's work, but some people find it too emphatic, too cartoonish, too caricatured. The fact is that if you do what Leigh does all the time – walk around Wood Green, travel on buses, hang around Soho, lurk in the inner cities, stalk the suburbs, listen and talk to anyone you meet, breathe in the metropolitan climate – no physical tic or mannerism of any actor is too exaggerated, no apparent oddity too abnormal. People, normally speaking, are very peculiar, and Leigh and his actors set about celebrating that peculiarity, not patronising it, with relish, gusto and imaginative flair. And in that profound sense, his work can be said to be Dickensian.

Alison Steadman's Beverly dominates *Abigail's Party* not because she acts everyone else off the stage/studio floor but because the character itself takes over the sitting room. Michael Billington describes her as 'some Southern Region Rita Hayworth', a phrase which certainly catches Beverly's mixture of vulgarity and sexiness. She used to work behind a perfume, or make-up, counter in a big department store like Selfridge's, or perhaps, before it closed down, Swan and Edgar. Hence the bossiness of the lipstick lecture, one of the ways in which she asserts both her dominance and social ascendancy over Angela in a manner worthy of Dame Edna Everage in full flight: 'A pinky red! Now, can you take a little bit of criticism? Please don't be offended when I say this, but, you're wearing a very pretty dress, if I may say so; now, you see that pink ribbon down the front? If you'd chosen, Ang, a colour slightly nearer that pink, I think it would have blended more with your skin tones; d'you know what I mean?' She suggests Angela sits in front of the mirror and says to herself, 'I've got very beautiful lips.' This psychology always worked with her customers, she tells her, and means that she will be applying the lipstick to every corner of her mouth. 'Will you try it for me next time?' she concludes, clinching her status as hostess in the know, and the driving seat. But it is the appetite with which Beverly sets about her evening that keeps us guessing. She's ready for a good time, and the guests will have to come up to scratch. And to scratch her back.

There are echoes here of Edward Albee's *Who's Afraid of Virginia Woolf?* (1962), in which the cocktail party of George and Martha becomes a marital wasteland, and their guests, pawns in the struggle. But Beverly's sluttishness is of a lighter, funnier vintage than Martha's, and Laurence's discomfiture less tortured than George's. Beverly's instinct is to turn the evening into a showcase for herself, and the comedy turns vinegary when the plot undermines her attempts to control the cabaret as easily as she controls Laurence. The famous flame-orange dress proclaims her intentions: a three-tiered taffeta arrangement with a low-cut neck is not the dress of someone expecting to be left with a dead husband on the carpet. It reeks of slap and tickle, kitchen cuddles and woozy whoopee.

All of the costumes and most of the properties on a Leigh project are bought in shops where the characters themselves would go shopping. Beverly's dress was no exception. The costume designer, Lindy Hemming, had lately worked at Hampstead Theatre on a Michael Frayn comedy, *Donkeys' Years*; she went shopping with Penelope Keith in Harrods. For Beverly and Angela, Hemming went shopping with Steadman and Duvitski in C&A. (Leigh points out that Beverly would never shop in

C&A; she would aim a bit higher, Richard Shops, or Miss Self-ridge, perhaps, but he was constrained by the limited production budget.) In C&A, the flame-orange dress – could it be dark peach or shocking salmon? – was one of the first they saw. The tier effect was created by a panel which hung loose in a V-shape at the front, with the useful, but unplanned, effect of concealing Alison's pregnancy as the run continued and indeed the television recording was made. Her changing condition transformed the speech about lacking a maternal instinct – 'all that breast-feeding, and having to change nappies, would make me heave' – into a giggle-rich minefield for the actors to negotiate every night.

Beverly wore the dress with a white bra, and Alison recalls almost coming to blows with a costume designer at the BBC who wanted her to match up the dress with a flesh-coloured undergar-ment; when she bent forward over the onyx table during Laur-ence's heart attack, the audience would cop an eyeful of clashing white bra clamped round the increasingly large and heaving Stead-man bosom. This was how Steadman saw Beverly, but the BBC costumier said that the clash was 'visually unacceptable'. The actress's response was tart and final: 'Well, I don't care about that. It will just have to be visually unacceptable. People do wear the wrong coloured bra under a dress, and they do lean forward, course they do.' She had her way, and Beverly sailed on, unim-peded and unimproved.

Alison Steadman's Beverly, which rightly won her the *Evening Standard* Best Actress Award in 1977, is one of those career-defining performances that are no better than many others but which associate her with a certain type of role in the public's mind: the comic, brassy, pretentious suburban hostess. But the portrayal is rich in specific, filigree definition: the rising finality, and public tone, of that 'please' at the end of each instruction to Laurence, the braying laugh to signal jocular filth, the dead-eyed look of disapproval and its concomitant lusty gleam, the cloying, recep-tionist-style whine of welcome to new arrivals, the front-door banter – 'go through' is what all guests have to do, eventually, and the irritating use of 'little' as in 'Have a little sandwich,' 'And I'd like a little top-up, okay?' or 'Tone, d'you fancy a little dance?'

Above all, the incomparable sound of a brilliant performer striking a rich new territory and claiming it as her own private domain. And because so much of Beverly derived from what Steadman knew of other people, and indeed of herself, any other interpretation must needs appear either a pale imitation or an inadequate substitute.

Abigail's Party is performed by professional and amateur companies all over Britain and around the world. It provides a slow trickle of royalty payments to Leigh and the original cast, but nothing life-changing. Leigh has always maintained an understandably wary attitude towards other performances of work he has devised and written in close contact with a particular group of actors, bending and absorbing their own impulses and idiosyncrasies towards the finished production. But since he has sorted out the confusion in his own mind over the labelling of his artistic function – at first he 'devised and directed' his productions, now he 'writes and directs' them – he has also conquered his reluctance to have his scripts published. *Abigail's Party* was first published in a 'Plays of the Year' collection in 1979 and later collected, with *Goose-Pimples*, in a new Penguin edition in 1983. Although there exists an informal nationwide fan club for the piece, rather like that which exists for Richard O'Brien's *The Rocky Horror Show* (1973), another surprise popular hit which was spawned informally and unexpectedly on the London fringe (in the Royal Court's Theatre Upstairs), *Abigail's Party* is a genuine modern classic which deservedly attracts both kitschy enthusiasm and critical applause. Unfortunately, the staginess of the original is unsuited to the television camera. But Steadman's Beverly, and the play it adorns, will survive for as long as people are interested in truthful vulgarity, cheese and pineapple chunks skewered on cocktail sticks, and the finest comic acting which is at once merciless and revelatory.

Through his chance commission at Hampstead, Leigh had both consolidated his theatrical reputation and added a new dimension of recognition and popularity to his work. He cherishes the collaboration – which engendered two more pieces – because he clicked so well with Rudman and Aukin, and their feedback was crucial when he found himself running, as usual, madly against the clock. He also liked the informality of the bar where cast and audience mingled after each performance, the flea-market outside on Saturday afternoons and, when he started work there with Rudman and Aukin, the strange old European atmosphere of the Cosmo Restaurant nearby. Above all, he liked the scale of the place: 'People-sized. Occasionally during auditions I've been terrified of accidentally ensnaring an innocent punter who only wants a ticket.'

'We all had some similarities in our backgrounds, Rudman, Aukin and I, we were all of the same age, knew many actors in common to our work, and we shared the same sense of humour. Rudman was brilliant, very perceptive. I remember him saying after a run-through that the thing about Laurence's death was that I hadn't properly focused the pointers towards it that run through the play. He was absolutely right. I went through the whole piece doing just that, so that when it happened, it was inevitable. It was a great working atmosphere, and I suppose the only time that I've ever felt really at home in the theatre.'

SEVEN

Melt-Down Means Ecstasy
for Grown-Ups

Trevor Nunn and Terry Hands had just announced their joint artistic directorship of the RSC in 1978 when they were hit by their first major problem. Mike Leigh cancelled his new piece for the company after ten weeks of rehearsal. The play, codename 'Ice-cream', was to be presented on the Aldwych stage in London in early 1979, cementing Leigh's association with a company he admired and where he had enjoyed one of his biggest successes, *Babies Grow Old*. Nunn and David Jones had both written encouraging letters in response to Leigh's request for another production. There were several contributory factors to the melt-down of 'Ice-cream': Leigh was at the cutting stage on another film for the BBC (*Who's Who*) while darting in and out of casting meetings at the RSC, where actors were traded like cattle between directors; the dubbing on *Who's Who* was completed late, the day before he started rehearsals, due to the BBC experimenting unsuccessfully with a new kind of sound stock, leaving him unprepared, or at least under-prepared, for the first day at the RSC; and the rehearsal room in Battersea was cold, inconveniently situated and devoid of local cafés. Excuses, excuses!

In addition, Leigh says that he and Chris Dyer, the designer, had together evolved the idea of a great set for something, and that Dyer had responded to that idea 'very well'. But it finally amounted to nothing Leigh recognised: an arrangement of abstract, interconnecting, interlocking cubes that must have reminded him uncomfortably of *The Box Play*. The cast included Lesley Manville, Jill Baker, Gwyneth Strong, Ron Cook, David

Threlfall, Bob Peck, Geoffrey Hutchings and Ian McNeice. Not a bad crowd. They were all involved in other RSC London productions, so that arranging rehearsals was difficult. Research had involved a works outing to Marine Ices on Haverstock Hill, north London, to learn about the mysteries of the ice-cream trade. Lesley Manville was playing a barmaid brought in to a new wine bar which had displaced a greengrocers' shop on the same premises. The theme was small-time capitalism, and Leigh's governing idea was that of a shop changing its identity, and ownership, in the blink of an eye. The wine bar was going to be doubled up as an ice-cream parlour.

Leigh now realises that he was mistaken to have taken up the challenge. His way of working – all hours, on his own terms, with total freedom of actors' availability, in a place where the performance is constructed through habitation and the security of common purpose – was impossible to achieve at the ever-expanding RSC, though everyone tried their best: 'I blew it, definitely, and they were terrific about it. I had asked for uninvolved actors – that is, actors not appearing in any other productions, fully available to rehearsals – as I'd had on *Babies Grow Old*; but that show had been at the start of a season and Trevor said, "Come on man, I can't give you everything," and I accepted that.' He also accepts that the failure of 'Ice-cream' has ensured that he has not worked since at the RSC. Leigh's resentment at not having ever worked at the Royal National Theatre, or ever having been invited to create a major piece for the main stage of the Royal Court, goes much deeper. He has some reason to suppose that cowardice and personal envy are at the root of that impasse; why else would every writer and director of national consequence have been commissioned and performed, but not him? The system is simply unprepared to accommodate him, and you could certainly argue that it is scandalous that the RNT has never turned over the facilities of the small Cottesloe auditorium to a Mike Leigh project.

At least the RSC and the RNT maintained a minimal correspondence with Leigh over the years, with Trevor Nunn and Terry Hands at the former establishment making much more encouraging sounds than either Peter Hall (who took no interest at all in Leigh) or Richard Eyre (who makes diplomatic but non-committal noises) at the latter. But apart from Hampstead Theatre and, more recently, the Theatre Royal, Stratford East, managements have been either too nervous or too unsympathetic to employ Leigh. Terry Hands now says the problems over 'Ice-cream' were chiefly to do with the 'exclusivity' demands on the actors, and he sums up Leigh's career with dispassionate intelligence:

'He went through a patch when he was putting forward clichés. Then he lifted that through a kind of language to art. In that language and poetry, especially with an actor like Timothy Spall [who had first come to attention in leading roles at the RSC before he worked with Leigh], you had characters completely involved and obsessed with themselves who do not develop, any more than do Ben Jonson's. Mike then very sophisticatedly refined the situation around these characters who never changed, but the story did, and that's pure Jonson. Peter Barnes [the playwright, author of *The Ruling Class* and *Bewitched*] at his peak is like that but he's more Jacobean, though he does have moments of revelation and breakthrough. I'm sure Mike will go further, as Ben Jonson did in his later plays, for instance, putting someone on the stage who offers to define Love for us. The world has become so sordid that someone has to tell us about those things. I blame our system, economic and cultural, which makes us part of a set-up that does not allow financial resources to people like Peter Barnes, Peter Brook and Mike Leigh.'

Hands rightly points out, too, that Leigh's method of co-writing with actors is an Elizabethan principle, and exactly comparable to the manner in which Shakespeare and his contemporaries wrote their plays. Nothing was written down, beyond the prompt copy. Hands' choice of unaccommodated geniuses (my word) is interesting, too. It is as if he is admitting the failure of the subsidised theatre to have promoted the work of its most talented practitioners. The funding principle has always been slanted in favour of the institutions, not the artists, and the most talented people tend to be the awkward buggers who start things off. Which is why George Devine had such a life-draining struggle in the early days of the English Stage Company at the Royal Court, why Joan Littlewood was never really supported by the Arts Council, why Peter Brook left Britain to establish his Centre International de Récherches Théâtrales in Paris in 1970, and why the short list of geniuses in the contemporary British theatre – to those proposed by Hands I would add (apart from a question mark against Peter Barnes) Philip Prowse, the director/designer of the Glasgow Citizens', and Ken Campbell, the Ilfordian playwright, director and solo performer – operate as peripheral mavericks in a critical and consumer culture that prefers the safe, the grandiose, the tawdry, the slick, the trendy and the necrophiliac.

The outsiderism of many of Leigh's main characters – Sylvia in *Bleak Moments*, Trevor in *The Kiss of Death*, the drifting, displaced lodgers in *Ecstasy*, Muhammad in *Goose-Pimples*, Johnny in *Naked* – all reflect this alienated aspect of Leigh's status in the British cultural establishment. He has had to knock on doors, write grovelling letters, fill the gap in somebody else's schedule at the last minute, apply for financial pittances, endure endless humiliation and rejection, and not just from the critics; all of this has taken its toll and indeed gone towards defining his subject matter. His plight, of course, is no different to that of many writers, actors and directors, but the failure to deliver at the RSC in 1979 was a particularly bitter blow for an artist on the brink of underpinning his reputation in the theatrical heartland.

Within a year, the RSC set sail on its great *Nicholas Nickleby* adventure, which prompted Ken Campbell to initiate his famous spoof Royal Dickens Theatre wheeze, in which he wrote, as 'Trevor Nunn', to various writers, actors and directors announcing the temporary eclipse of Shakespeare by Dickens as the company's new inspiration. The new RDC had a proposal for Leigh: 'Let bygones be bygones, Mike, and let's really try to put your inimicable [sic] style to work on this new venture. I can offer you twenty-three actors for a seventeen-week rehearsal period in the spring of 1982 if you are prepared to take on the challenge of *Bleak House*. Looking forward to your reactions, Love, Trev.' Leigh appreciated the humour of this, and the wheeze in general, but, unlike many other recipients of RDC offers, he was not fooled for a minute. Apart from the careless amalgamation of 'inimical' and 'inimitable' – a slip Nunn would never make – Leigh knew that 'Ken simply hadn't researched the signature, because I'd had so many letters from Trevor over the past few years.' He never signed himself 'Trev', and the 'T' of Trevor was always a sort of crossbow signifying perhaps a fraternal, or even affectionate, kiss.

To compound Leigh's misery over 'Ice-cream', the film he had been completing for Margaret Matheson, *Who's Who*, another BBC TV 'Play for Today', was not one of his best, though it is intermittently hilarious. Matheson wanted Leigh to venture more boldly into unknown territory, and he came up with a plotless Stock Exchange comedy – interestingly timed at the very start of the Thatcher years, and way ahead of Caryl Churchill's 'greed is good' satire *Serious Money* (1987) – in which the pivotal character of a fawning, middle-aged desk wallah, Alan Dixon (Richard Kane), creeps round his superiors, collects autographs of the royal and the famous – a signed postcard from Russell Harty, the TV chat show host, has lately been consigned to a desk drawer with the boiled sweets – and ministers at home to his wildly eccentric, cat-loving wife, April (Joolia Cappleman). He tells young Kevin at work – the intense, ferrety, blond-haired Philip Davis, one of Leigh's favourite actors – that Petula Clark is a person he very much admires, while at home, surrounded by a proliferating pride of chinchilla cats, several budgerigars and his wife ('Sherry, cherie?'), he proudly fondles a missive from Dr Christiaan Barnard, the heart-transplant pioneer. A partner in the stockbrokers goes to advise rich clients in Kensington, two of the younger upper-class bloods attend a dinner party for yuppies, and Alan's wife entertains an animal photographer called Shakespeare and a prospective cat purchaser, a Sloaney Miss Hunt played by Geraldine James, who has been badly let down by Harrods. 'Do you stretch very far back, Miss Hunt?' asks the blazered Alan (as well as, 'Do you ride, Miss Hunt? Do you hunt?'), diving into his readily available Debrett's to check out her mother's family name of Somerton-Friars. The whole confection is a spirited compendium of sneering snobbery and what, as Richard Last of the *Daily Telegraph* noted, Nancy Mitford would have termed 'linguistic and behavioural class indicators'. But having assembled all the various components and situations, Leigh fails to contrive a pulling together of the strands. There is no dramatic convergence. As work started, Alison gave birth to Toby, their first son, in February 1978, and Leigh contracted a mysterious headache which was only relieved when an osteopath in Greenwich pummelled it out of him. The shape of the film was never discovered and it drifted along, slightly out of control.

The close work is good, though, and there is nothing wrong with Richard Kane's performance, a Leonard Rossiter-style turn of suburban subservience and oleaginous mania. He quizzes the uninterested Kevin on who said 'The work you do is the rent you pay for the room you occupy on earth.' Answer: Elizabeth Bowes-Lyon, aka The Queen Mother. One night's task at home is to write to Lucinda Prior-Palmer, the show-jumper, and a fingerless piano player called Rhythmic Roberto who uses his toes: 'He won't be able to write back, then, will he?' drawls April. The smarmy, heritage-fixated pariah is of course excluded from the top snobs' table, where the hooray Henrys, including two of the young stockbrokers, and their screeching girlfriends, decry this horrible new 'punk thing', get in a tangle over the *'placements'*, drink themselves silly and throw bread rolls. The host is Nigel (Simon Chandler), first seen back-to-camera, seated in a comfy chair, smoking a pipe and listening to John of Gaunt's 'sceptred isle' speech from *Richard II* while some hearty heritage music rolls soothingly underneath. Nigel's dinner party is, Leigh says, 'more improvised than almost anything else that I've done, and it shows', and he reckons one more week would have knocked it into shape. 'The actors were terrific.' A less important scene, but more tightly worked, is the one where Jeffrey Wickham as the partner goes to Kensington for an intensely convoluted discussion about his client's assets and family arrangements. The scene is deliciously set by Lord Crouchurst's wife, played by Richenda Carey, the campsite manageress in *Nuts in May*, checking the diary ('Philip at his club, dinner at the Savoy, polo at Windsor'), while the noble

Lord (David Neville) intones drab nothings in an excruciatingly mannered accent that anyone who had never heard Brian Sewell, the art critic, on the radio, would dismiss as exaggerated beyond the limits of plausibility. A virtually invisible child is hustled upstairs by Lavinia Bertram as a nanny with a funny little baby gait of her own. There is no heart to the piece, and no clinching structure, and one is left merely enjoying – merely enjoying! – the clinically arranged composite of tics, jokes, sneers and exposures.

Leigh had to pull himself together and bounce back more convincingly from the RSC débâcle. His response was unusual and unprecedented: a radio play, *Too Much of a Good Thing*, recorded entirely on location, as if it were a film, in which the central incident was something that could not be done as authentically on film or on stage and had never been done before on radio: an act of sexual intercourse, with full realistic detail of foreplay, after-play and all the sticky bits in between. The midwife on this occasion was Liane Aukin, a BBC radio producer who knew Leigh through her brother, David, the general manager at Hampstead Theatre. She had at first invited Leigh to revive *Abigail's Party* on the airwaves, but he stated a preference for supplying an original play. Ronald Mason, the head of radio drama, was enthusiastic and allocated £5000 – a huge amount in those days for a radio play – from the Radio 3 controller, Stephen Hearst's, experimental programme fund.

Leigh rehearsed for three weeks, in his usual way, with furniture, properties and costumes. His three actors – Lesley Manville, Philip Davis and Eric Allan – learned all their lines. Leigh was blessed, he says, with two 'brilliant quadrophonic sound engineers', and they went out in the fourth week and 'shot' the radio play as though it were a movie. It was completed in May 1979. Mason was thrilled with the result, and so were his fellow producers. However, Ian McIntyre, who had by then succeeded Stephen Hearst as Radio 3 controller, found *Too Much* too much, although, in censoring the broadcast, he never once said that his objections were anything to do with the sex scene. His rejection was based on 'literary grounds'; the play was 'boring' and 'not good enough'. The rumpus became a *cause célèbre* within the BBC, and Richard Imison, a leading producer, wrote an internal memo comparing the play to Beckett (perhaps Pinter, and some of the sketch writing of the late Peter Cook, might have been worth mentioning, too). Leigh was invited to the 1980 Edinburgh Festival by the journalist Jonathan Coe, who was then the radio editor at *Time Out*, and he played a tape of *Too Much* to Coe and Nicholas de Jongh, then arts correspondent of the *Guardian*, in a hotel bedroom: 'When it got to the sex scene, some people next door started banging on the wall. I never thought I'd find myself in a room with Nick de Jongh while giving the impression that a fuck was going on!' De Jongh has no recollection of this incident, and suggests that Leigh's story, in so far as it concerns him, betrays wishful thinking on Leigh's part. The play was finally broadcast in July 1992, to considerable critical acclaim.

Too Much of a Good Thing is probably the least-known example of Leigh's best work, a script of unremitting black and greasy grottiness in which a fat girl, Pamela (Lesley Manville), who works in an estate agents and lives with her equally fat, widowed father, Mr Payne (Eric Allan), in Barking, east London, loses her virginity to her driving instructor, Graham (Philip Davis). Mr Payne is a rat-catcher for the council, and talks with a verminous croak, non-stop, about what he has recently eaten, what he's eating now and what he'd like to eat quite soon. It is already established that Graham and Pamela are courting; in giving Pamela driving lessons, Graham feels like a schoolteacher going out with a pupil. There is an interesting undertow of an abused teacher/pupil relationship, a betrayal of trust. They go for a Chinese meal – 'a touch of the Orientals' – and Pamela tells Graham she has left her Dad some pilchard and tomato paste sandwiches. Graham tells her about a giraffe in the zoo who fell over and died of high cholesterol. They go rowing in the park and Pamela reverses roles by taking the oars and handing over her nutty bar to Graham. They go home for tea: ham and veal pie, Branston pickle and salad cream. They eat Maltesers in front of the television, Mr Payne calls out for six faggots (fresh, not frozen). We also hear about prawn cocktails and rump steak *garni* in the Berni Inn, cheese and pickle sandwiches, banana sandwiches, marshmallows, and corned beef sandwiches. Mr Payne's boss is a mason, and is taking his wife to a dinner-dance. Is he a stonemason? No, a Freemason. Mr Payne has been down to the sterilisation unit to deal with a delivery from the hospital of clothes and stuff belonging to a vagrant who has been run over by an ice-cream van, and is tickled pink: 'I haven't had a night as good as that since your mother died!' In the final scene, when it is clear that Graham is not going to elaborate on his relationship with Pamela after bedding her, Mr Payne walks in with a dead rat which turned up in some woman's bedroom. The woman was a filthy whore, he says, a smelly old tart. He spots his disconsolate daughter: 'Cheer up, Pamela, it might never happen.' No, it never will.

Later on, Leigh would return to rat-catchers in *Smelling a Rat*, and construct a more complex web of food imagery in *Life is Sweet*. But for sheer, unadulterated grubby sensuality, *Too Much of a Good Thing* is hard to beat, and leaves you wanting to jump into several cold showers, scrub your fingernails and check your hair for infestation. You can smell these characters, and they don't smell very nice. But a shiver of affection, edginess and tentativeness runs through the sixty-minute play, too, with its fixed rituals of courtship and afternoon teas, of watching television and being discreet on the sofa, of nightcaps and cuddles. Above all it's the realism that is so startling, even in a medium that goes out of its way to match sound effects to actors' speech. The difference here is that the actors really are *in situ*, and not skilfully turning pages in front of a microphone as they do in every single radio drama from *The Archers* to Tom Stoppard, Howard Barker and serialised Dickens or Kipling. Lesley Manville, usually as thin as a rake, went into training by eating her way through bags of mini-Mars bars and mini-Twixes, and managed to put on a little weight, but finally opted for 'acting fat' without any padding. Philip Davis had recently passed his own driving test, and had an uncle who was a driving instructor with whom he went out a couple of times, so his command of the instructional jargon on gear changes, PSL (position, speed, look) and MSM (mirror, signal, manoeuvre) was spot-on. Leigh would crouch on the back seat as Manville and Davis drove off for their lessons and improvisations.

He was not quite so close when it came to recording the fifteen-minute seduction scene. This was done, when it was finally performed, like the fish paste and banana sandwiches, and the rowing on the lake, for almost absolute real, with Manville and Davis stripping down naked by night in an Islington bedroom wired for sound, and Leigh lurking outside with his sound recordists in the van. The expectancy of sexual activity comes without any of the embarrassment one inevitably experiences in the cinema or the theatre. The intimacy is powerful almost beyond endurance, as the couple fumble down to the dirty deed in Graham's bedroom. His parents have gone out. We hear two full minutes of oscular clicking and grunting, puffing and panting, relieved only by Pamela's 'I've lost my hairslide!' They get undressed, turn the lights off, climb into bed, Graham tries to help Pamela off with her tights: 'Lift your bum up!'; '*I*'ll take 'em off, Graham.' Then the scrambling for the condom ('Graham, where's the things?'), Pamela rushing and panting, and coming, collapsing like a big air-filled tent, then Graham coming as well, more practised, in little short sharp jabs of exhalation, like an athlete doing press-ups. Subsidence, detumescence, silence, traffic noise, bathos, trite conversation. Pamela, for whom the earth must have juddered, if not exactly moved, lets slip that it's her first time and says she feels 'funny'. Graham says he too felt a bit funny earlier on: he had a Wimpy at lunchtime and it left him with a touch of the wind. 'Do you still like me?' she asks. 'Yeah. Course I do. You'd better be going soon.'

Leigh had asked Manville and Davis how far they felt they could go without 'doing it', and they readily agreed to go to the limit. Manville recalls that the foreplay was enacted, on the take, right up to the moment of penetration, when it was decided that Davis would grab a little cushion which he placed between the two of them so he could, as Manville says, 'do the thrusting and carry on'. Condoms were indeed required – a real trouper, that boy Davis! – but the props department had overlooked this detail. 'Luckily,' says Manville, 'it was Friday night, and one of the sound guys was going away for the weekend, so he had a packet of three. We did three takes, and we used them all!' Davis was playing a character who was very shy but who never stopped talking, with a physical awkwardness that the actor translated into saying everything twice: 'One of the difficulties with the love scene was that Lesley is extraordinarily attractive, and trying to imagine her as a fat lump was a problem. Graham had zeroed in on her for this very reason; it was a measure of his own lack of self-esteem that he would target the ugliest bird around.'

These two bright young actors were the sort of performer Leigh is always happiest working with: intelligent, inventive, basic, working-class. Pamela and Graham in *Too Much* are coarse-grained characters drawn with sympathy and inside knowledge. The only people who could possibly think that Manville and Davis were patronising, or condescending to, their creations would be middle-class liberals with guilty consciences. Manville's background was untheatrical but her training was in traditional showbusiness, starting as a child singer in her home town of Brighton, attending the Italia Conti stage school and progressing to pantomime and 'dolly girl' parts in television comedy shows. She joined the RSC by accident to do a new play, and fell in with Mike Leigh on the aborted 'Ice-cream' project. While working on that, Leigh told her that she was very good at what she was doing, and should stick with it. 'It was the first time anyone had said anything positive to me about acting. Usually you just feel like a pawn. I'm good at working with Mike because I'm very organised, I've got a logical mind, and I love making lists and filling in background.' Like Davis, she was in Leigh's next film, *Grown-Ups*, and when it went out 'it changed my career overnight'. She became a Royal Court actress and closely affiliated with Max Stafford-Clark, another director with a distinctive, but very different, way of working: 'Mike serves the actors who will then create the play; with Max, the primary thing is the play. Max begins with the text and breaks down each sentence and thought for which you have to supply a transitive verb, or "action". You "action" the text. It takes a long time, but it gives you an incredible foundation for performing. You never sink, even on a bad night. I work best, I know, with these two directors. I'm very lucky.'

Davis actually hails from cockney Essex, so he knew all about Barking, Graham's milieu. He was raised on a big housing estate in Thurrock, between Grays and Dagenham. Dad worked in a soap factory, Mum was a canteen supervisor in a hospital. Davis is the middle of three sons: the elder brother is a teacher, the younger a social worker. He joined the National Youth Theatre from school and worked with Joan Littlewood when she returned to Stratford East in the early 1970s. 'With Mike, it's not improvise *what*, it's improvise *who*. It's to do with characterisation, and you do all this other work and research to make this character as three-dimensional as possible. It's very important to know where the sugar goes, otherwise the improvisation breaks down; you're supposed to be at home and you don't know where the sugar goes? That's not on. With Joan, it was a matter of showing off, really, and it was to do with "the theatre".' Davis made his first big impression as a furiously agitated schoolboy holding a lit cigarette over the petrol tank of his motorbike in Barrie Keeffe's *Gotcha* (1976) at the Soho Poly, and graduated to a rich diet of plays and films, including Franc Roddam's *Quadrophenia* (1979, with Sting, Toyah Wilcox and Phil Daniels) and Alan Clarke's violent football film, his last (*The Firm*, 1989, with Lesley Manville and Gary Oldman). He took to writing his own plays, very good ones, and has completed his first feature film as a director, *id* (1995), about an undercover policeman in the late 1980s required to infiltrate a mob of football hooligans. 'The experience of working with Mike is so creative that you come away buzzing, wanting to do something. There's no way you can work in the same way as him. But without working with him, I would never have leapt over that fence and got on to other things. People get the impression that it's all very serious. It isn't. It's a real hoot. He can be a bit peppery, old Mike, and he's not at all averse to giving you a bollocking. But you never get a bollocking for laughing.'

One of the Royal Court directors, William Gaskill, once said that an artistic policy is the people you work with, and Leigh would subscribe to that maxim, creating conditions whereby his colleagues are broadly sympathetic to the way he views the world, and also, very importantly, blessed with a similar sense of humour. Only such people could possibly have come up with the grimly unremitting *Ecstasy* (1979), Leigh's return to Hampstead, and a stage play of a stark, cheerless intensity similar to *Bleak Moments* and *Babies Grow Old*. 'By the time they got it on,' says David Aukin, 'some of the cast were close to breakdown.' One night, Jim Broadbent was indeed taken ill and excused himself from the arena, 'in character', leaving the bleak Kilburn bedsitter on the stage for the loo in the dressing room, where he promptly passed out. Sheila Kelley and Julie Walters turned to the audience, assured them that this was not part of the play and asked, 'Is there a doctor in the house?' Leigh says that fourteen men stood up, a revealing statistic in terms of the Hampstead audience composition. Leigh's new three-hour play – with an unusually long second act – was underrated, partly because it was so stunningly, and depressingly, different from *Abigail's Party*, and partly, David Aukin suggests, because the critics had enjoyed themselves so much the night before watching Danny La Rue camping it up in a revival of *Hello, Dolly!* There is humour in *Ecstasy*, in the same sense that there is humour in *Naked*, but the mood is desperate. And there are scenes of anxiety-inducing sexual violence between Jean (Sheila Kelley) and Roy (Ron Cook), a furniture-smashing incursion by Roy's girlfriend (Rachel Davies), and an eerily hypnotic, dead-of-night, post-pub singalong and booze-up that drove audiences crazy, not with pleasure exactly, but with either shock or dismay, or a mixture of both. It was a hard evening.

Hampstead was hoping for another zingy comedy that might transfer to the West End, but Leigh told Sheila Kelley, just after rehearsals had started, that he was going to do the play he wanted to do 'for my own sanity', and that it certainly would not go into the West End. Kelley considers that Leigh's best work emerges when his back is up against the wall. She may have a point in that *Too Much of a Good Thing* and *Ecstasy* are certainly the products of an artist bouncing single-mindedly back from the 'Ice-cream' meltdown. 'When he's comfortable, and got money, I don't like the work so much. I don't think he pushes it hard enough.' Kelley played Jean, a suicidal garage attendant who sleeps with unsuitable men, drinks heavily and has abortions. Jean's Brummie friend, Dawn (Julie Walters), who has had three children, brings back her husband, Mick (Stephen Rea), an Irish labourer, and his taciturn friend, Len (Jim Broadbent), and their second act ensemble trumpets the dark night of the soul, in what is at once one of the best and gloomiest party scenes in contemporary drama. Leigh felt happy in the misery, investigating this sad, real world just up the road from the theatre itself; the title was nearly 'One Mile Behind You', because of the situation of the Kilburn High Road literally one mile behind the audience's heads.

For Kelley as Jean, nude at the start with Ron Cook, beaten about, humiliated, spurned, spiralling into a nervous breakdown and edging pathetically towards a renewed and understanding friendship with decent, sensitive Len, this was the best part she had ever had; but no one had given it to her on a plate. She had created it from scratch with Leigh. 'We did an improvisation just after Roy had left, and the room's been turned upside down, and she's had a third abortion, and there's a knock on the door from Dawn who's come to take her to the pub to meet Len. But I had taken an overdose and killed myself. In the rehearsal, I took two aspirin and lay down. That was it. Jean was dead and there was no second half of the play! So Mike had to sit me down and we went through it all until we found a reason why Jean should answer the door before she took the pills, and we carried on from there . . .'

Julie Walters says categorically that working on *Ecstasy* was 'one of the happiest experiences of my career'. She has since been thwarted in her determination to work with Leigh again, but has not given up yet; nor has Leigh. For both Jim Broadbent and Stephen Rea, this was the first of several collaborations with Leigh. Broadbent found the experience 'like going on a huge acting course, with a wonderful play at the end of it. Len is a really nice man from rural Lincolnshire, as I am; my best friend to this day is a dairy farmer, though he's not the character on whom I based Len.' Rea, too, found the work invigorating – 'a training that's required if you're going to get into all the corners of acting'

– and, unlike Broadbent, who wipes the slate clean each time, he lives with the character in perpetuity. He says that Mick is now living with Dawn in Milton Keynes: 'I was never nervous in *Ecstasy*. I used to go in and drink seven cans of Carlsberg lager on stage every night. We were in complete control of everything. I had no idea Jean was having those abortions until the last few performances. Anyone who plays Mick now, from the published text, would give a performance unavoidably shaded by the knowledge that Jean is a tragic figure. To me, she was just a girl in a room. I had no idea she was having a hard time. That's what's so interesting about the process, not knowing anything your character wouldn't know. In all other work, I've always believed that an actor should have a panoramic view of the whole play. Mike's stuff is the exception. It's quite different. The text with Mike is just the result of everything you've investigated before. Which is the other way round from how it works in a conventional play.'

This important point is corroborated and further qualified by Antony Sher, who worked with Leigh a year or so later: 'I found, when we transferred *Goose-Pimples* to the West End, it was quite difficult to sustain over a continuous long run. Unlike some of the scripted plays which I have done in the West End, like *Torch Song Trilogy* and *Travesties*, where one can continue to dig away at what the author has written, and constantly mine new depths, this was not possible with a script that one had helped to devise oneself, and where one knew every minute detail of every motivating force behind everything which one's character was saying or doing. This is not meant as a criticism of Mike's way of working, but is simply an observation of the problems of doing the stage plays for a prolonged period of time. On film, I shouldn't imagine it's a problem at all, and is probably quite the opposite.' Broadbent and Rea agree with that, though *Ecstasy*'s run was limited to the Hampstead season, and each considers the play his definitive Mike Leigh experience.

Rea's Mick McSweeney, an invented name, was from Cork, and the actor knew all the guys like him who had come to work in north London, misplaced people in a strange ghetto. 'My character

Mick, we decided, actually came from Macroom, about twenty miles west of Cork City. One of the details of the character, which we also invented – but which did not surface in the play – was that he had a brother who owned a garage on the right-hand side of the road as you drove out of Macroom towards Cork. In 1980, just after the playwright Brian Friel and I had formed the Irish company, Field Day, I was touring with our inaugural production, Friel's *Translations*, and we drove from Limerick to Cork, through Macroom. As we drove out of Macroom, on the right-hand side of the road there was a garage called McSweeney's Garage. It completely knocked me out. I took Mike there a year later and showed it to him. It was just one of those magic things. The characters do have an intense reality for me.'

However much Rea may speculate on how another actor might play Mick, the question as to whether Leigh's plays could be performed convincingly by actors other than those who had conceived the roles with him was partially answered by a London fringe production in 1991. *Ecstasy* is arguably the most difficult of the stage plays to reanimate, but both Leigh and Sheila Kelley, who saw the Dark Horse company's revival, claim it was entirely successful. To Kelley, 'it suddenly looked like a very good play, an extraordinary experience with so many virtuoso performances going on.' Exactly the opposite effect was achieved by another fringe group, Raindog in Glasgow, whose 1993 revival mistakenly supposed that *Ecstasy* was 'loose enough in its structure to enable us to use an improvisatory rehearsal process'. The company added five peripheral characters, and relocated the action in a 'home town' of Glasgow, when Leigh's whole point is that nobody really belongs in this disorienting bedsit territory: the characters come from Birmingham, Lincolnshire and Cork. The lesson to be deduced is that while it may be difficult, and sometimes impossible, to revive Mike Leigh's stage plays, the best policy in so doing is to stick by the received texts and treat them like regular scripts, while somehow trying to recover the first cast's impulses and subtextual motivations without merely reassembling known mannerisms and inflections.

The 'Ice-cream' affair was almost licked. Leigh was up and

running and firing on all cylinders, and he came to the last year of the 1970s with yet another stop-gap commission which he turned to his creative advantage. Louis Marks, the BBC TV producer, had commissioned a David Mercer film to be co-produced with Israeli television, but the censor in Menachem Begin's new coalition government created problems and the film was scrapped. Marks, like Margaret Matheson before him, was left with a slot to fill at short notice. And like Michael Rudman and David Aukin at Hampstead demanding an instant 'Yes' or 'No' before *Abigail's Party*, he was in a hurry. With *Ecstasy* still running at Hampstead, Leigh said 'Yes' and got going. Leigh's usual procedure on a film (not a play) is, roughly, to start work with a couple of actors, arrange for others to join in gradually, start structuring, then schedule the departure of some cast members during the shoot while keeping some money on the side to extend contracts if necessary. 'In *Grown-Ups*, uniquely, I decided to have six actors who would be there all the time, and that we'd do something more intimate.' The density and finished quality of *Abigail's Party* and *Ecstasy* had increased Leigh's dislike for the erratic, uncontrolled elements in *Who's Who*. He was determined to make a precise and utterly controlled film. 'And that's what we got, I think. It was also the first time I worked with far and away the best lighting cameraman I'd had up to that time, Remi Adefarasin, who subsequently shot *Home Sweet Home* and *Four Days in July*.' Another key collaborative friendship, and one crucial to Leigh's sustained success in recent years, was forged with Simon Channing-Williams, who worked on *Grown-Ups* as first assistant director.

The BBC had a rule stating that within thirty miles of Charing Cross, a film crew was in London; beyond thirty miles, they were on location. Leigh wanted to be on location but as near to London as possible, and whimsically decided to shoot his new film, *Grown-Ups*, in Canterbury, having thought seriously about Harlow New Town ('I'm fascinated by Harlow, it's so depressed and bleak'). His resolution was stiffened when he discovered that Brenda Blethyn, whom he had cast in a role that was to be one of his most inspired creations, hailed from nearby Ramsgate (where she was the last of nine children reared in a council house). He also wanted two adjacent houses, one semi-detached and privately owned, one a council house. Two such houses were found, and we stay in and around that location for most of the film, apart from a couple of scenes by a bus station and in a pub, in places of work and in the opening sequence in which we follow a removal van around Canterbury in the shadow of the cathedral (and some awful flats), with the cathedral choir singing in the background. Dick and Mandy (Philip Davis and Lesley Manville) – school chums, sweethearts and newlyweds – are moving into their first house.

Their new council-owned abode turns out to be next door to 'old Butcher' (Sam Kelly), their Religious Knowledge teacher at school, who still grunts and makes strange noises. Butcher is married to an earnest fellow teacher, Christine (Lindsay Duncan in specs and angora cardigans). Theirs is a joyless, arid union, fuelled only by sarcastic exchanges at the meal table. Dick and Mandy are locked in disagreement over whether or not to have children (the same debate is reprised in *High Hopes*). They are visited by another old school chum, dour, unhelpful Sharon (Janine Duvitski), and pestered throughout their settling-in period by Mandy's older sister, the fussing, spinsterish, and increasingly desperate Gloria, whom Blethyn projects as a pathetic monster in the same class of performance as Alison Steadman's Beverly.

Gloria is a typist and general lost soul who has found her vocation in clamping herself to Mandy and Dick with hopes, some day soon, of extending her visits into a permanent baby-sitting arrangement. She arrives with a gift-wrapped Hoover and immediately starts trying to use it, her bum pushing into the camera. She precipitates a series of mini-crises and protestations, especially on Dick's part ('Yap, yap, yap, all through *Grandstand*,' he complains on the fateful, climactic Saturday afternoon), by her unscheduled appearances, popping up at the front-room window with a 'Whoo-ooh' and a run for the sofa before anyone can dive for cover, let alone slam the door in her face. The motor of this magnificent performance is sheer panic. Gloria cannot stand being stuck at home with her tyrannical mother. She keeps chattering, and turning up, and keeping busy, and coming back, so that no one can undermine, or punctuate with reasonable objections, the utter banality and pointlessness of her activity, or question her long-term prospects for domestic peace and personal fulfilment. Even her eyes refuse to stop still in case they meet an honest look or a straightforward question. Blethyn's external acting is all flutter, gibbering and movement, but its vivacity and brilliance indicates conclusively the vacuity and sadness within.

Gloria makes herself useful by helping Mandy unpack her china animals in the new house ('It's like a farmyard in 'ere'). In discussing this scene, Leigh notes how the camera never pans by itself, or goes ahead of the discussion; it is always motivated by what the actors are doing. Mandy lollops around the room in another version of that old-before-her-time arthritic waddle of Linda in *The Kiss of Death*. The animals are placed on various surfaces, with reminiscent comments ('Dick's Mum used to like it' justifies one particularly horrible piece), and a convenient nail is discovered on a wall ('There's a nail 'ere, Glaw' is not a line, Leigh justly remarks, that would readily occur to a desk-bound writer). As they work, the two sisters move rhythmically back and forth in a single panning shot while Gloria brings the conversation round to her future in Mandy's house by developing the story of how she went baby-sitting for somebody else's sister in Dover: 'One of the kids liked pilchards and not the tomato sauce and the other liked tomato sauce but not the pilchards, so there I am separating the pilchards from the tomato sauce . . . you should hear that little Rod's language, Mandy, he kept saying the "F" word, then he kept saying things about my bust. I didn't know where to look.' The various strands in this scene, Leigh explains, were created separately in rehearsal, entwined in controlled improvisation and knitted together in action: 'It all had to be worked out so that the paper coming off each prop was timed with the baby-sitting story, and of course one of the advantages of working in this plastic, organic way, i.e. not from a script that some other bugger's written down that you have to stick to, is that you can expand and contract both the dialogue and the action, so that it all works together. And the scene must serve the camera, and the camera the scene. In this instance, we're in a tiny space, lit for night, so you've got one source light (instead of a flat light for daytime). And you've got a sound boom hovering over the action and you don't want any boom-shadows. So you have to construct the shot carefully to accommodate all that as well.'

In *Grown-Ups*, Leigh is battening down the hatches, refining the vitality and exuberance of his actors with the control and contrivance that marked *Abigail's Party* and *Ecstasy*. The transference of his rigid stage structures to screen he attributes not only to his own maturity, but especially, in the instance of *Grown-Ups*, to the editing of Robin Sales. Sales was the best editor Leigh had worked with up to this point; he would develop a similarly creative, but more long-lasting, relationship with Jon Gregory, who began editing with Leigh on *The Short and Curlies* (1987).

This structuring process is applied with literal savagery to the farcical uprush which connects all six characters in a human chain of restraint on the Butchers' staircase. Gloria says her mother has finally thrown her out (this may or may not be true), and insists on staying with Dick and Mandy. Dick will have none of this, and in the ensuing fracas, Gloria rushes from the house and, seeing the Butchers' front door invitingly open (Christine is outside washing the car), runs into *their* house, up the stairs and locks herself in the bathroom. This brings Dick and Mandy, and Sharon, into the Butchers' in pursuit. Gloria is talked down and is just leaving peaceably when she lurches around and charges back up the stairs, and the whole company is embroiled in an elasticated rugby scrum, Gloria at the top, tears streaming and nose dripping. 'She's a bit aeriated,' offers Dick, a garbled diagnosis good enough for his ex-teacher.

The entire sequence was worked out in a five-day break during the shoot – a break made possible by Simon Channing-Williams, whom Leigh had recognised immediately as 'a fantastic organiser', persuading the crew to trade all their bank holidays and weekends at this stage and leave the location. This innovation became a practice on all subsequent films: Leigh demands a breathing space in the shooting schedule as a matter of course in order to stand back from the work thus far and devise, or deduce, the appropriate conclusion. At this climactic point in *Grown-Ups*, Gloria's choice of action lay between boarding a bus back to the housing estate where she lived with her mother, or rushing next door. Leigh knew what he wanted to happen, but Brenda Blethyn, having wavered for a time, decided for herself, in the improvisations, that Gloria would indeed run next door.

From this point, the film subsides in scenes of reconciliation and adjustment. Gloria starts to ingratiate herself with the Butchers. Christine makes her a cup of tea and offers biscuits: 'Gingernut, bourbon or Garibaldi?' 'Haven't we got any Penguins?' asks Mr Butcher, harrumphing quietly in the corner. Sam Kelly had first made his involuntary stretching grunt one morning in rehearsal after a late night and had incorporated it in the 'running condition' of his character without anyone reacting to that aspect of his performance until, in an improvisation for this tea and biscuits scene, Blethyn suddenly said, 'Got tummy ache, Mr Butcher? A drop of magnesium would sort that out,' and of course Kelly corpsed until his tummy really did ache; it's a perfect placement for the malapropism, a misconstrued observation which brilliantly defines Gloria's shifting alliance as she pinpoints her new victims and their alternative haven.

The two neighbouring couples are symmetrically juxtaposed at bedtime. Butcher sits up, marking his school essays on the *Marie-Celeste*, or reading a book called *Life Before Man*. 'What do you want?' he asks his wife. The reply is stunning, the one moment Lindsay Duncan brings Christine to full emotional self-exposure. 'I want sex. I want love. I want a family. That's what I want.' Checkmate, and lights out. Butcher thought it might have been something he could do something about. Next door, Dick and Mandy make love. Mandy is off the pill. The film cuts to Christmas a few months later. Gloria is re-established in her sister's house, helping to make up the tree, head pressed in excited expectation against Mandy's pregnant bulge. Life goes on.

Around this time, as the 1970s drifted into the decade of Mrs Thatcher, Leigh was becoming more fashionable and increasingly written about in magazines covering alternative lifestyles, rock music and 'the look' of contemporary youth. In some ways, he became a representative poet, the voice of critical dissent in the identifiable suburbs, not unlike Ray Davies of The Kinks, whose songs exerted a similar appeal to a previous generation. The bric-a-brac and the petty rituals of the everyday appealed to *Blitz* magazine, who computed the following references in *Grown-Ups*: twenty-nine to tea, twenty-three to alcohol, eighteen to babies, four to milk-bottles. In addition, the film contained forty-five cigarette-to-mouth movements. Mervyn Jones wrote more soberly in the *Listener*: 'You wouldn't think it possible to create a richly enjoyable entertainment with characters who rebuff all sympathy, but Mike Leigh does it. The secret lies, I suppose, in his endless curiosity about human beings, his refusal to condemn or deride, and his precise judgement of authenticity.'

The London Film Festival had just changed its rule about not admitting television films to the annual showcase, and *Grown-Ups* was the first television film to be included. After that screening, Maurice Hatton, Leigh's fellow film-maker (best known for *Praise Marx and Pass the Ammunition*) with a lower-middle-class Jewish background in Manchester, asked Leigh from the back of the auditorium, 'Is this film autobiographical?' to which Leigh replied 'No.' Hatton, without saying anything, winked heavily in Leigh's direction, implying that this kind of carry-on with people shouting at each other and misbehaving on the stairs could only have been fully realised by someone tuning in to their own Jewish domestic background. Hatton was of course quite right. Gloria was undoubtedly incorporating memories of Leigh's Auntie Janey – the widow of his maternal grandmother's eldest brother, killed in the first week of the First World War, who used to pop round to visit the family in Cavendish Road at unexpected moments, peering through the window in her thick spectacles. But the shouting and the brouhaha was exactly the sort of domestic babble he had grown up with.

'Auntie Janey was left with two tiny sons, Ellis who became a furrier, and Monty who was a tallyman, and a source of research for Louis Raynes when he played the tallyman in *Hard Labour*. Monty was a bachelor who lived all his life in the same little terraced house in Cheetham, first with his mother, then alone after she died. His one treat each week was to go to a Chinese restaurant by himself and have a steak; I only discovered this after we made *Bleak Moments*, incidentally. He died a few years ago in poverty, and his body was found a couple of months later, rats having eaten away half his remains. It was Auntie Janey who used to ask me, "Are you still at the university for a doctor?", mixing me up with my Dad. So yes, there is something autobiographical about *Grown-Ups*, and not just the screaming on the stairs. The whole atmosphere of people coming round, coming into a house. I now see that, after the RSC abortion, I was plugging back into a world I knew about, things that directly concerned me: hell in the suburbs.'

EIGHT

Salesmen and Postmen:
Rows over Special Delivery

Jean Renoir, one of Leigh's heroes, said that however many films you make, you are really making just one film. 'The point of it all,' says Leigh, 'is seeing how far away from that one film you can get.' One important distinction Leigh makes between his stage work and his film work is that the plays are self-consciously theatrical, in the sense that they acknowledge the form, and the place, in which they are made. Thus *Abigail's Party* was a subverted form of boulevard comedy, and his next two plays for Hampstead, *Goose-Pimples* and *Smelling a Rat*, challenge West End farce conventions by first of all invoking them.

Even starker plays, like *Babies Grow Old* and *Ecstasy*, are imbued with a playful sense of a non-referential theatricality which subliminally acknowledges the exact topographical circumstances of performance. *Babies Grow Old* is clearly a response to the fact that *King Lear* was simultaneously playing in the RSC's repertoire, while pointedly bringing issues of old age right up to date within a company that prided itself on making the classics new-minted. And *Ecstasy* invoked a north-west London bedsit land just beyond the comfortable 'new work' audience at Hampstead Theatre. Commissioned to work in Sydney, Australia, Leigh produced *Greek Tragedy*, dealing with issues of ethnicity and the labour market on the theatre's doorstep. *It's a Great Big Shame!* at Stratford East was specifically geared to the local surroundings and the refurbishment of the beautiful Victorian theatre in which it played. Films, on the other hand, to Leigh, even if they suggest other films and have cinematic pedigree, are the pure business: 'When

I make a film, I don't think that I'm "making a film" and that therefore there has to be a statement about the nature of film.'

His next two pieces, produced almost back to back, sustained his healthy schedule of shuttling between Hampstead Theatre and the BBC. His third play for Rudman and Aukin, *Goose-Pimples*, was always more likely to transfer to the West End than was *Ecstasy*, and promptly did so. In the 1982 *Evening Standard* Drama Awards, *Goose-Pimples* was adjudged Best Comedy ('Anyone can knock off a tragedy,' said the avuncular John Mortimer, presenting the award to Leigh at the Savoy Hotel), alongside Andrew Lloyd Webber's *Cats* (Best Musical), Peter Nichols's *Passion Play* (Best Play), Peter Hall's *Oresteia* at the National (Best Director), Maggie Smith in Edna O'Brien's *Virginia* (Best Actress) and Alan Howard in C.P. Taylor's *Good* (Best Actor).

Home Sweet Home (1982), about postmen, parenthood, social workers and sex – what more do you want, feathers and dancing girls? – was Leigh's lucky thirteenth project for BBC TV and a second happy collaboration with 'Play for Today' producer Louis Marks, cinematographer Remi Adefarasin and composer Carl Davis. Both pieces were highly successful, and both led to controversy: *Goose-Pimples* reopened the argument about condescension and contempt towards characters and nearly precipitated a diplomatic incident in its portrayal of a Muslim Arab who thinks he is visiting a brothel and consumes vast amounts of alcohol while waving bank-notes at his hostess; *Home Sweet Home* figured in an essay about contemporary drama by the playwright David Edgar as an example of what goes wrong when characters speak truthfully in situations not of their own making but of the director's – 'contempt' comes in here, too, and 'elitist views of human beings'.

Leigh's natural instinct is to keep audiences guessing, to follow the unexpected with the dissimilar. Of all his plays and films, *Goose-Pimples* is probably the most relentlessly hysterical and shamefully funny. Brenda Blethyn was not in the cast, but her breasts were on the poster, because her partner, Michael Mayhew, designed it: a photograph of her inviting upper slopes seemed to guarantee some tingling flesh and shivers down the spine. This was a mischievous publicity ruse, for the hyphenated title was not to be construed in the 'goose-bumps' pleasure sense, but as a single, unfunny yoke of 'goose', as in placing your hand uninvited on, or in, somebody else's nether regions, and 'pimple', as in something you squeeze if found either in those aforesaid regions, or on your face, or in the general likeness of a nasty piece of work.

Such as Vernon, who is an unmitigated walking pimple. The play's setting is Vernon's flat in Dollis Hill, a residential area further north from Hampstead than Kilburn, but not that much, merging with Neasden and Cricklewood. Vernon is a house-proud car salesman who lives on his own, with a lodger. The lounge and dining area – shockingly well designed by Caroline Beaver – is a riot of tigerskin wallpaper, chrome dining chairs, an imitation leopardskin rug, an elaborate music centre, fitted wall-units containing a few books, school trophies and models of vintage cars, and a fully operational bar, with bar-stools, on the side. Vernon is entertaining his fellow car salesman Irving Gammon, and Irving's wife Frankie, to dinner, and he first of all buzzes around busily.

The two friends see filthy innuendo in everything they utter, but the camaraderie is itself a back-slapping, ball-squeezing sham. Vernon is having a secretive affair with Frankie. After the first course of melon (which should have had ginger sprinkled on it, advises Frankie), the supermarket steaks prove an inedible disaster; they are well past their sell-by date – 'I'm going to report those bastards to the Area Health Authority . . .' yelps Vernon (or 'Vern', or even 'Ver') as he whips out his pocket calculator to tot up a rip-off cost of six pounds, nine pence for 'putrefied bloody horsemeat'. The party decamps to a steak house in Wembley, shouting, as they go, of underpasses, 'bloody Neasden' and cutting through to the Harrow Road.

Vernon's lodger, Jackie Scragg, a nightclub croupier with a North Circular buzz-saw accent that guillotines some words and strangulates others ('That's whisky,' for instance, would come out as ''ts whiskoiy'), brings home Muhammad, who has strayed into her West End casino, assuming that he is an oil-rich sheikh. But he's merely a small businessman who imports livestock for Islamic sacrifice and fancies a good time. Single-minded and self-absorbed, Muhammad speaks only in limited broken English and sawn-off Arabic phrases with the odd interjection of 'Okay', 'Abdullah' (the friend he's lost touch with in the pub) and 'girl'. He becomes more excited the more Jackie fails to understand what he means or wants: 'Okay, urugsi, urugseely, make, er make – okay, make, er, dance, make, er okay, take er, okay, tsallakhy! Tayyib! Okay! Urugsi! Urugseely! Hadoum!!' (the gist of which is an invitation to Jackie to get on with the floor show, to start dancing and remove her clothes).

When Vernon and co. return, the bewildered Muhammad assumes Irving is the barman and Frankie a second whore. He desperately tries to extricate himself from Vernon's hell-hole, with stuttered signals of 'orange-juice', 'barman', 'taxi'. Jim Broadbent's Vernon makes his position reasonably clear: 'I'm not a barman!! I'm not a barman!! I'm not a barman!! I'm not a barman!! I'm not a barman!! I'm not a barman!! I'm not a barman!! I'm not a barman!! I'm not a sodding barman!!' Muhammad has become a butt for a stream of racist abuse, and a conduit for Irving's disgusting outburst against his own wife (shortly after he has been caught trying to touch up Jackie): 'You slut! You cow! . . . WHY DON'T YOU JUST SUCK HIM OFF, EH? . . . GO ON – GET INSIDE HIS TROUSERS! – WE ALL KNOW WHAT YOU'RE AFTER – WHY DON'T YOU JUST GET ON WITH IT?' Muhammad is plied with so much orange juice heavily laced by Vernon with spirits that he is finally sick on the sofa and passes out. His terrible comic predicament is a vicious variation on Goldsmith's Charles Marlow treating his prospective father-in-law as an inn-keeper in *She Stoops to Conquer*, but without the genial untangling of 'the mistakes of a night'. Muhammad's nightmare is not one that lifts for the sake of dramatic convention or of sending the audience home happy. As the Gammons leave, Vernon denies that he is having an affair with Frankie ('Irving, I wouldn't stoop so low' – to conquer?), and suggests that Jackie might feel safer staying in his bedroom for the night. She thinks about it as the lights dim, and follows Vernon into his room.

As an artefact, *Goose-Pimples* is as highly wrought and, in its own way, as unsettling as *Ecstasy*. The acting was outstanding, from the salesmen of Jim Broadbent and Paul Jesson to the quivering, lush Frankie of Jill Baker and the hilarious, yet patently vulnerable Jackie of Marion Bailey. The targets are not just the crudity and tastelessness of Vernon and his friends, but also their hypocrisy, xenophobia and profound cultural oafishness. Muhammad is not a figure of fun – though his helplessness and delicious misreading of the situation are inherently funny – but an extreme example, the most extreme in Leigh's canon, of the alienated outsider. The role was taken unforgettably by Antony Sher, an actor for whom outsiders were to become a speciality over the next few years at the Royal Shakespeare Company. Even before he launched his Stratford-upon-Avon performances of Richard III, Malvolio, Shylock and Vindice in *The Revenger's Tragedy*, Sher was adept at showing a character writhing in nets of his own and others' devising.

Sher had been isolated from the other actors during rehearsal to such an extent that an anxiety about the size of his role began to affect his confidence. He worked alone on Muhammad for nine weeks, and told Gordon Burn in a *Sunday Times* Magazine feature in May 1981 that the experience had been 'absolutely terrifying. The feeling that I was being left out and forgotten made me horribly insecure.' When he joined the other actors for his first improvisatory rehearsal with them, he was force-fed real liquor and vomited in front of everyone, an accident as much regretted by Leigh – 'If I'd realised how drunk he was, obviously I would have stopped' – as by a temporarily furious Sher: 'No real damage was done. I was just deeply embarrassed and angry the next day. It is very startling to find yourself the raw material of somebody else's creative process, but you've got to trust Mike absolutely. He's not to be worked with at all by anyone of a paranoid disposition.'

For a time, as a Jewish South African, Sher was worried that the play was racist; every time he turned up to rehearsal, he was assaulted by Vernon and Irving. Leigh had to go round to his house and talk him down. In performance, it is obvious that the play deals with the racism of the car salesmen but is not, in itself, a racist play. Sher also went out 'in character' with Marion Bailey, who played the croupier, and they took a taxi home from the

West End as an improvised enactment of a prelude before their first entrance. They chatted in character on the back seat, and the taxi-driver was obviously one step ahead of even Muhammad's game, for as they paid the fare, he winked at Bailey and said, 'Is he your first one, love?'

There were plans at one stage to go even further afield for research purposes. Leigh told David Aukin that Sher was having trouble finding Arabs who would meet him, so could Hampstead underwrite a trip to Saudi Arabia? 'You have to be quick on your feet with Mike,' says Aukin, 'so I said, what made them think an Arab would be prepared to meet them in Saudi Arabia if he wouldn't meet him here?' Which sounds like the start of a bad joke, but the pay-off line went missing. 'Instead, Sher tried to see the Saudi cultural consul. He was kept waiting for hours and eventually told the secretary that he was an actor preparing a play about an Arab. There had recently been an uproar in the Arab community over a programme called *Death of a Princess* on British television. [This showed a woman being ostracised and punished for daring to be an individual in a repressive, male-oriented society.] The secretary swept in to the consul and told him that he certainly would not want to see this man who was playing an Arab. But the consul was so offended to be told by a woman what he should or should not do, that he called Sher inside immediately.' *Death of a Princess* had caused Saudi Arabia to cut off diplomatic relations with Britain, but Mrs Thatcher, the Prime Minister, mended fences by going to Riyadh, wearing a long dress, making a trade agreement and arranging a state visit for King Khaled in the following year.

Goose-Pimples transferred from Hampstead to the Garrick Theatre at the end of April, and the producers simultaneously received a letter of protest from the Union of Muslim Organisations, pointing out that the consumption of alcohol and consorting with prostitutes was forbidden in the Koran. The Foreign Office warned that a consequence of the show going on in the West End might be the cancellation of King Khaled's visit. The Foreign Office demanded tickets for the opening night at the Garrick, reviews were sent in a diplomatic bag to Riyadh (Ian Christie in the *Daily Express* helpfully, and accurately, declared that Muhammad was the only sympathetic character on display), and Leigh appeared on a couple of BBC TV current affairs programmes. The objections evaporated, and the run of the play continued.

Most British plays and films, when they are produced or shown abroad, travel with their British titles. The sole exception among Leigh's films was *Bleak Moments*, which the American distributors renamed *Bleak Moments, Loving Moments*, in an attempt to sweeten the pill. *Goose-Pimples* turned up eventually in Singapore, performed in Singapore-Chinese patois. This was only accidentally discovered by Leigh on a stop-over during his Australian jaunt a few years later: 'I was feeling a bit lonely and went along to see what the Raffles Hotel was like. I bought a newspaper and sat on the loo and read an announcement for "*Be My Sushi, Tonight*, based on *Goose-Pimples* by Mike Leigh." I nearly fell down the toilet. I went to see it and it was very extraordinary indeed. It turned out that the same company had already done *Abigail's Party* without procuring the rights, which is the usual piratical procedure in Singapore. They all took me out for this incredible Chinese banquet which went on all night, and I didn't feel lonely at all. So when I got back to London I told my agent to waive the rights.'

The critical controversy was more interesting than the aborted political one. Michael Billington in the *Guardian* concluded that Vernon and Irving are damned 'purely because they are car salesmen'. To which the only possible response is: *sua cuique sunt vitia*, in as much as we all have our shortcomings; the play doesn't appear to have a general 'down' on car salesmen in general, though it might well not be too keen – in so far as a play *has* an attitude separately identifiable from those of the characters enacting it – on these two car salesmen in particular. Another possible response would be: come off it, old bean. Billington also held the visible, surface nature of the play against Leigh, as though poking fun, in his book, was an even bigger mortal sin than being a car salesman: 'In a good play, every person is seen from his own point of view: here, you feel people who eat at chain restaurants, have bars in their living rooms and vintage cars on their shelves, are utterly beyond redemption.' Well, they are, aren't they, Michael? And why, because they strike you in a nasty way, should you deduce, if that's your fetish, that they are not being seen from their own point of view? And who cares, anyway? It's only a play, and these horrible people have a horrible lifestyle, and we all have a jolly good laugh at it. Even people who have bars and models of vintage cars at home themselves might have had a jolly good laugh at it if they had been bothered to go along to Hampstead (they weren't). The theatre was anyway clogged up with its elderly local Jewish audience (who loved the play and laughed themselves silly) and *Guardian* readers who went along to tut-tut *à la* Billington and not be caught out laughing at their social inferiors. Irving Wardle in *The Times* was left wondering whether Leigh 'is disappointed that actors should select such defenceless targets; or whether he encourages them to select easily despised stereotypes so as to flatter his public into a sense of superiority'.

The only times I am ever aware of a sense of superiority slurping around the stalls is when I am at a brilliant Tom Stoppard play, where audiences are congratulating themselves on getting half the point or on tuning in to some heavily crafted, gleamingly witty dialogue. But the minute Mike Leigh comes along, critics come out with all this superiority mallarkey. I simply cannot believe that people sit and watch *Goose-Pimples* in the state of suspended intellectual animation required to form a judgement about people *such as* Vernon and Irving, rather than a judgement about Vernon and Irving *themselves*. Audiences do not adopt those sorts of political positions in the theatre, though of course I concede that some critics, myself included, frequently do. Vernon is an irredeemably ghastly person and he is a car salesman. But he is not ghastly *because* he is a car salesman. He is ghastly *and* he is a car salesman. Which is like saying he is ghastly *and* he is theatre critic, or he is ghastly *and* he is a professional footballer; the two qualities are not mutually dependent, though of course in some people's minds they might well be. Safer to say, perhaps, he is ghastly *and* the most distinguished brain surgeon in Europe.

The controversy also arises because of our old friend 'caricature,' a sloppily-used pejorative these days, and a word which, in some critics' view, as we have already seen, is both dirty and detrimental to the fine old cause of 'character'. This is not the case with the drawings of Gillray, Cruikshank or Hogarth, or indeed of Ronald Searle, Ralph Steadman or Gerald Scarfe, all of whom draw caricatures that also convey the essence of a character. 'Distillation of character' is Paul Clements's useful phrase, while Leigh himself is fond of the notion of 'heightened reality' as a definition of his work's relation to what you might term 'humdrum reality'. It is a question of putting the reality of people into an aesthetic frame; otherwise, what is the point of composing films and plays? What would be the point of a drawing, or a cartoon, if you could just take a photograph? 'Only the arty intelligentsia are worried by social caricature, which is what a lot of my work obviously is,' Leigh wearily told Gordon Burn in that same *Goose-Pimples* feature; 'Real people aren't.' And I think he's right.

At the time of *Goose-Pimples*, the poet James Fenton was half-way through a three-year stint as theatre critic on the *Sunday Times*. He wrote a fine column about Leigh's work in March 1981 in which he reported the complaint of a colleague that 'Mr Leigh always made his cast act badly because he filled them with hatred of the characters they were portraying.' Apart from being codswallop, that observation will not survive a close examination of any of the major performances. In applauding Leigh's psychological discoveries beyond the savagery, Fenton noted an element of the pathological in Marion Bailey's depiction ('depiction' is a good word) of the croupier 'who is torn between her intense desire for money, and her perfectly genuine sexual fear of the Arab she has brought home. The terror she shows at the idea that her Arab might not be the oil-sheikh she has imagined, her brave attempt to reconcile a cosmopolitan with a distinctly suburban conception of morality, her inability to get what she wants and to be the kind of person she would respect – well, if such perceptions derive from a hatred of a character, then hatred cannot be too bad a thing.'

The complex nature of what Leigh does was readily appreciated by Timothy Spall, who worked with him for the first time as a hopeless postman in *Home Sweet Home*. There were three hopeless postmen in the film, which was shot on location in Hitchin, Hertfordshire. Spall played the second most hopeless postman, Eric Richard the first most hopeless postman and Tim Barker the third most hopeless postman, so hopeless that he was, as Clive James wrote in a memorable review, incapable of taking in the news that his wife was having an affair with the first most hopeless postman. Spall spotted straight away that Leigh illustrates the incongruous in normality, the quirkiness in the apparent banality of everyday speech. Spall once overheard a girl refusing to take her grandfather for a haircut in a wheelchair. 'No, no,' she was protesting, 'he can walk, he can walk; he can walk in small doses.' That is pure Leigh. 'Verisimilitude' is the word Spall likes to use (now that he's learned it from Leigh, he says): 'His area is the glory of everyday nothingness which he elevates to great drama. The minutiae of people's repetitious lives becomes of the utmost importance. And his people are never seen anywhere else, except when they are destroyed in the tabloid newspapers or in patronising documentaries. If you were to tell me you think Mike's patronising, I'd accuse him of the dead opposite: of elevating, and of making amusing and tragic, what most people in life go through. Which is nothing to do with glamour.'

Spall was born and bred in south London and, curiously enough, his father was a postman. Young Timothy once took Christmas casual work with the Post Office, but 'I did fuck all. I went in at nine and sat on a sack and went home at five.' So he did have to do some research on the role of Gordon Leach, a slothful, slobby couch potato in permanent dispute with his svelte and brassy wife, Hazel (Kay Stonham), who has lost four stone, works part-time in British Home Stores in Stevenage, and is offering to entertain the first most hopeless postman, Stan (Eric Richard, a wonderful actor, now a familiar, hook-nosed face on TV's *The Bill*), when his shifts don't coincide with Gordon's. 'The thing about postmen,' says Spall, 'is that they are rather eccentric characters. It's changed a bit now because of technology, but they used to be a sort of hotchpotch of blue-collar workers moving towards admin. You may have thought the postmen in our film were a bit odd, but they weren't nearly as bizarre as the ones you encounter in Hitchin. Or anywhere else, probably. There was a lot of goosing going on, a lot of arse-pinching and talking in tongues, which was a bit of a revelation. My Dad was an original, interesting sort of bloke, and he thought it was pretty accurate. The whole culture of postmen is a bit unusual.'

The third most hopeless postman, Harold Fish, tells terrible jokes and mutters the lines of songs (without the tunes) almost without knowing that he is doing so. He rattles off stinkers while sorting mail or confronting his beans on toast at teatime, with Gloria Hunniford prattling on the radio in the background. 'Does your wife make good toast? That's a burning question. Why is Prince Charles a postman? Because he's the royal male.' Even Harold doesn't think these quips are funny, though there must have been a time in his life when he did. His snaggle-toothed, bespectacled wife, June (Su Elliott), shuffles around in pink fluffy slippers and house-clothes, not just ignoring him but not even noticing him. Their marriage is as dead as Gordon's, who sits burping and grossing out downstairs while Hazel goes upstairs alone. In this film, it's the women who are straining at the sexual leash. Gordon and Harold are cringeing blobs.

Stan's wife ran off with another man when their daughter, Tina, was six. She is now fourteen. As the film progresses, Stan and his domestic arrangements assume a pivotal importance. He is pestered by a social worker (Frances Barber) who talks more about herself than about his daughter, and he misses an important Sunday visit to Tina by going to the laundrette, where he picks up a strange, limping, waiflike creature, takes her to the pub, then back to his bed. The woman is played by Sheila Kelley, who was called in at short notice by Leigh when a vague plan to have Stan become sexually involved with the social worker did not materialise. Kelley is only on screen for a few minutes – in the pub, then dressing after sex with Stan and leaving, never expecting or wanting to see him again – but in this desolate, polio-stricken creature she paints a whole life of someone who haunts laundrettes, not to wash clothes, but to make human contact. When the veteran film-maker Michael Powell attended a showing in San Francisco in 1986, he asked Leigh, 'She's not an actress, is she?', so disturbingly real did Kelley's performance seem to him.

Stan's sex drive is nothing abnormal; when, with a slight shock, we learn late in the film that he has been having an affair with June Fish, they have not achieved congress for six months. The secrecy and furtiveness of the affair on a housing estate is achingly well caught when June, repelling Stan's first lunge at her bottom, says, 'Don't; the neighbours can see.' Our shock, though, is nothing compared to Harold's when told by his wife of her affair with Stan. His helpless, humiliated 'Why?' conveys the following: why would you want to do something like that; why would anyone want to do that with you; why is this happening to me; why was I born? In the improvisations, of course, the actor Tim Barker really did not know about the affair. When Su Elliott as June confessed the affair to Barker as Harold, Barker himself simply did not believe it. He told Leigh it was not true. Then he discovered that in fact it *was* true. 'He was devastated,' says Leigh, 'and he tapped into those real feelings, which is why it's such a good scene.'

Eric Richard's Stan is attractively valiant and horny. He drives a wedge of solid integrity through the film which is totally characteristic of Leigh in having both a watertight symmetrical structure and a fascinating, shifting quality, as we speculate on Hazel's libido, and her marriage, or the situation at the Fishes, or whatever is going to happen to young Tina. The elements are pulled together in a Sunday lunch at Gordon and Hazel's which is extended into a walk back to Stan's for tea and a series of confessional revelations starting with a shouting match on Stan's garden path between the lunch hosts: 'bleedin' fat' and 'bleedin' whore' are a couple of the insults exchanged. Wanting or not wanting children emerges as another major issue, personified in the sad sight of blank, pushed-about Tina.

The camera does most of Tina's talking for her. Indeed, the camerawork on this film is wonderfully precise: Gordon gets off his bike, parks it, the camera pans with him as walks up to a front door, and we hear the bike fall over out of shot; Stan drives under a viaduct on his way to see Tina and the camera waits for a train to complete its journey from right to left and cuts instantly to Stan's destination; a long-shot of Stan and Tina in the scrubland of Stan's back garden, with a full view of the grim, pebbledash back wall, supplies the eloquent vacuum for their halting attempts at communication. These are just small reminders that 'making films' is not necessarily about special effects, non-stop action and crazily energetic camera movement. It is necessary to state this obvious truth only because there are people who think that, because Leigh's films are undoubtedly 'performance-led', what he does is therefore not 'cinematic'.

One merry little snippet is the medium long-shot of a man in a dressing gown dashing from his house to snatch a brown envelope from the postman, which he smuggles into his car. The furtive recipient is played by Paul Jesson, a genuine son of Hitchin who could not participate in the film more fully because he was appearing in the West End in *Goose-Pimples*. The slightly 'in' joke is that this man is in fact Irving Gammon, Jesson's *Goose-Pimples* character, intercepting his pornography order while Frankie is still lying in bed upstairs.

The social worker, Melody, high-tails it from Hitchin to London and is replaced by her boyfriend, another social worker, Dave, who wears round spectacles, and who ends the film with a cascade of jargon about Melody's 'quiche lorraine attitudes', peripheral sub-structures in a society catering for social greed, not social need, and the evils of commodity fetishism. Stan looks bemused as Dave babbles on and the soundtrack amalgamates the traditional workers' anthem, 'The Internationale', with Carl Davis's witty, plangent score for double basses. The credits roll, and Tina is alone.

This last scene infuriated the playwright David Edgar who, in the course of an interesting essay pondering the strengths and weaknesses of the fringe generation of alternative theatre, and a possible way forward in a marriage of intellectual commitment and performance-art visual imperatives, struck out at Leigh's methods. The technique, he averred, of allowing actors to develop their characters apart from each other, and then introducing them into conditions of conflict with each other, produced 'work of extraordinary, naturalistic perception; but it also appears to produce an attitude to the character of little more than rank contempt'. The implication behind the poor environment, he said, was a poverty of spirit. Such a response, surely, can only be that of a middle-class intellectual who finds no joy in the humdrum. For Stan is not a sad or deprived creature, nor is he bitter and twisted. Things have not turned out all that well for him, and he has fewer words than the social worker, but his spirit is harsh and resilient. He is patently a good man with many failings, a definition most of us, including, I imagine, David Edgar, would be only too happy to be in a position to deserve. Contempt I do not detect.

At the NFT retrospective of Leigh's films in May 1993, after a showing of *Home Sweet Home*, a middle-class woman in the audience accused Leigh of 'cruelty' in showing Hazel shaking out her synthetic orange doormat with a ferocity that implied, and indeed conveyed, that she was doing something an audience should find amusing. So, was the carpet cruel? Leigh replied: '"Cruel" is your judgement. You are colluding in this film. We gave her what the character requires. We did not make the rug. We're not looking out for something "cruel" to give her at that point, or ever. It's just who she is.' We are back at the 'laughing at' issue which presumes an attitude of contempt. We laugh at Shakespeare's Malvolio in his yellow stockings making a fool of himself, but we do not despise him. We laugh at Ben Jonson's Master Morose for soundproofing his house with ludicrous precautions in his quest for a silent life, but we do not despise him. We laugh at a chattering housewife in carpet slippers shaking out a fake orange rug . . . who despises her? Suddenly, modern costume causes a problem. Good Lord, we could be unfortunate enough to live next door to such a person.

As with the Dennis Potter reaction to *Abigail's Party*, the only basis on which to deduce a motivation of hateful caricature is the one of sentimentalising the working class to a pitch where their 'cause', in the middle-class view, precludes the possibility of absurdity or phoniness. If there is one guiding principle in Mike Leigh's work, it is that sentiment is a non-starter. Edgar's particular gripe, having laid out his general objections, is finally aimed at that last scene between Stan and Dave: 'The model for the social worker probably did talk just like that, in the pub or at home or wherever, but I cannot believe he would have done so in the first, or I suspect any subsequent, meeting with a client, and thus a perceptive piece of observation turned into a contemptuous caricature.' (Note how Edgar has cleverly switched his attack to defend not the spiritually impoverished postmen or their wives, but a middle-class comic turn in the last reel.) There is no doubt that Dave is a figure of fun, though whether he would be less of one in the pub or even at home is surely open to debate. The assumption you make most easily about the character is that he would talk like this wherever he was, *pace* David Edgar's intimate knowledge of the species. The other thing is that films are films and plays are plays and not always responsive to the demands of one particular aesthetic rulebook – in Edgar's case, in this essay, the rulebook of social realism. The last scene of *Home Sweet Home* is powerful precisely because Dave represents a continuum of institutional indifference to the domestic plight of people like Stan and his daughter, not out of malice or even incompetence, but out of a social and cultural separation which compels him to erect, in the hastiest and most insensitive manner, the language barrier of professional certainty. Dave has no doubts, whereas Stan has only fears.

Although Stan's predicament emerges as the strongest thread in the film, you are never sure, or really concerned, that it will do so until the end. The question of dominance in Leigh's work is interesting because the structure and thematic content depend to such a large extent on what happens, chemically, in rehearsal. Reviewing *Goose-Pimples*, however, Michael Billington said that it was Billington's Law that 'in improvised plays one character always romps off with the evening', and that this law was triumphantly confirmed by Antony Sher 'crashing through the farce-barrier to create a character who is bewildered, truthful and credibly alive'. This is a fair enough comment given Billington's response to *Goose-Pimples*, and it may be true that he could command the examples of Anne Raitt's Sylvia, Alison Steadman's

Beverly, David Threlfall's Trevor, Brenda Blethyn's Gloria or David Thewlis's Johnny as grist to his mill.

You could easily argue that strong characters dominate plays much as they do in life. And the democratic nature of Leigh's process allows, of necessity, for the strongest performances to swim to the fore and the top. In the end, it is all down to how Leigh, as the dominant artist himself in the creative process, absorbs and responds to what the actor brings into the discussions and the rehearsal room. But Billington's Law clearly cannot be illustrated by reference to *Nuts in May*, *Ecstasy*, *Home Sweet Home*, *Meantime*, *Four Days in July*, *High Hopes* or *Life is Sweet*. In other words, improvised work, or work using improvisation as a means to an end, is as likely to lead to dominating characters as it is to ensemble equality, and usually to something of both.

As in all conventionally written plays. Leigh admits that 'you obviously exploit people who have a lot to offer, and people who have less to offer, less so,' but his decisions about that are invariably made much later in the process of production than is usual, for the simple reason that rehearsal is where the play or film, and the performances, happen. Johnny in *Naked* would undoubtedly have been a major player whatever happened; but Leigh is adamant that the film could just as easily have been concentrated on the vile landlord Jeremy, or on the three girls in the Dalston flat, as on the detail and dynamic of Johnny's odyssey. Eric Allan felt unhappy about his performance as Rex Weasel not developing more in *Smelling a Rat*, Leigh's next play at Hampstead, but he blames no one but himself for that. So he spent the first act in a wardrobe. Rex Weasel could theoretically have been the central focus of that play (though it is hard to see how, with Timothy Spall rampaging around as Vic Maggott); whereas there was no way Allan's quarryman in *Nuts in May* was going to take the limelight, however conscientiously he researched the role, or however brilliantly he improvised in rehearsals. And his was, no question, as Leigh is the first to attest, an outstanding performance in a peripheral role.

Because of all the mystique surrounding Leigh's working methods, he is taken too often, and too superficially, to be some kind of guru. Like all good directors, there is something of the teacher in him, and he is a forceful and persuasive communicator. In the early part of his career, especially, his impact on others was such that they wanted to work in the same way. Something of that must surely apply in the case of Les Blair. Blair is inclined to say that his working method came out of the atmosphere, the *zeitgeist* of the late 1960s, but Leigh, who says his view on all this has 'evolved', remains sceptical. 'It is simply not true that you can just work how I do, or adopt my approach, because what I do is too complicated and too personal.'

One or two of Leigh's assistant directors have achieved success in their own right. Mike Bradwell had met Leigh at the E15 Acting School, where he says he was taking 'a non-existent course' as a director. They hit it off. In the summer of 1968, while Leigh went back to Manchester to write the play he promptly destroyed (*Monsters*), Bradwell went home to work with the Scunthorpe Youth Theatre. He hung around on *Big Basil* with the Manchester Youth Theatre, and then played Norman, the folk-singing hippie lodger, in both the play and the film of *Bleak Moments*.

As *Bleak Moments* became a film, and Leigh struck out into *Hard Labour*, Bradwell diverged with the remnants of their joint plans and, after a short spell with the Ken Campbell Road Show, managed to found Hull Truck Theatre Company: 'I was concerned to do plays about people of my age for people of my age. We were dreadful hippies, really.' Maybe, but the work was terrific, starting out in obvious imitation of Leigh but developing a distinctive and individual style of bedsit epic with original music. In due course, fine writers such as Alan Williams and Doug Lucie, who were aware of the Leigh/Bradwell process of discussion and improvisation, happily absorbed elements of that process into the way in which they wrote.

At the same time, Bradwell would take a received script and break down the characters' histories with the actors and build that information and any pertinent discoveries back into the script. It was like stripping down an engine and then reassembling the parts. 'An awful lot of this stuff is just commonsense. It's all there in Stanislavsky. It's all about getting down to the truth; in rehearsal,

I provide a framework for actors to do the kind of research they *think* they do on their own but never really get round to.' Bradwell ran Hull Truck for ten years and was succeeded (briefly) by Pam Brighton and then John Godber, whom Bradwell head-hunted at the National Student Drama Festival. Godber has remained with Hull Truck ever since, transforming the outfit into a phenomenal producing factory of mostly his own plays. 'I lost faith with Godber,' says Bradwell, 'when he went on Terry Wogan's TV chat show and said he wanted to do shows his Mum and Dad would like. That was never our purpose. I suppose it was the times, but we were supposed to be an irritant, an in-yer-face alternative. Yeah.'

Phil Young was another assistant director (with Leigh at the RSC) turned disciple who produced one unforgettable piece of work on his own account, *Crystal Clear* (1983), which transferred from the Old Red Lion into the West End, where it was produced at Wyndham's Theatre by Robert Fox, who had produced *Goose-Pimples* at the Garrick. A powerful 'disability' play about blindness (Tom Kempinski's *Duet For One*, about a crippled musician, had lately been a West End transfer from the Bush, and *Children of a Lesser God* brought deafness to romance in the West End), *Crystal Clear* took a gruelling, funny and unsentimental look at a burgeoning friendship, then fall-out, between a diabetic picture dealer losing his sight and a blind girl. The dealer's short-sighted ex-girlfriend also figured in five punchy scenes with not an ounce of fat on the text. Improvised on a single-room set ransacked from jumble sales in north London, *Crystal Clear* was a notable addition to the illuminating repertoire of blindness stretching from *Oedipus Rex* to *King Lear* and Milton, via Ghelderode's Beckettian sketch for blind beggars, *Three Blind Men* (revived in 1993 by Cheek by Jowl), and Synge's *The Well of the Saints* to Brian Friel's *Molly Sweeney*. Young never really repeated that early success. These days, he teaches at drama school.

For a time, too, the actress Sheila Kelley devised and directed 'improvised' plays with Sarah Pia Anderson, but the partnership floundered after one or two reasonably successful efforts at the Bush Theatre, and Kelley realised that she should write fiction,

The writer/director on location with producer Simon Channing-Williams
during filming of *High Hopes*, 1988.

Ruth Sheen, Edna Doré and Philip Davis in the last scene of *High Hopes*, on top of the flats, if not the world, beside St Pancras Station.

Saskia Reeves and Greg Cruttwell in *Smelling a Rat* (1988), Leigh's fourth Hampstead Theatre play, a rabid anti-farce in a pink boudoir.

Stan Kouros and Evdokia Katahanas in
Greek Tragedy, Leigh's play for the
Belvoir Street Theatre, Sydney, in 1989;
it later visited the Edinburgh Festival
and Stratford East.

Timothy Spall as Aubrey tries to enthuse his kitchen assistant, Paula (Moya Brady), before the opening of the Regret Rien restaurant in *Life is Sweet* (1990).

Jane Horrocks as the anorexic Nicola, and Alison Steadman as Wendy, her mother, in *Life is Sweet.*

Paul Trussell and Wendy Nottingham, the long and the short of it, in the grisly first-act climax of *It's a Great Big Shame!* at Stratford East (1993).

On location with *Naked*: Leigh, director of photography Dick Pope, boom operator Loveday Harding and focus puller Garry Turnbull.

David Thewlis as Johnny in *Naked* (1993), the lingering image of a film about alienation, sexual violence and the city.

Greg Cruttwell as Jeremy, the repellent landlord, and Katrin Cartlidge as Sophie, the victimised punk Goth, in *Naked*.

Leigh and Dick Pope on location in east London during the filming of 'Untitled '95', which was to become *Secrets and Lies*.

Mother and daughter getting to know each other after years of separation. Marianne Jean-Baptiste and Brenda Blethyn in *Secrets and Lies*.

while Anderson moved into television. At one point, Leigh told Kelley that she should join the Theatre Writers' Union: 'I remember,' says Kelley, 'David Edgar got up at one meeting and said "I think there are some people here who shouldn't be here because they are not playwrights."' This anecdote provides another clue, perhaps, to Edgar's attack on the Leigh method in *Home Sweet Home*. He was not only suspicious of the way Leigh worked, but he refused to recognise that what Leigh did was in fact 'writing'.

But as Leigh himself came to realise, and as his pieces became 'written and directed by' as opposed to 'devised and directed by' – the first to be so labelled was *The Short and Curlies* in 1987 – he was writing not merely with pen and ink, but with actors and technicians. He acknowledged the reality of the film and theatre media to an extent unexplored by David Edgar: the practical, pragmatic reality was that actors had to speak what he wrote, so he paid them the democratic courtesy of involving them from the off in that process of composition. Their liberation fuelled his creativity. And if Leigh's was not the governing voice, and Edgar was right in alleging that he merely organised the efforts of his actors in a spirit of objective contempt for the characters they devised, how was it that every Mike Leigh play or film was so palpably bursting with concern for humanity and so easily recognisable as bearing his own personal stamp?

NINE

Mean Times, Irish Times and Difficult Times

A few years into the 1980s, Britain started to feel the effects of Thatcherism and, according to the British film industry, the effects were not all beneficial. The decade was a turbulent one for many people, with rising unemployment, sudden wealth in the City creating a generation of super-rich yuppies, increasing violence and disaffection on the inner-city streets, political disenchantment in the student population, the nation at war in the Falklands and Northern Ireland, the proliferation of satellite television stations and mediocrity in the media, the collapse of any shared sense of moral, ethical or political propriety. For Leigh, the decade was a difficult but highly dramatic one. He made two fine films, *Meantime* and *Four Days in July* (his last film to date for the BBC, shot in Belfast) and, while working in Australia in 1985, was hit for six by the death of his father. Deeply affected, and suddenly unsure of his professional future, he extended his absence from Britain for a few months.

He returned in a deeply troubled condition and started work on a new film for the new Channel 4, codename 'Rhubarb'. The project was abandoned after eight weeks in an unnerving replay of the RSC 'Ice-cream' débâcle, although this crisis was perpetrated more by Leigh's own personal circumstances than by the crowding demands and hassle of any umbrella organisation. Once again, but this time after a longer gap of two years, he bounced back and launched the latest phase of his career with his first full-length feature film since *Bleak Moments*; *High Hopes* (1988) not only completes a trilogy of 1980s political films – though the trilogy was not planned as such – but also marks the maturity of a film-maker with the skill, passion and confidence to speak for himself, his nation and his characters together. Thanks in large part to the new creative optimism engendered by the founding in 1982 of Channel 4, which took over from the old BBC the challenge of nurturing and producing new British film, Leigh rode his luck, and his resurgence, right through to *Naked*. He was now unquestionably a leading British film-maker, and increasingly recognised as such in Europe and America.

David Canter, Leigh's friend the psychology professor, claims that these political films of Leigh, from *Meantime* to *Naked*, 'are really just about how difficult it is for the individual to be part of a community and survive effectively when you have the state driven by people in power who have their own particular qualities. The films are political in a subtle sense, not a party political sense.' That is certainly true. Most of Leigh's memorable characters are up against it in some way, but they battle on. I once asked Pam Brighton, the stage and radio drama producer now based in Belfast, why she disliked the work of Mike Leigh. 'Because it's nihilistic,' she replied. While it is true that there is little prospect of kinetic salvation or liberation from their grim circumstances for most of Leigh's characters, his work is really about the qualities of the soul as manifest in the everyday routines of survival and companionship. And in that respect, it is not nihilistic at all. *Meantime*, an exceptional film by any standards, is possibly the exception, with a disturbing smog of defeatism spreading from the East End council flat of the Pollocks right through to Mavis's sister's home on the Chigwell housing estate at the Essex end of the Central Line. Leigh would defend such pictures of nihilistic defeatism by saying that 'that is how life is for many, many people.' And he is right.

Meantime in embryo came to Leigh in the bath. 'When I was shooting *Home Sweet Home*, I had this terrible flat, with a bath, no shower, over a shop in the barren Bedfordshire countryside. (I always tell film students, you *must* have a shower or a bath when you're on a shoot because you don't want to pong.) I was in the bath, listening to the radio very early in the morning, and this story came on about two unemployed kids in Warrington or St Helens or somewhere who had committed suicide. And I thought – I always go through something like this – what we're doing is irrelevant. *That's* what we should be doing. Something about unemployment. We were two or three years into Thatcher, it was already an issue, and it lingered at the back of my mind.'

Meantime was made as a 'Film on Four' by Central Television, produced by Graham Benson, on 16mm film. A few months later, Channel 4 films started to shoot on 35mm, with a view to feature film distribution. So *Meantime* was slightly too early to benefit from this crucial change-over. This unlucky timing, in fact, held up Leigh's return as a feature film-maker for another five years. Every film since *Bleak Moments* had been made for BBC TV.

Meantime was his thirteenth film in all, and his thirty-sixth piece of work evolved and scripted through improvisational rehearsals. It was shown at the London Film Festival in 1983 and on Channel 4 a few weeks later, on 1 December. Three days earlier, three extraordinary films had been shown on British television *on the same night*: on BBC 1, Alan Bennett's *An Englishman Abroad,* a film about the spy Guy Burgess, starring Alan Bates and Coral Browne, and directed by John Schlesinger; on BBC 2, William Trevor's *The Blue Dress*, starring Denholm Elliott; and on ITV, David Hare's *Saigon – Year of the Cat*, starring Judi Dench and Frederic Forrest.

But only *Meantime* was the subject of extensive features in the *New Musical Express* and *The Face*. The Mike Leigh retrospective on BBC TV in 1982 had helped to focus his career, but the unemployment issue in *Meantime*, together with the visceral, compelling performances of a fairly unknown but remarkable young cast – Gary Oldman, Tim Roth, Phil Daniels, Tilly Vosburgh, Pam Ferris, Peter Wight, Alfred Molina and Marion Bailey – ensured media interest not just in the 'serious' newspapers but also in the music and style magazines. 'I've chosen, quite consciously,' Leigh told the *NME* in the course of a five-page interview, 'to say, this is that world where everybody's unemployed, which is the primary condition of what's going on.' The 'cultishness' of

Mike Leigh really starts here, and the actors were still talking about the film several years later. Gary Oldman, who played the ferocious skinhead Coxy, achieved his first real prominence as Sid Vicious in *Sid and Nancy* (1986), and told *Blitz* magazine in 1987: 'Coxy was such a kid. He had that childish idea that through behaving aggressively in front of a girl you can find deep love or emotion . . . That's how I felt, myself, doing wheelies as a kid – that *somehow* it would get a girl into bed.'

The film still exerts a special appeal to the young. As the costume designer Lindy Hemming says, 'I see those kids, in those clothes, every day on the street in London today.' And Phil Daniels, a rock musician in his own right (after *Quadrophenia*, he played in the group Renoir, later the Cross), was invited to appear on Blur's 1994 chart-topping album, *Parklife*, because, he says, 'They're all *Meantime* freaks! Ditto, Suede. Maybe it's one of those films. Kids of fifteen and sixteen, maybe they want to nostalge a bit for the late 1970s, early 1980s. Whereas we find it hard to. It felt a natural film to make at the time. Also, young people like films about young people, and they like to see reality about themselves. Kids who play bass guitars don't like all that American teen-wolf shit. They like something a bit more sort of bleak, a bit blacker.'

Oldman's Coxy is a bovver boy, layabout friend of Daniels's Mark. 'You're thick, I'm 'ard,' says Coxy as they disappear along a towpath, kicking cans, a scene of acrid beauty typical of a film where a dole queue in a packed Social Security office exudes an eerie, smoky, 'Depression-era' atmosphere. Even the desolate housing estate, where litter blows shoulder-high through the open air, and Coxy bursts violently around the graffiti-infested lifts and threatens an innocent lamp-post with random head-butts, is photographed by Roger Pratt with a careful, mournful, never sentimental dignity. Coxy is a pathetic sideshow, banging around the pool table in the pub, scissor-kicking like a sitting-room psychopath on the sofa, taunting a black neighbour and finally (our last sight of him) rolling around in a tin drum, like one of Beckett's doomed dustbin-dwellers in Leigh's beloved *Endgame*, bashing it noisily in a self-absorbed lather of pointless, energy-consuming bravado. The sapping, debilitating and demeaning state of unemployment, the futile sense of waste, has not been more poignantly, or poetically, expressed in any other film of the period.

Coxy, and to a lesser extent Tilly Vosburgh's Hayley, the gang's pub pal, operate in the margins of the domestic story of the Pollock family: Mavis and Frank and their two sons, Mark (Daniels) and Colin (Tim Roth), live in the East End, and visit Mavis's sister, Barbara (Marion Bailey), and her husband (Alfred Molina) in Chigwell. All three Pollock men are unemployed. Barbara offers Colin some casual decorating work in her own home in a well-meaning gesture which Mark interprets, or misinterprets, as patronising. The Pollocks have been visited by a politically do-gooding estate manager about a broken window ('Windows are good: light, space, yeah'). He squats on his haunches and, egged on by eager Barbara, who is also visiting, discusses economics and self-help, illustrating his argument with an ill-chosen mixed metaphor. 'It helps us if you tell us about the grain of sand. Don't wait to tell us about the anthill. Okay? Yeah.' Roth's lethargic, severely myopic and slow-witted Colin stirs on the sofa as if coming out of a deep coma: 'We got ants?'

The estate manager is played by Peter Wight almost as a spoof preview of his night-watchman in *Naked*. Wight is one of the few actors Leigh allows to break some of his most precious rules. Matthew Guinness, who played the farmer in *Nuts in May*, used to turn up three hours late for rehearsal with the excuse that he had been milking cows. Leigh would berate him thus: 'We are rehearsing a film here, and you are only doing research.' Wight, in a more complex variation of this syndrome, is prone to ring up and wheedle his way out of rehearsals on the grounds of pursuing increasingly recherché avenues of research, but Leigh knows he is invariably onto something worthwhile. 'He's a complete magpie. The trouble is, he's also obsessive. He finished all his scenes in the film and then rang up to ask if he could continue researching anyway and be paid to do so!' Wight is also the only actor Leigh allows to talk about his character in the first person: 'I've given up with him saying "I wouldn't do this" and "I can't do that" when the cardinal rule is that an actor must talk about his character in the third person, once he's come out of character.'

On Colin's first working day in Chigwell, Mark goes ahead of him on the Central Line and turns down Barbara's offer on his brother's behalf out of innate political resentment and sneering disapproval of his aunt's suburban lifestyle. Colin makes a sad attempt at becoming a skinhead like Coxy and shaves his head, having been repulsed by Hayley. Mark promises to look out for him, but the atmosphere at home is claustrophobic, destructive, acrimonious. He says he is leaving, he can't handle all this, 'it's doing my brain in.' Meanwhile, in Chigwell, Barbara hits the bottle and is invaded by depression, which her impatient husband puts down to pre-menstrual strain. She tells him to 'fuck off,' a mini-triumph of sorts, but the outlook is as grim for them as it is for the Pollocks. Pam Ferris as Mavis seems to lard the earth with lassitude as she rolls along, several stages beyond caring, none of her biros working in the only public place apart from the Social Security that is packed to the gills – the bingo hall.

The film's charged authenticity undoubtedly comes from the actors tapping into people and backgrounds they knew all about. Daniels was a 'King's Cross boy' who trained at the Anna Scher school in Islington at the same time as such other cockney aggressors as Kathy Burke (who worked with Leigh in *It's a Great Big Shame!*) and Pauline Quirke and Linda Robson of the hit TV comedy series *Birds of a Feather*. He based Mark on someone in the flats where he grew up. A lot of this background sub-culture of darts, pubs and pool was glamorised by Martin Amis in his novel *London Fields*; Daniels, for instance, and the others, did 'a lot of heavy pub improvisation, playing pool in the middle of darkest Hackney'. They are the sort of actors, however, who would not have been out of place there. In fact, it was probably their natural environment, though Daniels says, 'I had to be careful in character, because Mark would always say something to top someone else.'

His colleagues were not so careful with each other. The rehearsal space was a factory in Homerton. One day, Roth and

Oldman were throwing a milk bottle around. Suddenly Roth threw it up and it smashed into a fluorescent lighting strip. Leigh remembers seeing 'Gary's shaven head erupt into a thousand red blotches; in the film, you can see the stitch marks'. He rushed Oldman to hospital in his car. 'As I drove him there, all done up in his skinhead stuff, covered in blood, Gary said to me, "For fuck's sake, tell 'em I'm an actor!" He could easily have lost his eyesight in the accident, and I do not know to this day what I would have done if that had happened.'

Physical danger was not usually a factor in the rehearsal process, but within a year Leigh was preparing and shooting a BBC film on the streets of east and west Belfast. He had never worked abroad before and jokingly refers to *Four Days in July* (1984) as his first 'foreign-language movie'. The cast was drawn exclusively from the north of Ireland, with the exception of Shane Connaughton, the actor and writer who had followed Leigh into repertory at Stoke-on-Trent, who comes from County Cavan, a border county technically situated in ancient Ulster but, since partition, facing south. Connaughton had seen an advertisement in *The Stage* seeking Northern Irish actors. As he hails geographically from the north but lives in the south, Connaughton at least wanted to go along and have his say on the subject. He was cast initially as a Belfast plumber with a Belfast accent, and was out on the streets 'in character', practising the accent, and speaking to a woman at a bus stop who asked him, 'Oh, what part of London do you come from?' Although they did not feel unduly defeatist about this, Leigh and Connaughton finally decided that the actor should revert to his own soft southern brogue and became a plumber called Sean Maguire.

Four Days in July is already a period piece, as well as a valuable document of life before the British Army stopped patrolling the streets of Belfast in daylight hours following the peace initiatives and IRA ceasefire towards the end of 1994. Twenty-six years of troubles cut deep into the local psyche, and although Leigh's film is symmetrically arranged to culminate in the birth of two babies in neighbouring hospital beds – one to a Catholic couple from the Falls Road, the other to the wife of a soldier in the Ulster Defence

Regiment – its heart is in the Republican camp. As Connaughton says, 'The Protestant side, and some of the Protestant actors, felt they didn't get a fair crack of the whip.' Or, indeed, a fair crack of the crack. All the jokes and all the communal spirit dance along the Falls Road, whereas the loyalist soldier and his chums are a pretty dire and dour bunch, keeping fit, twirling batons, singing 'The Sash' and getting sombrely drunk on cans of lager. Stephen Rea says that Leigh's position was resented in some Protestant quarters – there were, indeed, questions asked in the House of Commons – 'but there is a community that polices and a community that is policed. That's very broad, maybe, but it's a fact. There is one community that feels outside the law and one that feels they can impose the law. This means that the legitimacy of the state, the whole constitutional question, is a part of the fabric of everyday life.'

The four days, 10–13 July (including Friday the thirteenth), covered, as for real in the film, the Battle of the Boyne festivities, the Protestant marches and the bonfires. The fictional manipulation of that 'footage' was expanded to include a tale of two families with the arrival of a new baby in each. Leigh had sat next to Kenith Trodd, the BBC producer and longtime colleague of Ken Loach, at a dinner after a screening of David Puttnam's first co-production with Channel 4 (Michael Apted's *P'Tang Yang Kipperbang*, scripted by Jack Rosenthal, with a lovely leading performance by Alison Steadman as a schoolteacher with a crush on the groundsman). Leigh suggested a film about Northern Ireland. At the NFT 1993 retrospective, Trodd said that Leigh telephoned him in a panic after a few weeks and said, 'Get us all back, I haven't got any ideas.' But he knew Leigh well enough to be confident that this was just a routine procedure; besides, he was too busy on another project. The film started to gel.

Leigh found Belfast incredibly friendly, but filming there was traumatic. 'We had started research in the summer of 1983 and went to shoot it in the following July. There was some scepticism at the sight of a film crew, but no real obstruction. The best thing was that we had no script, so no one could accuse us of doing anything; that's always worked to my advantage. We were fantastically lucky; in east and west Belfast, we rode with the hares and hunted with the hounds. Trodd was adamant that I should not just do another domestic piece. And of course it is an *entirely* domestic film. He got a bit annoyed at first, but was very happy with it in the end.' Filming the Orange parade, Leigh caught a wonderful shot of a baby at an upper window sucking on a bottle of orange juice, mother's milk to a new generation of Protestants. And on the eve of the twelfth, the big day, Des McAleer as the crippled Eugene was framed in a door on his crutches, the light behind him, a potent image of the isolation of a Catholic in west Belfast with all the noise of the bands and fireworks ringing in his ears. This shot was the very last in that location. A big crowd had turned out, so Leigh contrived a party turn with McAleer: he stood in the doorway, and the call went up for 'Quiet, please,' for a rehearsal. Then Leigh shouted, 'Action!' and McAleer suddenly threw away his crutches and danced wildly down the street like Mighty Mouse. The crowd roared, then the scene was shot 'for real'. Trodd recalls that, during the bonfire, he talked to a sixteen-year-old boy who announced proudly that his grandfather had fought with William of Orange at the Battle of the Boyne (1690). Connaughton, an admired novelist and screenwriter (*My Left Foot* is a notable credit) and now very much a 'former' actor, thinks that the film *is* a fair reflection of how things are: 'It is easily the most interesting picture I've seen about Northern Ireland since the troubles started. Apart from John Arden and Margaretta D'Arcy's *The Ballygombeen Bequest* [1972], I can't think of any play or film that has gone into it so successfully in any deep way at all.'

And the troubles were funny, too. McAleer's Eugene recounts how he was going nowhere in particular when he stopped a bullet in 1973, was hit by a bomb in 1976, and shot by a soldier in 1979. Bad luck, eh? 'Apart from that, you're rightly!' says Dixie, the itinerant window-cleaner played by Stephen Rea – another of his 'comic Irishmen', he admits – who turns up in a straw hat, replacing the usual feller, who's under arrest, 'cardiac arrest'. Dixie, a former political internee at Long Kesh, has eight kids, the Kesh special recipe for making poteen in the lavatory, and a fund of appalling jokes such as 'What's the name of the ship in *The Mutiny on the Bounty*?'

Rea based Dixie on a man he knew who really *was* a comic Irishman. He picked up the Bounty joke in a club in west Belfast and was later told it by someone in the same club who had picked it up from *Four Days* on television. In the waiting room at the maternity hospital, we meet a lovely mad Ulsterman, Mr Roper (John Hewitt), railing against doctors ('They've got it all sewn up!') and offering a condensed justification for not having children: 'Years of not sleeping at night . . . by the time you get any peace, you're too old to enjoy it . . . what is there for them in this country? . . . I'm not going through this again! . . . You're better off never being born at all.' When called by a midwife, he jumps to his feet with, 'It's not a girl, is it?'

All the actors used their personal backgrounds to telling effect. Bríd Brennan, who plays the Catholic housewife, Collette, is the daughter of a Belfast publican and, as a child, used to visit her elderly aunt and uncle just around the corner from where she acted in her scenes on the Falls Road: 'I remember standing in their little front room when I was eight years old, singing "The Patriot Game", the only song I knew then or know now. So when Mike asked me to sing a song in bed with Des, that's what I had to sing.' As part of the rehearsal, she went to witness a birth in Tooting (she has lived in London for over twelve years): 'I found it really disturbing, all those people in one little room, so I've had my two children at home. I always felt I should have a go at writing, but now I know I don't have the discipline. That film was the nearest I came. It was a great release, and very creative, because Mike was tapping into a whole system of language used by people living on top of each other. He loved all the turns of expression.'

Belfast, as Connaughton confirms, is a great place for people 'slagging each other off', but the best jibe, he says, wasn't even in the film: 'I was sitting on the lavatory [which he had come to fix], talking to Des McAleer, complaining about going off on my holidays to Bundoran in Donegal Bay without having done all my tax returns. And Des said, "Why don't you bring them with you?" and I said, "You can't do tax returns in a caravan," and Mike couldn't resist stepping in with, "As every self-respecting tinker knows." We were on the floor at that.' In his research as a plumber, Connaughton worked for a firm who went round replacing radiators and floorboards after army raids. 'The drama of it all is incredible. A character called Bonzo McCann was shot by the army when I was away one weekend. I knew his girlfriend because I had been working in her house as "a plumber" on quite a big job, having tea there every day. She was a stunning woman, and when I went round afterwards, she was coming down, all dressed in black, surrounded by other women. Like a scene in a Greek tragedy. We were stopped and searched by soldiers with rifles all the time. It's weird when they drop the rifle on you. They say, "It's all right, I've got you in my sights." The west Belfast people cope just by ignoring them, not even looking in their eyes. It's an extraordinary thing.'

With the advent of Channel 4, and the decision of David Rose, who was appointed head of drama and senior commissioning editor for fiction, to shoot films in 35mm as opposed to 16mm, Leigh knew that he had a better chance than ever of making another feature movie. But the next couple of years suddenly clouded over. He had agreed to attend a screenwriters' conference in Melbourne at the start of 1985 and had accepted a subsequent invitation to teach at the Australian Film School in Sydney. His father, Abe, now seventy-one, was extremely ill at this point, having suffered a stroke a few years previously. He had already suffered three heart attacks since the age of fifty-nine or sixty. His mind now flickered in and out of the past. Over this last four or five years, Leigh had seen much more of his father than before he was incapacitated. It was if a barrier was removed. Abe began to open up to his son and, according to Leigh, 'became extraordinarily garrulous'. Lying in bed, Abe put a hex on any of his four grandchildren – Leigh's two boys, his sister's son and daughter – becoming doctors because, he claimed, it was a curse to know what they're doing to you when you are old and ill. Before Leigh left for Australia, he went to the flat in Salford to say goodbye: 'We both knew it was the last time.' They gave each other 'a spontaneous hug', probably the first since Leigh's childhood. Not unusually among fathers and sons, 'that sort of thing was not part of the culture of our relationship.'

While Leigh was teaching in Australia, Abe's condition deteriorated to critical, and he was moved first to a mental hospital and then to a heart unit, then back to another mental hospital. He died at the end of February 1985. Alison rang Leigh with the news in Sydney, and he promptly rang his mother in Manchester, just as the funeral was leaving for the Jewish cemetery in Oldham. 'I felt completely lost and alone. I was staying in a very small room with a very fancy, oversized electric fan. I lay on the bed just looking at the fan, playing the one Mozart tape I had in my possession back and forth all night. Ours had been such an unresolved relationship, and now there was nothing I could do about it. I was just turned forty-two years old.'

He needed to clear his head, but he felt he also had to carry on. He fulfilled his teaching obligations and did some promotional work on *Meantime*, which was receiving its only theatrical release in Australia. He went to Melbourne and Perth to give lectures, and so first of all buried his solitude and sense of loss in a busy round of people, publicity and talks. But the extended sojourn was now changing into something even more profound, a quest for the meaning of his work, or at least a period of self-assessment. He went to an island off Tasmania with an old friend and visited other friends in Adelaide. He took the train to Alice Springs and then hired a car and drove to Ayers Rock over the Easter weekend, an experience he found terrifying. He drove towards the rock with his eyes fixed on the red and golden natural monument and, on arrival, walked around its ten-kilometre circumference in the middle of a very hot day.

All this time he was in constant touch with Alison by telephone, but he was gradually extending the long journey home. He drove to Darwin for a few days. 'You sign a kangaroo clause with Avis, the hire car firm, which makes you responsible for any damage caused by kangaroo collisions. You see them bounding across the road but, statistically, you are driving the only car that kangaroo will ever see in his life; and that road is the only road he will ever see. There is no one and fuck-all forever. And you are warned very seriously to stay in your car and never leave the road for two reasons: you might go walkabout in the heat and go potty; and there are deadly snakes around.'

Travelling alone, Leigh had booked cheap flights in Sydney through to Hong Kong. The forty-two-year-old backpacker, afflicted by what later turned out to be a bilateral hernia, flew from Darwin to Bali, and took an overnight bus to Surabaya on Java, followed by a week in YogYakarta. Thence to Singapore (where he saw *Be My Sushi, Tonight*, aka *Goose-Pimples*) and Hong Kong for a few days while arranging an instant visa to go on to China, where he spent four weeks. 'My arrival in Beijing on a cheap flight was a totally surreal experience. It was dirty, grey and dusty. I found myself in a hotel for overseas Chinese, none of whom spoke English. I certainly didn't speak Mandarin. I was having trouble checking in when a young French guy materialised who was working for a French company and waiting for his boss to turn up. He spoke Cantonese, Mandarin and English and offered to share his twin-bedded room with me, which was bloody brilliant. On top of which, he had time on his hands and proceeded to act as my guide for nine or ten days.'

The cultural impressions were coming thick and fast, and Leigh found himself meeting a wide range of people and immersing himself in everything the country had to offer. On May Day, he joined the massed throng on the Great Wall of China. He found the Peking Opera, despite the reluctance of the tourist authorities to admit there were any performances, and the People's Theatre where Arthur Miller had lately directed his own play, *Death of a Salesman*. He took a twenty-four-hour train journey to Xian, 'where the terracotta warriors were an incredible, fantastic experience, not least for someone concerned with characterisation and detail'. His enquiries about theatre in Xian were stonewalled, but he found by stealth a company performing little satirical playlets. His new-found enthusiasm for Chinese train journeys took him on another twenty-four-hour expedition down to Chengdu, the capital of the Szechwan province, where he 'pottered about and fell in with more people'.

His next stop was the holy mountain of Emei-Shan: 'You climb up into the clouds and while sitting on the holy lavatory in the temple, your dung falls thousands of miles into oblivion.' He stayed in the Temple of the Thousand-Year-Old Elephant where a priest cooked 'incredible vegetarian meals', which no doubt explains the popularity of the celestial toilet. He returned to Chengdu, took a flight back to Canton, spent a couple of days there, took a hover ferry back to Hong Kong where he boarded a flight to London and returned to the family home in Wood Green.

'The whole thing was an amazing, unforgettable period in my life. But it was all to do with personal feelings, my father, where to go next, and my desire to make a feature film. In Australia, where I had to talk about my work a lot, I was distanced from everything. You do feel as though you are at the other end of the planet. Because you are. I felt I was at the end of one stage of my life and at the start of another. And apart from anything else, I returned home a serious Australia-phile, and to this day there's a funny part of me that really would like to be there a lot.'

There was a possibility brewing of a feature film. Before leaving London, Leigh had sat in the office of his agent, Anthony Jones, at A.D. Peters (later amalgamated to form Peters, Fraser and Dunlop), and, painfully aware that he had just missed out with *Meantime*, said it was high time he made a feature film. Jones agreed but had no positive suggestions. Leigh left the office and turned the corner into John Adam Street just off the Strand, where he bumped immediately into the director Jack Gold, who was on *his* way in to see Anthony Jones. With the advent of Channel 4, a number of new independent companies had been formed in order to supply the new channel, and the British cinema, with co-productions. Gold (the director of *The Naked Civil Servant* and *The Bofors Gun*) had joined forces with the playwright Willy Russell, director Mike Ockrent and producer Victor Glynn on one such company, Quintet. They later amalgamated with the much older established Portman Productions, and the new company assumed that venerable name. In John Adam Street, Gold said to Leigh that he must do a film with Quintet.

That film was codenamed 'Rhubarb', and Leigh returned from Australia to get cracking. Instead, he cracked up. First of all, he had to undergo his hernia operations. In the spring of 1986, he cast and gathered twenty-six actors in Blackburn, Lancashire. They included Julie Walters, Jim Broadbent, Jane Horrocks and David Thewlis. After seven weeks' rehearsals he withdrew, and the film was cancelled.

His friend Sheila Kelley was in London, working at the Royal National Theatre, during the Blackburn episode. She stayed two or three nights a week in Wood Green with Alison while Leigh was away, and saw clearly what was happening: 'I think at that stage Mike felt his home life was compromising his work and that he had to make a choice. The boys were young and there were demands being made on him as a father which he felt he could not meet while also making films. Then he discovered there was no point in making films if you didn't have that life outside of it. So he went from thinking that his films would be better if he devoted all his time to them, to realising that films were always better when you brought the *whole* of your life, with all its complications, to them, as a writer and director.'

At the time of the cancellation, Leigh hit rock bottom. 'I was all over the place,' he now admits. 'I was under a lot of pressure and when I went to a doctor it was agreed I was suffering from a nervous breakdown. Which I was. Luckily this enabled them to get back the insurance on the film. It was a *force majeure* clause; I had to be declared ill, and I had to be treated and so, on the recommendation of Antony Sher and David Threlfall, I went to see the famous Monty Berman – the South African psychotherapist, *not* the theatrical costumier. I saw him regularly for seven months, and that was designated the cure.

'The nature of what I do is totally creative, and you have to get in there and stick with it. The tension between the bourgeois suburban and the anarchist bohemian that is in my work is obviously in my life, too. The heroine in all this, of course, is Alison Steadman, who was, and who remains, fantastic. She is as anarchic and cheeky as anyone, but she is also very sensible and down-to-earth. I started to pull myself together. I didn't work, I simply stayed at home and looked after the boys. But I was told that unless I received some treatment, I was unlikely to be insured on another film.'

At which point, Channel 4 put up some money for a short film and, pending that project's success, agreed to co-produce, with Portman Productions, Leigh's first feature film since *Bleak Moments*. All went perfectly to plan, and Leigh bounced back, yet again, to make first *The Short and Curlies* (1987, 18 mins) and then *High Hopes* (1988, 104 mins). His darkest hours were behind him. After a relaxing holiday with Alison and the boys in Sardinia, he dug deeper than ever before and launched himself into an amazing new stretch of artistic endeavour, on screen and stage, that took him into the 1990s and towards his own half-century.

Channel 4's contribution towards *High Hopes* would be £745,000 in a budget of £1.27 million, i.e. 59 per cent. David Rose and his associates produced an astonishingly high standard of work for the 'Film on Four' slot over the next decade. The careers of major directors such as Stephen Frears, Peter Greenaway and Derek Jarman, as well as Leigh, all received an important boost. The idea, as the critic John Pym expressed it, was 'to encourage new (and not so new) independent film-makers by offering them not only money, but the chance (if a distributor could be found) to exhibit their work in the cinema, where it might gain a reputation and an identity, before its television transmission.' Such a policy, tried and tested on the Continent, was new to Britain, and it would be impossible to say today that it has not been triumphantly successful.

David Rose says that, right from the start, he fought shy of adaptations and anything about the Second World War. 'It turned out, of course, that a couple of the films I really admired were adaptations, such as Pat O'Connor's *A Month in the Country* [1987, adapted by Simon Gray from a novel by J.L. Carr]; but I was always looking, in the first place, for original work. In the 1980s, we were looking for the younger generation with something to say about what was going on around them and in the world at large. And we couldn't find them. We were turning, in fact, to Ken Loach, Mike Leigh and David Hare. Loach and Leigh, in particular, are welcomed by the Europeans, who always have a place for the real *auteur* in their film culture. Their energy has been such that it is impossible to ignore their work.'

In 1990 Rose was succeeded as head of drama at Channel 4 by David Aukin, Leigh's old friend and collaborator at Hampstead Theatre, who had spent an interim period of seven years first as director of the Leicester Haymarket Theatre and then executive director of the Royal National Theatre alongside Richard Eyre. Aukin is much more confident of new work emerging from a new generation, while expressing the hope that he would be involved in some way with any film Leigh made, 'and I hope he feels the same about me.' (Channel 4 was not involved, however, much to Aukin's disappointment, in the financing and preparation of Leigh's latest film, 'Untitled '95', although the channel has since secured the television, theatrical and video rights in Britain.) Aukin operates an annual budget of £10 million. He and his staff of eight produce or co-produce 'ten to fifteen films a year'. Half of the films Channel 4 commissions each year are from first-time film-makers – most recently these include Nancy Meckler's *My Sister in this House*, Danny Boyle's *Shallow Grave* and Nicholas Hytner's *The Madness of King George* (based on Alan Bennett's hit National Theatre play, starring Nigel Hawthorne).

'When David Rose initiated the Channel 4 commissions,' says Aukin, 'he was doing so in a context of a commercial film industry to which he provided an alternative. Now, there hasn't been anything of late for Channel 4 to be an alternative *to*. It is a lot easier for the commercial big boys like Rank – our equivalent of Warner and Paramount in the United States, who are at least making movies and investing in them – to buy in American films that have already had a success and not help all that much in creating their own. It is no coincidence that *Four Weddings and a Funeral* [the most spectacularly successful of all recent 'Film on Four' co-productions] will receive a much wider release in this country after its American release and critical and popular acclaim. Such is our lack of confidence at the moment that we need the Americans to tell us we have a good movie before we believe it ourselves.'

Aukin knows as well as Leigh that for a film to succeed internationally, it has to be absolutely specific in its location and universal in its themes and emotions. One of his first commissions on arriving at Channel 4 was *Naked*. The budget was £1.5 million, of which Channel 4 supplied two-thirds. 'I've never thought of *Naked* as a film with a statement about contemporary Britain,' says Aukin. 'It's clearly placed in contemporary Britain, but I've always been convinced of its universality. It's like Dante's *Inferno*, a journey into hell. It happens to be set in London in the 1990s. Without those specifics, you get Euro-puddings or transatlantic nonsense.'

Ironically, as Leigh floundered in 1986, his reputation was growing steadily in America. The 1986 San Francisco Film Festival presented a season of new British films, including five of Mike Leigh's: *Meantime* and *Four Days in July* as well as the American premières of *Nuts in May*, *Grown-Ups* and *Home Sweet Home*. In his introductory essay to the festival programme, David Thomson made the important point that, 'More even than Cassavetes or Jacques Rivette, Leigh is as good as his actors,' and he mentioned his detached, medical watchfulness with the camera. The press reactions in San Francisco were generally appreciative. His suburban world was directly linked by some commentators to the pop lyrics of the Who, the Kinks, the Clash and the Sex Pistols. In *Meantime*, Frank and Mavis were said to 'look like twenty years of dirty tea dishes', while one critic fastened on to a key factor in Leigh's anatomy of British life: 'Much of Leigh's appeal lies in the fact that his is the Britain which American audiences never see except from behind the sophisticated Oxbridge-infected [inflected?] put-downs of John Cleese, Michael Palin, Eric Idle, and the rest of the *Monty Python* school.'

It was three years since Leigh had been behind a camera. The 'short' he promised Portman was *The Short and Curlies*, by which he would be definitely caught if he failed to deliver the goods. The little film he made after just three weeks' rehearsal was a delightful *bonne bouche* about a chatty hairdresser, Betty (Alison Steadman), her withdrawn daughter, Charlene (Wendy Nottingham), and one of her customers, Joy (Sylvestra Le Touzel), who

works in a chemist's shop and is chatted up over the Durex counter
by Clive (David Thewlis in the first of his three Leigh roles), a
lanky, persistent customer. Wendy Nottingham had been cast in
'Rhubarb' and, like everyone else on the film, received a letter of
apology from Leigh, saying that he would try and work with
them all again at some point in the future: 'That was brilliant. So
many directors say that sort of thing, but they just say it. Mike is
incredibly loyal, a man of his word. I'd been offered, and accepted,
another job just before I heard he wanted me for *The Short and
Curlies*. There was no question of not turning it down in order
to work for Mike.'

The tight, taut narrative moves swiftly towards Joy and Clive
getting married, and the morose, lonely Charlene getting pregnant. Betty is more excited about her client's love life than her
own daughter's well-being. The hairdressers, 'Cynthia's', is in
Willesden, north London, and the exterior locations were in
nearby Harlesden. Thewlis's Clive is an incipient motormouth,
though clearly not in the Johnny in *Naked* class. He is another of
Leigh's bad-joke merchants: 'What's round and really violent? A
vicious circle.' The imagery of this film is particularly interesting:
the rubber helmet Betty pulls savagely over Joy's head before
plucking her hair through in thin strands for streaking unavoidably
suggests the contraceptive latex items Joy herself sells, one of
which Clive wears in bed with her: 'Might have had my cap in
upside down,' she says. 'I had the Durex on the right way round,'
counters Clive. 'The Durex was for AIDS,' says Joy, accusingly.
On the one hand, there is ritual, physical indignity, rubber, pre-
vention; on the other, new life, love, marriage. Charlene slips
sadly and silently between two stools, like a victimised blob.

Joy's hair is a different colour and style in each scene, one
minute frizzy, the next dyed and permed, the next coiffed and
piled high. All done by wigs. She is a self-transformer, while
Steadman's bunch-backed, hypochondriac, waddling Betty with
a whining, twangy voice and direct, nosy manner on the job ('Do
you have trouble with your periods, Joy?' is one of her more
discreet enquiries) tugs at her restrictive underwear at home and
regales her sullen daughter with a catalogue of her ailments and

twitches. Joy's home is a dark haven of loud furniture and a fish tank. Alison Steadman, who has a hairdresser sister, which came in handy, loves Betty as much as any of her characters: 'If Mike said I could do one of my parts again, that's the one I would choose. I loved her from the word go, the minute I got the curlers and the scissors in my hands. It just clicked. Sylvestra is a terrible giggler, and we just giggled the whole time, it was terrible. Great fun, though.'

Now, at last, it was full steam ahead on that feature movie. The chief location area for *High Hopes* was King's Cross, where Cyril and Shirley live in a top-floor flat.

Cyril's mother, the lonely old lady so beautifully and quietly played by Edna Doré, lives in the last council flat in a 'gentrified' Islington street although, as cooperation was not forthcoming in Islington, Leigh and his crew had to move down to Bethnal Green to find the two adjacent houses, one privately owned by the stuck-up, 'opera-loving' Boothe-Braines, the other Mrs Bender's – a new version of the domestic juxtaposition in *Grown-Ups*. Cyril's sister, the vulgar, incipiently hysterical Valerie – described by Nigel Andrews in the *Financial Times* as 'a walking colour clash with a hyena laugh, a philandering husband and a home designed like a hairdressing salon' – lives in a suburban area beyond north London (those scenes were shot in Radlett) which bears the same sort of jumped-up relationship to King's Cross as Chigwell does to the East End in *Meantime*. As in that film, *High Hopes* contrasts the economic and spiritual conditions of siblings. And in developing some of the themes in *Babies Grow Old* and *Grown-Ups*, it presents a brilliantly organised dramatic résumé of attitudes towards parturition and old age.

Sammy Cahn's cheery Oscar-winning ditty 'High Hopes' was crooned by Frank Sinatra in Frank Capra's optimistic *Hole in the Head* (1959) and used as John F. Kennedy's campaign song in the 1960 presidential election. Leigh's appropriation of the title is deliberately ironic. His film builds towards the increasingly helpless and amnesiac Mrs Bender's seventieth birthday, celebrated in a nightmarish family gathering on a ghastly housing estate. Another strain is the meditative comparison of shallow lifestyles triggered when Mrs Bender locks herself out of her house and is reluctantly assisted by her upper-middle-class neighbours over a cup of tea in the next-door kitchen. 'Have you kept all your original features?' drawls Lesley Manville's killing Laetitia Boothe-Braine. The camera searches the parched, lined, confused face of Edna Doré for an answer. In vain. This iconic confrontation between the two extremities of Mrs Thatcher's political legacy dares to control, in a few sharply-etched frames, the spirit of the age. The film does this so consistently, and so brutally, that the old complaints of 'over the top' and 'caricature' were bound to be heard again.

The Boothe-Braines imply a routine of kinky sex games behind their nursery banter on the stairs. It is not even dark, and Rupert, a bow-tied wine merchant, is tearing his clothes off while Laetitia in silk undergarments fondles her scrawny teddy bear, 'Mr Sausage', an impure descendant of Candice-Marie's fluffy Prudence in *Nuts in May*. Extremely portrayed as they are, these representatives of the brainless classes are no more grotesque than – or, rather, just as grotesque as – their upwardly mobile working-class counterparts, Valerie and Martin Burke. Burke is 'the jerk in the Merc', 'the wanker in the tanker', 'the weasel in the diesel', a dealer in second-hand cars and hamburgers whose vowels, walk and slobbish, lecherous demeanour in Philip Jackson's superb portrayal are every bit as repulsive as the yuppies. Heather Tobias's Valerie, too, who pathetically steals fashion tips from Laetitia – a swish pillbox hat with a diamond-shaped decoration is shamelessly imitated in a mail-order style – and sticks her nose into the 'done-up' house, uninvited – Rupert's basement study is greeted with 'Ooh, look what they've done to your coal-'ole, Mum!' – has converted the venial sin of pushiness into a full-scale preparation for the inevitable hysterical breakdown.

The images of Britain perpetrated by the movies of this decade are not flattering. Vincent Canby of the *New York Times* drew some gloomy conclusions about the Thatcher years from Lindsay Anderson's *Britannia Hospital* (1982), a satirical metaphor for a nation under siege in a strike-bound hospital; Richard Eyre's *The Ploughman's Lunch* (1983), in which Jonathan Pryce as an overweening journalist writes a book about the Suez Crisis during the

Falklands War, and Eyre's cameras smuggle footage of a triumphal Prime Minister out of the Tory Party conference; two collaborations by director Stephen Frears and writer Hanif Kureishi, *My Beautiful Laundrette* (1985), with Daniel Day-Lewis as a gay, reformed racist punk, and *Sammy and Rosie Get Laid* (1987) reporting deftly from the front line of a painfully integrating society; as well as from *High Hopes*. By the time *Naked* appeared, right-wing journalists in this country even started to suggest that Leigh's portrait of Britain was prejudicial, lopsided and irresponsible.

No film-maker has an obligation to be fair, or balanced, about the society he by rights claims as his material. His only obligation is towards the truth as he perceives it, and Leigh perceived a divided and demoralised nation. So it was no surprise when the critical jeremiads of 'unfair' and 'exaggerated' directed at Leigh's methods of characterisation were applied with equal gusto to his political temperament. Even the eminent, usually sensible Pauline Kael of the *New Yorker* fell into this trap, wondering if the film's 'violent contempt' for Martin Burke dated from 'the bohemian left's traditional snobbish hatred of the prospering middle class (and people who move to the suburbs)'. Maybe it does. Or maybe Burke is just one helluva contemptible character. Any rule against that? Kael, in her first and only statement on Leigh, clung to the idea that his style was an aesthetic manoeuvre undermining his talent: 'The film is never drab, never ordinary. Leigh is a real film-maker, and his political vision gives his work substance and conviction. But he's shaping sentimental screwball microcosms. If an artist can be said to be corrupting absurdism, that's what he's doing. He uses absurdism to modernise realism, to syncopate it. It still drags its feet.'

'Absurdism' seems to me the last thing on Leigh's mind, but Kael's way of writing about Leigh's heightened effects is certainly original. Does the realism drag its feet? Burning on a slow fuse throughout the film is the central relationship of Cyril, the motorbike despatch rider, and his plant-loving partner, Shirley, whose biggest cactus, Thatcher ('a pain in the arse'), dominates a cabinet of lesser spikey species – Bollocks, Dick, Willy, Brains and Turd.

Cyril and Shirley are played by Philip Davis and Ruth Sheen with consummate tenderness and sincerity. They love each other deeply as an insurance against the cold climate of the times, but that relationship is continuously modified and buffeted by the debate over whether or not to have children.

At first, we see them helping out a lost, clueless new boy in the city, Wayne from Byfleet, who is trying to find his sister. Wayne left home after a row with his mother; he went out and bought pork pies instead of steak and kidney pies. The wrapping comment on this episode is Shirley's: 'I hope I don't have a kid that's a bit thick.'

Cyril, like Wittgenstein, is reluctant to advocate bringing children into a life of misery, a sentiment which also echoes the powerful speech of Kirillov in Dostoevsky's *The Possessed* about the mess of the world we have made for the unborn. Cyril is a quiet, unruffled, decent man whom Philip Davis, shaggy-haired and blond-bearded, manages to make interesting. And Ruth Sheen as a buck-toothed, physically relaxed Shirley only has to open her big brown eyes slightly wider to make all sorts of unspoken comments on the subject, and the man, closest to her heart.

They visit Karl Marx's grave in Highgate Cemetery. 'Without him,' Cyril says, looking reverentially up at the great stone head of the monument, 'there would be no unions, no Welfare State, no nationalised institutions.' You half expect Mrs Thatcher to leap out from the shrubbery yelling, 'And a good thing, too!' Shirley reads the Marxian inscription at the foot of the statue: 'Philosophers have only interpreted the world in various ways. The point, however, is to change it.' Back at their flat, they are visited by a zealously 'politicised' and emotionally chaotic friend, Suzi, who blazingly, and simplistically, denounces Thatcherism and advocates power to the people. She plans to go to Nicaragua. Cyril and Shirley appear to have grown out of all that. Cyril softly derides Suzi's 'meetings about meetings' and states his deeply felt desire for everyone to have enough to eat, places to live, jobs to work in – 'and then you can have babies,' he adds, looking across at Shirley. He offers to knock their relationship on the head. She takes him in her arms.

That scene is the emotional centre of a notably well structured film. Bedtime contrasts in three households are yet another development of a stylistic ploy in *Grown-Ups*. In the Boothe-Braines' bedroom, Laetitia lies immobile with restorative cucumber slices on her eyes while Rupert boasts of having consumed 'Two steaks, same day, totally different.' She patiently explains to him the plot of the opera they have just sat through (*The Marriage of Figaro*), of which he has no sensible recollection whatsoever. Next, Valerie writhes around in her lingerie next to Martin, asking him 'to start' and then suggesting that 'You're Michael Douglas, I'm a virgin.' Martin giggles, snorts, coughs, and turns over to go to sleep. Then, in a more serious rerun of the bedtime scene in *The Short and Curlies*, Shirley says she does not want to put her cap in, after a warm, cuddly, sensual interlude; all families are a bad idea, Cyril sums up. Even the slightly worrying false start, the unlooked-for extended encounter with Wayne which concludes with the hapless, harmless sponger waving goodbye on a Green Line bus back to Byfleet, finds its symmetrical, charitable counterweight in the decision of Cyril in the last scenes to see more of his mother from now on.

On a personal level, Leigh was here exorcising some of the guilt over his father's missing years while simultaneously expressing the new relationship he was trying to forge with his widowed mother in Salford. In terms of the film, Cyril undergoes a sea-change: in the final, quietly exhilarating scene on the roof of the flats, he points out the London landscape to his mother: the gas works, St Pancras station, 'where Dad worked', St Paul's, the Post Office Tower. 'It's the top of the world,' whispers Mum, pleased to be up there. Life could be worth living. A child would enjoy this view. People have each other. All in all, Cyril's lucky.

On a political level, *High Hopes* expresses part of the confusion many members of Leigh's generation feel about being a socialist. He supports the Labour Party on a regular basis through his bank account, but he has never been a party member. He has been confused by the debate over Clause 4 in the party's constitution, and admits that the film attempts to discuss the impossibility, or at least the difficulty, of realising in practice the socialist aspirations he espouses. These ambivalent feelings were perfectly expressed by Leigh in his own 1994 foreword to the published text, and are worth quoting in full:

> How the world has changed since we made this film only six short years ago! Communism has all but collapsed, which may not be a wholly bad thing, sadly. And what has happened to real Socialism, not least here in Britain? Does it survive?
>
> Cyril, by now doubtless a happy if concerned parent, must be more deeply frustrated than ever by the gulf between how things are and how they ought to be, and how ever-increasingly hard it has become to do anything about it.
>
> *High Hopes* was of course born of my own such feelings of inertia. These were thrown into even greater turmoil when, in 1990, courtesy of the British Council, I accompanied the film to Poland. In Warsaw, some people were outraged by it. To see the goodies espousing Socialism was disgusting enough, but their visit to Karl Marx's grave was nothing short of obscene!
>
> In Krakow, well after midnight, when the public transport had long stopped, and the November snow was still falling, a sizeable chunk of the audience was still slugging it out in debate; the pros using the film as a metaphor for any number of ideological positions (most sensible, though some daft) and the antis flatly refusing to believe my bizarre claim that there were actually folk sleeping rough on the streets of London!
>
> This often violent battle was most confusing and dis-orientating for me. But that was just the beginning. Things seem to have got worse in this crazy world. And, like so many of us, I'm more confused than ever.
>
> And *High Hopes*, whilst not, I trust, having dated in any real sense, now seems oddly innocent in its way.

The London-ness of the film is as crucial to its 'metropolitan feel' as it is in *Meantime* and *Naked*. We see Cyril delivering a parcel to a blank receptionist in Richard Rogers's Lloyds building (incipiently blue in the late afternoon), descending in the exterior, transparent lift with two equally blank identical lady twins. Lesley Manville returns home with a Harrods shopping bag, a souvenir of the day she and David Bamber spent in the Knightsbridge emporium 'in character': 'If you think Laetitia is over the top, you should meet some of the women *we* found researching in the country, at the opera, at Harrods. I overheard a woman ordering a sofa in Harrods; she was so posh, I just wanted to die. I couldn't believe I lived in the same society as this woman.' The Boothe-Braines went undetected, indeed unremarked, in Harrods. Manville, as Laetitia, bought a snooker cue for a friend.

One improvisation did not go uninterrupted: Philip Davis and Jason Watkins (as Wayne) were improvising outside the rehearsal room in King's Cross; Wayne was trying to find his sister's place with the address written on a scrap of paper and had been told by Leigh that he should, 'in character', ask the way if he came across anyone else in the cast. 'I had invented a fictitious street so that Phil definitely wouldn't know where it was, which was the necessary outcome of the scene. Just as Phil as Cyril said he did not know the street, a mounted policeman appeared on a really huge horse and Jason, absolutely properly, asked, "Excuse me, do you know where this is?" And the copper said, "Let's have a look," and said he didn't, then got out his walky-talky and proceeded to get through to the cop shop. So I popped out from behind a wall and said "Come out of character" and explained to the copper that we were rehearsing a film. He believed us, eventually, but he didn't much like the sound of it.'

Street credibility was an issue, too, for the composer Andrew Dickson, who had first worked with Leigh on *Meantime*. Coxy and co. rattled around to a metallic accompaniment of treated piano (stuck with drawing pins) and soprano saxophone. For *High Hopes*, Dickson provided a more lyrical, melancholic sound of blues harmonica and double bass, with viola and saxophone as back-up. It is a good city sound – less urgent and less memorable, perhaps, than his subsequent tumbling, serial music score for *Naked* – and one ideally suited to the reflective, philosophical core at the heart of the film. He was named Best Composer in the European Film Awards, honoured alongside Ruth Sheen (Best Actress) and Edna Doré (Best Supporting Actress). This formal acknowledgement of Leigh's status as a *bona fide* feature filmmaker after all those years meant a lot to him. He was equally 'chuffed' to receive the Peter Sellers Comedy Prize for *High Hopes* in the *Evening Standard* Film Awards. He was back. Over the worst, but not over the hill.

TEN

Rats, Greeks and East-Enders

It is convenient to summarise Mike Leigh's career as a steady progression towards his current distinction as a film-maker. This achievement has been his primary ambition. In his early days, however, it was easier to work in the theatre, and he has never completely lost his taste or his enthusiasm for the medium, though it is fair to say he would now be perfectly amenable to the idea of never creating another piece in the theatre again. This, I believe, would be regrettable. But the point is, Leigh really only wants to make films, and has only ever really wanted to make films.

The Hampstead Theatre connection, however, means a great deal to him, so one of the first possibilities he discussed with his agent as *High Hopes* was underway was a return to the boards in Swiss Cottage. The Michael Rudkin/David Aukin partnership had been followed by a period of artistic control by Aukin alone. When Aukin went to Leicester in 1983, the succession fell to Michael Attenborough, with Dallas Smith staying on as general manager. Leigh suggested another play. By the time *Smelling a Rat* was programmed, Attenborough, too, was on his way: first, for a brief sojourn in the commercial sector, and then to the RSC as executive producer. He was succeeded by Jenny Topper, who saw *Smelling a Rat* safely on to the stage.

For once, however, Hampstead failed to find suitable and congenial rehearsal rooms for Leigh and his cast. 'We fetched up in the headquarters of the National Youth Theatre; we had to pass through their offices all the time, and there were loads of kids around doing a Christmas show. One of my first and last requirements, every time, is a closed, real workshop environment where we can rehearse, uninterrupted, at any time of the day or night. And we didn't have it.'

Nonetheless, *Smelling a Rat* was a desperately funny play, with maybe not quite enough action, or events, to sustain the farcical structure it so cleverly subverted, but with a fantastic clutch of buttonholing performances led by Timothy Spall as Vic Maggott, a pestilential, belching and jabbering north London rat-catcher (next Tuesday's appointment: 'Cockroaches in Colindale') and Saskia Reeves as a tremulous, knock-kneed, virginal retard called Melanie-Jane Beetles, with a lisp and red glasses. Seven years after *Goose-Pimples*, here was another robust anti-farce, a prime candidate for a West End extension, but the production did not quite detonate as Leigh had hoped, and the Robert Fox management declined to take up the transfer option.

As in the then still-banned radio play *Too Much of a Good Thing*, Leigh was down among the rat-catchers, a tribe that obviously exerts a peculiar fascination for him, as it did for Henry Mayhew in his accounts of the Dickensian London poor in the mid-nineteenth century. In *Naked*, Johnny has a speech about one's never being more than ten feet away from a rat at any given time in London. The audience's incipient state of entomological paranoid psychosis, or fear of all insects and creepy-crawlies, is one that Leigh exploits by humanising the rats in the shape of their detectors: the rat-catchers are turning into rats themselves, just as some dog-owners (especially poodle-fanciers) grow uncannily to resemble their dogs. The difference between the examples of the species in Mayhew and Leigh, and exactly the kind of delicious incongruity Leigh relishes, is that rat-catchers nowadays work for, and own, private pest-control firms, aspire to respectability, millionaire status even, and play golf. Even the insalubrious Mr Payne in *Too Much of a Good Thing* called himself a 'rodent operative'.

They also, apparently, sleep in the sort of garish, livid green and pink boudoir owned by Rex Weasel (Eric Allan), who has returned unexpectedly from holiday on the black volcanic beaches of Lanzarote because his wife has taken up with a toy boy there. It is the day after Boxing Day, and Vic Maggott, Rex's employee, has popped round after a seasonal party, as requested, to keep an eye on the flat. Vic, full of grating good cheer and burping brazenly, brings his wife, Charmaine (Bríd Brennan), in tow, just to have a bit of a look around, check out the facilities. Rex, jerky as a ferret and quick as a flash, dives into one of his many fitted cupboards to overhear Vic denounce him as a bit two-faced, like 'a fork-tongued chameleon'. A second incursion is made by Rex's son, Rock (Greg Cruttwell, later the despicable Jeremy in *Naked*), at which point Vic and Charmaine dive into the wardrobe, reinforcing the structural 'feel' of a French farce. Rock resembles a traumatised, morose egret, and hardly speaks at all, but is hoping to seduce his girlfriend, Melanie-Jane, in the absence of his parents. Not all that surprisingly, Melanie-Jane, who chews her split ends like spaghetti, enquires of Rex, 'Will you be going back to Lanzarote, Mr Weasel?', a line that protrudes with a lovely incongruous rhythm and pokes you in the ribs like a tickle stick.

The whole script has a wild anthropomorphic provenance, so that you really do feel you are watching human beings in laboratory conditions. 'I saw Keith Chegwin the other day in W.H. Smith's,' offers Rock unexpectedly, as if he'd been wandering round a zoo. Even for those who do not know that Keith Chegwin is a particularly wearisome television personality, the line is a gem. Vic is offered a drink: Scotch, bourbon, rye? 'Got any whisky?' he retorts. Food comes up. Charmaine fancies a kebab. 'I could sink a sish,' exclaims Vic, rolling his hands round his stomach. Spall has a field day lolling about with language as Vic Maggott; he always knew he was Leigh's type of actor – in the National Youth Theatre he had become friends with Liz Smith's son, the writer Robert, and at RADA he and his chums became complete devotees when *The Kiss of Death* was broadcast, 'going around doing all those characters' – and Leigh regards someone like Spall as 'a gift'. They had not worked together since *Home Sweet Home*, and when it came to the issue of improvisation on the streets, Spall said, 'You do realise I've become a bit of a celebrity now [due to the overwhelming popularity of his performance as Barry, the hopeless electrician, in *Auf Wiedersehen, Pet* on television]?' And of course, he's the master of the put-down. 'Do give me some credit,' he said, 'I have worked with Miss Alison Steadman and Mr Jim Broadbent.'

Vic is an incredibly loquacious character who builds speeches with minimal syntactical foundations, so they rise and spiral like a peculiar baroque edifice wobbling about on sliding sand. Some of this effusiveness comes from Spall's own research – the rat-catcher he spent a day with actually did come out with, 'This is your common house-mouse, inasmuch mus musculus' – but he says that a lot of Vic Maggott was compiled sitting down with Leigh, 'half in, half out of character', trying to recreate and refine what was said in the original improvisation. Vic's outlandish philosophy of Christmas – 'sluff and glotteny' – was developed in this way, a quite usual manner of work in the Leigh process, as was his hilarious theory of evolution:

> Course, they're a bad design, ain't they, feet? They weren't built to take the weight of the body in a vertical position; they was designed to be used in tandem, with the hands, like a quadruped, scurrying and foraging in the bracken, in a position, thus. But, what with the Ascent of Man, inasmuch Evolution, 'e is now able to reach 'igh kitchen units, and change electric light-bulbs, without the use of too 'igh a step-ladder. Whereas once, we was as common as the Lowly Iguana, crawlin', with a vegetarian bent.

Leigh recalls having a lot of fun with the script, but Eric Allan, one of Leigh's longest-serving collaborators, who was not happy as Rex, says, 'We didn't do the usual kind of improvisations. There was an awful lot of sitting around and talking about things. With Mike, it works when you're doing what happens. I just wasn't in shape with it. Tim was terrific, though. I discovered later that he'd been investigating pests with the council, while I'd been doing it with a private firm; I never got off the ground with that. It was a most unhappy experience for me. That said, Mike is the strongest character I have ever met, and a genuine artist. He always has a blank canvas and never harks back, or makes references to anything else. I still feel I let him down, though, on *Smelling a Rat*.'

Rock, we learn, was always being ejected from his bedroom

while his father's colleagues checked for rats; one day he found himself permanently thrown out. So beneath this sleek dramatic veneer lurks an abortive attempt at reconciliation between son and father; another twist, no doubt, on Leigh's personal sense of loss after Abe's death. Terry Hands, in a congratulatory letter to Leigh after the première, felt 'the second half needed a little more for the boy and his father'. Rock is certainly touched with an Oedipal terror of invading parental territory. His chatting-up of Melanie-Jane therefore hovers on the far side of unease and disturbance even compared to that of Sylvia by Peter in *Bleak Moments* or of Linda by Trevor in *The Kiss of Death*. 'Where erotic body language is concerned,' said Paul Taylor in the *Independent*, 'Rock and Melanie-Jane speak broken Trappist.' Melanie-Jane, too, has intimidating parents. Her father once hit her on the head with a place mat from Stratford-upon-Avon, while a glimpse of Rock's mother's offstage toilet area sends her into ecstasies of lisping filial concern: 'My Mummy wants a bidet. She's agoraphobic.'

Something certainly lurked here of the essential futility of our condition. There was a sad, subtextual counterpoint to the comic abrasions of sharp encounters. Michael Billington in the *Guardian* opined that Leigh had found the right form for his talents: 'Like Ayckbourn, he uses the stock properties of farce to expose the dire consequences of emotional cruelty . . . Deep down, this is a political play about the new kind of sanctified entrepreneur who has wealth but no moral values.' Indeed it was. But as Leigh cast around for his next film, his sights were set further afield than the back yard of Hampstead Theatre. Since that first trip to Australia in 1985, he had conceived of a film about people emigrating to the continent, and then returning home, codename 'Whingeing Poms'.

It is not, incidentally, strictly true that Leigh has no conceptual or thematic fantasies before he starts work on a project; he just keeps them all to himself. But, apart from 'Whingeing Poms', it is widely known that possible subjects that have been kicked around include a piece about airline travel and air stewardesses, codename 'Flight Attendants'. Leigh knew that the 'Whingeing Poms' project would take two or three years to realise as a film, and would involve a lot of long-haul travel: 'It would be imperative in the film to see families here, and families there, and it would be very expensive.' An invitation now came through from Australia which Leigh thought might prove useful as pre-research on the film.

The Belvoir Street Theatre in Sydney (a radical set-up housed in the old home of the famous Nimrod, the Australian equivalent of the Royal Court), prompted Leigh's second trip abroad to concoct a new piece, this time a play. Sydney proved just as controversial a hotbed, in its own way, as Belfast had done during *Four Days in July*. Every actor in Sydney wanted to work with Leigh. He auditioned 180 of them in three weeks. At first, he thought he might do something with Aboriginal actors, but he noted that a small group of those auditioning had Greek backgrounds. He was intrigued. His next-door neighbours in Wood Green are Greek Cypriots who take in piece-work. He discovered that there was a rag trade in Sydney, too, populated by the Greek immigrants. 'So I decided to do this Greek thing, and apparently the shit hit the fan with all the big-deal actors, the well-known professionals, not because they were racist, but because they expected to be considered above any lesser-known performers.'

The Belvoir Street Theatre was funded for this production by the Australian Bicentenary fund, and it was always the theatre's intention to present something subversive and anti-establishment to mark the celebrations. Leigh certainly obliged. He produced *Greek Tragedy*, an eighty-minute suburban nightmare set in the Greek district of Marrickville among the mismatched sofas and ethnic trinkets of a pregnant seamstress, Kalliope, and her chauvinist husband, Alex, a volatile, discontented cutter in a garment factory who is failing to complete the repainting of the apartment. All the characters are Australian Greeks, except Kalliope (Evdokia Katahanas), who is native Greek and wants to go home. Alex (Stan Kouros) cuts his finger to the bone in an accident at work, which prompts the arrival of his vulgarian, bottom-pinching boss, Larry (George Spartels); Larry's grotesque wife, Vicki (Christina Totos), bursting out of a gold lamé sheath dress; and Vicki's sister (Zoë Carides), an air stewardess with Qantas (an embryonic refugee from 'Flight Attendants,' perhaps). The airport is nearby and the sound of overhead droning punctuates the proceedings with a frightful regularity. Larry returns from the loo to shout down his screeching wife: 'Take your teeth out, give your tongue a rest.' 'Don't talk to me like that, I'm not your secretary.' 'You couldn't be my secretary – you've got to be able to read and write.' In the terrible ensuing silence, Larry turns to his hosts and social inferiors with the ultimate non-compliment: 'I like this house . . . it's got a good *atmosphere*.' Which, as Allan Wright pointed out in the *Scotsman*, is about as accurate an observation as King Duncan's on entering the Macbeths' place ('This castle hath a pleasant seat . . .').

This relentless highlighting of one form of Aussie nightmare among an immigrant ethnic minority was hardly what the highest authorities were expecting. (Although what anyone *might* have been expecting from Mike Leigh in such circumstances is hard to imagine; this was never going to be *Neighbours* on stage, or 'God Bless Australia'.) Leigh relished the success of the opening, and the whiff of controversy surrounding it. During the run of the play, he went to the Melbourne Film Festival for a retrospective season in his honour, and the opening down under of *High Hopes*. The play was attracting packed houses, mixed notices, and an icy official response, which froze to solid when the Australia Council learned that Belvoir Street intended to export the play to Britain. Philip Hedley, the artistic director of Joan Littlewood's old haunt, the Theatre Royal, Stratford East, was in Australia on holiday and expressed an interest in bringing *Greek Tragedy* to London; that interest became a reality when Frank Dunlop, the director of the Edinburgh Festival, enthusiastically invited the production to Scotland as part of his 1990 programme.

Unfortunately, Dunlop booked the show into the cheerless, unlicensed (for drink; no pub for half a mile) premises of the Church Hill Theatre way out on the Morningside Road. But not even that bastion of amateur theatricals and graveyard of good intentions could entirely subdue *Greek Tragedy*. The stage glowed, especially in the piteous beauty of Evdokia Katahanas's performance as Kalliope, whose namesake in Greek legend gave birth to Orpheus, and who wants to return home to give birth, even as her husband kicks her in the stomach. The performance was re-reviewed in the more kindly and intimate circumstances of the Theatre Royal, where Jack Tinker of the *Daily Mail* recognised its surface wit and lethal undercurrent and Paul Taylor in the *Independent* 'the insecurity, the swagger, the bewilderment, the anger, the grief all too likely to emerge when people have been yanked out of their native clay and have yet to root themselves in the chalk to which they have been transplanted'.

Leigh loved the production most in the Belvoir in Sydney, an intimate 300-seater originally converted from a salt factory, which, it is alleged, Peter Brook once described as the most perfect indoor theatre space he had ever seen. Leigh enjoyed the show in the same way he enjoyed *Ecstasy*, in that he was tapping in to something 'so real and not so remote from my experience. The rag trade loomed large in my north Manchester childhood, even though none of my family was directly involved. There were always people clambering in and out of cars shouting, 'Have you got the gowns, Gertie?' and in the windows of tailors' shops on winter nights as I came home from school I'd see people with Hoffman presses: a world of piece-work, of coming and going.'

At a post-performance discussion in Sydney, Leigh dwelt on 'the sense of duality of what our identity is', and likened the Australian/Greek experience to his own Anglo/Jewish background. In *Greek Tragedy* he formulated the strongest statement in his work since *Ecstasy* of this idea of outsiderism on the very street where you live, the condition of denizens in an alien host culture. When asked, as he usually is on such occasions, about his methods of rehearsal and improvisation, Leigh impatiently cut his questioner off at the knees: 'I'm not interested in anything as much as the end product; I don't give a fuck about the processes.' He openly admits these days that the long period of preparation and incubation is 'a pain in the bum', but it is something he has to endure, even if it means arriving, in the case of a film, at the first day of shooting in a state of near-terminal exhaustion. That is how it is for Leigh, and he has no choice. He does not, and cannot, work in any other way. He summed up succinctly for a Belvoir Theatre customer who wanted to know which came first, creatively, the chicken or the egg, the actors or the director? Leigh was characteristically frank and generous: 'They [the actors] couldn't do this play if I didn't do what I did, and I couldn't do this play if they didn't do what they did.'

Leigh had been made to feel happily at home in Stratford East by Philip Hedley, and he returned there to create a new theatre piece in June 1993, after the great success of both *Life is Sweet* in 1990 and *Naked* at Cannes in May 1993. *It's a Great Big Shame!*, the title taken from a famous music-hall song of Gus Elen, and sung as a prelude by Kathy Burke in the guise of a sexless, soot-stained Victorian cockney waif, opened after a slight delay in mid-October, one month before the London première of *Naked*. It therefore generated a lot of interest and played to full houses, as well as to generally good reviews. The company kept a list pinned up in the Green Room of all the notables who had seen the show.

On my second visit, the last two names on the list were Holly Hunter and Jane Campion, star and director of *The Piano*. And among the regular weekday audience that night I spotted Leigh's fellow film directors Lindsay Anderson and Mike Newell. The bulk of the audience, though, was local, ethnic, working-class, and they responded with enthusiasm and great applause. A key factor in the production was the musical research and direction of Katherine Aughton, who contributed to the Victorian evocation by rounding up over eighty Gus Elen songs which permeated the rehearsal period and helped to define the authentic world of the final play.

The theatre had been completely refurbished during the rehearsal period, and Leigh's play was an imaginative response to the history and spirit of a building and its neighbourhood. New red seats had been installed, the original stencilled wood panelling uncovered, a black and gold frieze restored along the upper circle walls, and two floor-level stage boxes reconstructed. The play documented two murders – the first murders in Leigh's canon, though death and dying had always been a vital component – separated by a hundred years, but committed in the same address, 13 Manbey Street, just around the corner from the Royal. The occupation of the same house became a performance metaphor for the rehabilitation of a theatre building which had opened in 1884 and had served variously as a home of melodrama, variety, and rare classics, all of which traditions were buoyantly embraced by Joan Littlewood when her Theatre Workshop troupe acquired the lease in 1953.

The first act of *Shame!* was set in 1893. Katherine Aughton's mood-setting original music was complemented by the Victorian *verismo* of Alison Chitty's design – brick walls, a pub interior, the hardware shop, the street corners, a magnificent revolving wooden sculpture of drayman's cart, horses and barrels. After the interval, this scenography yielded to the more familiar Leigh-land of a 1993 domestic interior, where the new incumbents, a bickering black couple, the wife's sister and the husband's friend, enact a more familiar scenario of faddish behaviour, resentments, quirky conversation and quarrelling. The first act comprised thirty short-to-quickfire scenes, and played for ninety minutes; the second, four more sustained scenes playing for about fifty. Audiences were divided as to which half they preferred, if they did not like each half equally, which was rare. I loved the Victorian half much more than the second act on the first night, but enjoyed the second half more, if not as much as the first act, on my second visit. Alison Chitty brightly suggests that the first half is really a film and the second half is palpably a play.

For the first time, then, Leigh was trying to combine cinematic and theatrical techniques in the one piece of work. The technical provision at Stratford, excellent though it was, could not cope with all the demands Leigh and Chitty made for dissolving and cross-fading between locations in the first act. The waif Nellie fancies big Jim Short the drayman's mate (a throwback, perhaps, to Leigh's tall Mr Small at North Grecian Street Primary School?), but he ignores her. In the hardware shop, Jim meets little Ada Ricketts, whose father was ejected from Fanny Clackett's pub for pulling out his private parts (is it a mere coincidence that the highly popular little Ada Reeve, later a huge revue star with C.B. Cochran, performed at the Royal, with her father, in 1887?). Ada's a brisk opponent, and Jim walks straight into the trap, after giving her a jar of pickles, his idea of the perfect present: 'Do you want

to be me missus, then?' 'Yes, thank you very much.' 'Ta-ta, then.'
''Ere, Mrs What?' 'Mrs Short' (*Ada looks crestfallen*). 'Goodnight,
then.'

Their fate has been forecast in wistful Nellie's song:

> *It's a great big shame,*
> *And if she belonged to me,*
> *I'd let 'er know who's who;*
> *Naggin' at a feller wot is six foot free,*
> *And 'er only four foot two . . .*
> *Oh, they hadn't been married not a month nor more,*
> *When underneath her thumb goes Jim;*
> *Isn't it a pity that the likes of 'er,*
> *Should put upon the likes of 'im?*

Gus Elen's elegy for his newly wedded chum contained all the
elements of Jim Short's former life – the brewer's drayman with
a leg of mutton fist, playing pitch and toss along the Lea with his
pals of a Sunday morning – now exchanged for that of a bullied
drudge, cleaning windows and knives and scrubbing the floor.
Here, in a beautiful microcosm, was the classic Leigh tension
between freedom and domesticity. But the outcome was more
gruesome than in the usual Leigh fracas: Jim, worn down by
chores and nagging, announces that he is going home to Mother,
picks up Ada and throttles her in that casual, not-knowing-his-
own-strength manner of all such gentle giants; John Steinbeck's
huge farm labourer in *Of Mice and Men* is another example.

The show might be a deconstruction of the song, but none of
the actors knew that (except for Ruth Sheen, who sussed what
Leigh was up to at an early rehearsal; 'Keep your mouth shut!'
Leigh whispered to her, with a conspiratorial wink). Eventually,
three months into rehearsal, Leigh showed them all a video of
Gus Elen singing the song, and Kathy Burke was dumbfounded:
'I couldn't believe it. I'd been walking round in a flat cap with
the hammer and the pipe and doing my research into what sort
of jobs Nellie would do to make money; I even scraped the barrel
by suggesting lookout at a pitch and toss match, which of course
he wanted – it's in one of the verses of the song! I felt disgruntled

at first and manipulated – though I don't mean that in a negative way – because it meant I hadn't been quite as clever as I thought I had been.' Burke's second big shock in rehearsal came when she went down to Manbey Street – not on location, but to the improvised room in the rehearsal space in Toynbee Hall – for what she thought was going to be a showdown with Ada and found Jim covered in blood. Her first deduction was that Ada must have attacked him. In the play, as it turned out, Jim was eating the well-cooked head of his wife, just as he had relished the sheep's head broth she once cooked for him, nice and tasty, with the eyes left in.

There was one unforgettable moment in the first act when Jim brought Ada to the pub and Nellie saw them together for the first time. His new missus. And his nemesis. She just sat and looked, and said everything by saying nothing. The heart-breaking poignancy of it all was almost unbearable. Burke pulled this off each night by going through the scene as if she had dialogue, thinking through each stage of her reaction: 'With Mike, the most important part is the warm-up. You do spend most of the time warming up, but once the play starts, he leaves how much you want to do to you, though you are called for each performance ninety minutes before the curtain-up [as opposed to the usual thirty]. I've always wanted to work with him ever since I started acting. I just assume everyone does. I think he's brilliant, but he doesn't like any sign of lack of confidence. He sees that as a negative thing. People do get worried and scared in case they are letting him down.'

The actors in the Victorian half did more library research than walking around 'in character', though Paul Trussell as Jim did go out delivering beer with real draymen in Wandsworth, in a real horse-drawn cart, the last surviving dray in London. He observed the time-honoured tradition of drinking a pint of beer at each port of call, even at nine-thirty in the morning. Wendy Nottingham as Ada went to the Bodleian in Oxford and looked up hardware and advertising for ironmongery products of the period, having read out, much to her amusement, the declaration which bids all visitors to the library to promise not to burn the place down; she based the tartar in Ada on a shop-owner she knew as a child in

Norfolk. The woman sold sweets and little Wendy was caught stealing some. 'She didn't report me, but she said that if I ever went back in that shop again, she would tell my parents. That frightened me, and I never saw her again. But I have a strong physical memory. She had a beehive hairstyle and she wore high stiletto heels and had a very tall, hard image, although she was probably quite short, and she wore bright pink lipstick. She also sold toys. I started researching Ada once we decided that this shop should be a hardware shop. It seemed right for her, with things like nails, and everything well-organised and packed up in tight, mean, tiny packages and containers.'

The second half of *Shame!* is an example of the past revisited through the spirit of the place, though you feel Leigh might have made a lot more of the ghost of Ada finally returning to haunt – and comfort? – the distraught Joy who has strangled her inadequate husband in the very same room. But the reverberations are clearly registered in the wider context of the local community reinventing ancient squabbles and grudges in the afterglow of Gus Elen's old song, and in the revitalised, refurbished material circumstances of this wonderful, atmospheric theatre. The British theatre at large had several productions in 1993 which explored similar territory: Graeme Miller's *The Desire Paths* at the Royal Court, a dense performance-art piece which traced the history of a community through the ley lines of Birmingham; Tom Stoppard's RNT hit play *Arcadia*, in which a Byronic murder mystery and a love story came alive in the contemporary setting of the same Derbyshire country house; and Geraldine Pilgrim's *House*, an on-site reconstitution of a crumbling Victorian detached property in Salisbury, Wiltshire, in a guided tour through the rooms, re-animated by actors in period costumes suggesting all sorts of narrative scandals and mysteries. There must have been something in the air that year.

Joy has been nagging squeaky, hopeless Randall, who plays in a local football team and sometimes scores twice – once for each side – to knock out the old hearth in the sitting room: 'When you gonna mash down dis ting?' She is forever tidying, polishing, spraying and moaning. She is the spirit of Ada reincarnate, but with Jim's strength: Michele Austin presents a huge fat black woman with an unattractively surly disposition. She is the kind of character you simply do not meet in politically correct new drama at Hampstead or the Bush. She's a total pain. Her upwardly mobile sister, Faith (Marianne Jean-Baptiste), tells her she has a big face, but it's a lovely face: 'You don't realise, when people meet you, they meet your glasses.' Faith has a beautician's tip for Joy that she might have filched from Beverly in *Abigail's Party*: 'All you need now, Joy, is a little bit of make-up to pull out your features.'

Faith knows where she's going: luxury apartments, next door to a theatre – 'Shakespeare. Live actors – *talking*!' Joy works menially in a bank, but Faith works in foreign currency at Lloyds Bank headquarters. Jean-Baptiste researched the role at Lloyds HQ in Bristol, at Coutts Bank in the City, and in the stalls at Covent Garden. 'I took Faith to the ballet,' says Jean-Baptiste, 'to see *Job*, which is a really disgusting, terrible ballet by Ninette de Valois. Faith enjoyed it, however. I sat there, in these very good seats, thinking that Faith actually likes *this*, and it's like the Emperor's New Clothes.' Faith has a whirlwind, self-justifying exit speech, topped with a major laugh line which came from Leigh, in a typical creative ploy, goading her into finishing it off:

> I've moved on y'know. I've bettered meself, I don't live like this and no one, not no one is dragging me back down, family or no family . . . I'm an independent woman, single. I'm on twenty-two grand a year . . . Next year I'm going cruise up the Nile, Egypt, Luxor, see the pyramids, learn a bit about history. I don't 'ave to be sat 'ere on Sunday afternoons on cheap IKEA chairs. I could be eatin' in Quaglino's . . . (*she exits briefly and returns*) lobster!

In the first act, in the pub run by the quickfire yackety-yacking Fanny Clackett, a drunken Jamaican mariner, Amos Churchill, played by Gary McDonald, falls about all over the place, sings a shanty and starts a fight. He is subjected to a blast of biological ignorance from Fanny similar to that she lets rip on being told by Nellie that a dwarf has been sick ('Only a little bit of sick.' 'Well, he was only a little bloke'): 'Their blood's a different colour from ours which is why they can't hold their drink.' In the second act, the ethnic balance has swung right round, and the black inmates of Manbey Street are the new majority. Leigh's stories had never focused so intensely on black or Asian characters before, although the possibility has always lurked. A confused Asian lady is helped out by Liz Smith in the laundrette in *Hard Labour*, Alan Erasmus has a small role in the same film, and Ben Kingsley makes a wonderful impression as the Asian stall-holder and taxi-driver. There is a nice cameo by Hepburn Graham as an abused, dignified neighbour in *Meantime*, who also has a good scene with his girlfriend, played by Leila Bertrand. The sweet black girl in the chemist's shop in *High Hopes* grins sympathetically as Edna Doré fails to find her purse. McDonald, who was squaring up for a career as a soccer player with Wimbledon FC before becoming an actor, pops up in the second act as Barrington, a team-mate of Randall's and a painter and decorator by profession. Plastered in each half, you might say.

'Amos is based on an uncle of mine who used to live in Brixton. I never saw him sober.' Barrington, who paws the ground incessantly with his feet and has a gargantuan twitch, was based on a good friend of McDonald who really was a painter and decorator, 'so that was easy'. What about the twitch, though, when it comes to putting the paper on the wall? Wouldn't he miss the place it's supposed to land on? 'Well, it stops then. It's not a handicap, that twitch, it's an athletic twitch, like Mike Tyson's. He works out such a lot, Barrington, he can't stop still for a second.' Neither Marianne Jean-Baptiste nor Gary McDonald thinks it is any big deal working with a white director; they do it all the time in television. And Leigh makes no distinction between black and white: 'A good actor's a good actor, period. And this lot are all *very* good actors.' He had never made any conscious decision to work with black actors, or not to work with them. His Stratford commission just took him there for the first time, and was one aspect of a process in which the area and its community, and its splendidly refurbished theatre, were celebrated in a unique and original collaboration.

This was certainly a new departure in Leigh's theatre work. It remains to be seen, as his stock in the film world rises, to what extent he will continue his creative campaign on British stages. He is, like everyone else in the theatre, at the mercy of stringent economics and unpredictable management policies. But his theatrical work has such an immediate edge, and such an overpowering sense of danger and satirical purpose, that it would be criminal of our major, and minor, subsidised theatres not to open their doors to him again in the future. Leigh's career started in the theatre, and he is unique among his peers in having forged an output of such vibrant homogeneity, depth and quality on both stage and screen; the characteristics and demands of each discipline have undoubtedly complemented and fuelled the other.

ELEVEN

Life is Sweet, and Sour, and Going on

Leigh and Simon Channing-Williams formed Thin Man Films in 1989, after *High Hopes*, and opened an office in Greek Street, Soho. The nucleus of Leigh's production collaborators now have a geographical point of focus, and there's no doubt, according to Leigh's agent, Anthony Jones, that this new arrangement has provided him with comfort and stability. It remains to be seen whether Sheila Kelley's view that Leigh works best with his back up against the wall still applies. I suspect that he finds walls to have his back up against whatever the material circumstances.

Thin Man's first enterprise was the food and family comedy *Life is Sweet,* filmed on location in Enfield (yet another slippery, slightly anonymous point of call on the north London wall chart), in which Jane Horrocks as Nicola, the anorexic chocaholic, pipped Princess Diana to the post in advertising the disease of bulimia. Timothy Spall, having already played one reasonably hopeless postman and one fairly hopeless rat-catcher, played a *totally* hopeless restaurateur called Aubrey, who opens the Regret Rien (Très Exclusive) in an Enfield shopping parade and, on opening night, attracts not one single discerning customer so resorts to smashing the place up himself.

The essential day-to-day running of a new Thin Man film is lubricated by the secretarial ministrations of Deborah Reade and the go-between function of Heather Storr, Leigh's freelance continuity and script supervisor. Storr, like designer Alison Chitty, editor Jon Gregory and cinematographer Dick Pope, works elsewhere when Leigh is between projects. But Leigh's informal core team is now very important to his creative equilibrium. Storr first worked with him on *Meantime*, Pope succeeded the excellent, increasingly lionised Roger Pratt as Leigh's preferred cinematographer on *Life is Sweet*, and Chitty dates back to *Ecstasy* at Hampstead.

Storr liaises with Leigh on casting, correspondence, all office requests, and helps actors arrange research facilities. On *Life is Sweet*, the married couple played by Jim Broadbent and Alison Steadman – Andy and Wendy – wanted to meet their Enfield contemporaries, while their twins, played by Horrocks and Claire Skinner – Nicola and Natalie – needed to meet members of their peer group. Visits to schools and the local library were fixed up, while Claire Skinner researched her job as a plumber after leads taken up first by Heather Storr and then by Alison Chitty (who knew a friend of a plumber). Storr also contacted TAMBA (Twins and Multiple Birth Association) so that Horrocks and Skinner could pursue their twin sibling status more fully. Stephen Rea's character, Andy's pub pal Patsy, was declared a Catholic who had gone to school in Tottenham, and Storr was despatched to find just such an institution and arrange a visit. All of this carries on, over many weeks, while the actors are either rehearsing with Leigh or researching their roles in between being called to rehearsal.

Only in the last few weeks of rehearsal does Storr start writing anything down. Leigh never looks at this, but sometimes asks for a general prompt such as, 'What else did they talk about in that improvisation?' The structure, or scene breakdown, is always written by Leigh on three or four pages – his neat, discursive scrawl set out in neat lines and boxes – indicating the number of the scene, the location, the characters involved and a one-line summary of either what happens or what is discussed. The scenes are then rehearsed and developed on location in as chronological a sequence as possible. All the time during rehearsal the script is kept fluid as Leigh chips away, changes, the actors find something else, and so on. But Storr does finally write down each scene, usually on the night before it is shot: 'And I write it in longhand, a pretty fair copy. On the morning of each shooting day, we show that section of script to the crew and, while they are lighting it, we often change and fine-tune until we decide what is definite, and I type another quick fair copy with a carbon for the sound recordist.' A play is obviously fixed in a way similar to this before the first night, and the actors then repeat, or recreate, the play as achieved at that cut-off point; on a film, the whole process keeps rolling for each individual scene until the shooting. Then it is fixed. Then it is shot.

Jon Gregory, as film editor, is not involved in rehearsals. He moves much closer to Leigh at the early stages of assembling the first few reels: 'Mike's stuff is complex in its undercurrents with the actors, so it's not easy to put together very fast; which is why the extra length of shooting he always has is so important . . . when the rushes on any film first come in, I go through them on my own and I make notes so I'm ready for when the director arrives. I was falling about at *Life is Sweet*; you don't know what to expect and it's always so fresh and funny with Mike. The other great thing with him is that you don't have to keep showing it to other producers and money men – he's a law unto himself, and is left to do what he wants, which is wonderful from every point of view, not least mine.'

Something even more intuitive goes on between Leigh and Alison Chitty, who describes working with Leigh as 'like a sort of solidarity around a black hole; there's this complete trust and commitment and confidence in something that isn't there'. Chitty's background is theatrical, coming to Hampstead Theatre and the Riverside Studios during Peter Gill's initial incumbency after eight years with Peter Cheeseman at the Stoke-on-Trent repertory. She has become Leigh's closest creative confidante while simultaneously building her reputation in London's major subsidised theatres and international opera houses. Leigh was similarly reliant on Diana Charnley, the designer of *Meantime* and *High Hopes* (and assistant designer on *Home Sweet Home*), and now head of design at the National Film School.

Chitty certainly knew from the off about the Gus Elen song that Leigh was planning to unravel in *It's a Great Big Shame!*, and both she and Dick Pope had long discussions with Leigh during the rehearsal period about the mood, atmosphere and 'look' of how *Naked* might turn out. Chitty, too, is an essential part of the quest for locations. Residents of desirable (for film purposes) council houses are paid a handsome fee, lodged in alternative accommodation and often, as in the case of the Enfield tenants, finally returned to a newly redecorated dwelling that is in a far better state than when they left it. ('It's the neighbours who are more often pissed off,' Leigh says, with all the coming and going and working at strange hours of the day and night.)

Chitty found the house in Enfield for *Life is Sweet* and fell in love with it because of its garden shed. She also found the old mobile snack-bar, which Rea's Patsy sells on to Broadbent's Andy as a pig in a poke, in Northampton, and painted it up. Location pub interiors are either 'just all right', after a bit of dressing and alteration – the one where Natalie is seen playing snooker – or 'gifts from God' – the smoky dive, with glass and mahogany, where Rea's Patsy litanises the 1961 Spurs double-winning team deep in his tankards with Andy. Rea, an Arsenal supporter, admits he 'rather loved that bit of treachery. I loved hanging around White Hart Lane trying to find out what sort of evil it was that made you want to be a Tottenham supporter!' An awareness of, and interest in, street life is a prerequisite for actors and the creative team. Chitty has a lot of what she calls 'fish and chip locations, where someone can eat a bag of chips and say "I love you," which I feed in; there's always a joke with Mike, that he is making one film and I'm making another. The thing is, I'm making *both*, I think.'

Chitty says that her triple-headed passion as a designer is with actors, texts, objects; she has a 'surgery' with each actor, independently of Leigh, talking about the character and making a 'possession list'. On *Naked*, 'David Thewlis's list was just half a page, Claire Skinner's was longer, Lesley Sharp's was short – as she could only have what she'd brought from Manchester, and Katrin Cartlidge's was just one item: the big "S" for Sophie that had fallen off a shop front, which wasn't something she suggested but something we found in a fit of pure serendipity, which is important, too.' She second-guesses Leigh all the time, and particularly enjoys making an environment which can then prove a seedbed for the scene and a source of material for the actors. In *Naked*, she and Leigh 'invented' the two men who lived in the flat which the café girl is minding. They were an upper-working-class, slightly pretentious gay couple called Dave and David, who liked going to opera, travelling (especially to Morocco) and cooking with woks. One worked in the Vehicle Licensing office at Stratford in the East End, the other in the Keith Prowse ticket agency. 'Nobody else knew about Dave or David,' says Chitty, 'though of course I did send mail to that address, so we had franked envelopes all over the set. It is a form of madness, this, but you create these environments and little worlds at a point where you don't know *exactly* what Mike wants.' Another example of this sort of design input, in the costume department, occurs in *Life is Sweet* at the moment where Steadman's Wendy vacillates over what to wear for Aubrey's opening night in the restaurant. She pulls out of the wardrobe a fluffy pink angora jumper. As Steadman describes it, 'The dressing in the wardrobe is never just that. On most jobs you do as an actor, you've never seen what's in a wardrobe before you play the scene, but not in Mike's stuff. Nothing went in there without us all – Mike, Alison and Lindy Hemming – discussing what she might or might not wear. So the dressing of that wardrobe becomes a part of the scene and of the film.'

The whole approach was alarming at first for Dick Pope on *Life is Sweet*, his first collaboration. He had no discussion about the film, had no script, and had been unimpressed by the house in Enfield: 'I died a death when I saw it. A living room and a stairs, a bit of a kitchen, little bedrooms at the top and a patio at the back, and that was the film. I saw the interior of the Regret Rien, where I also died' (though not as dramatically as Aubrey's business prospects). Pope is well over six feet tall, and although cameras are smaller these days, they are not that small. And there's lighting equipment to fit in around all the bodies.

His mounting panic was not relieved on the first day of the shoot when Leigh, tied up with the actors, left him to look at the first shot of Wendy returning to the house from the children's dancing class where she teaches and where the opening credits roll. 'I set something up, feeling pleased with myself, and Mike joined me and tore it to pieces, questioning why the camera was cutting to certain shots, and from whose point of view. I was speechless, and embarrassed, because obviously there were other people around. He looked awful that day, like he'd been to hell and back, but I didn't know then how nervous *he* was. He said, let's investigate this shot, and we trooped all over the estate for the rest of the morning, something else I wasn't used to. Usually, it's nine o'clock and the first shot's in the can, thank you very much. And here we are, walking everywhere. Finally we found it, and it was incredibly simple: us across the road, the car draws into the frame, Andy's already stood in the doorway, we cut in closer, Wendy gets out the car, one twin is coming out and the other's arriving on her bike. It's almost proscenium arch. I felt I'd been on a therapy session, but he was testing me out, and also working his way back behind a camera after a couple of years since making *High Hopes*. Ever since, the whole process has been one of finding the right shots within the scene. Mike never comes on the floor with a film in his head. The characters are in place and very sure of themselves, so he doesn't have to fight for performances. What we do then is almost pure film-making.'

If *Naked* is conceived in blacks and blues and a dark, dilapidated grunginess, the contrast with its predecessor is all the more marked. *Life is Sweet* is bright, jaunty, primary-coloured. Wendy teaches dancing, but she also works in a kids' clothes shop called 'Bunnikins'. She is a chirpy, chivvying, cheerful character, and her marriage to Andy is rock solid, in spite of his chronic lethargy in the DIY department. The film is a story of the twins, Nicola and Natalie, and of two chefs, Andy and Aubrey, both of whom end up the worse for wear before we are wrenched back to laughter. Andy slips on a spoon at work in the large kitchen where he is the chief chef – the offending implement is hung on a wall at home, over the Dégas print – soon after he has been discovered in a recumbent posture in his burger van (a doomed hot-dog bar enterprise) after drinking too much in the pub with Patsy. Asked what he's doing down there, he nonchalantly replies: 'Tidying up!'

The dark side is the gnawing misery of Nicola, but even that is cleverly and light-heartedly done, without once selling short the seriousness of her condition. Nicola is an unreconstructed reflex rebel, screwing up her mousy face in the 'take that' brand of hearthside abuse of parents and bourgeois lifestyles we all recognise; as teenagers we dished it, as parents we ship it. As usual, Leigh pokes his camera right into the secret, awkward life of his characters, and we see Nicola feasting voraciously on her stash of chocolate bars and then making herself sick. In the next room, Natalie, poring over her American travel brochures, sadly overhears her sister's habitual bingeing and retching. Horrocks, who reacted hungrily to Leigh's suggestion that Nicola might be anorexic, discovered that the sexual appetite decreases with the condition but that, as bulimia develops, the repulsion turns itself into a disgusted gorging. This led to the famous sex and chocolate spread scene, where Nicola and her straggly, discontented boyfriend (David Thewlis), who continuously berates her garbled feminist posturing, engage in their startling but cheerless sexual activity. Dominant, and wielding a couple of flimsy silk scarves as accoutrements to bondage, Nicola commands her lanky slave to smear her taut torso with the contents of a jar of Nutella and lick it off in a sticky prelude to ferocious congress. As the *Evening Standard* wryly commented, Horrocks does here for chocolate spread what Kim Basinger did for honey in *Nine and a Half Weeks* and Marlon Brando for butter in *Last Tango in Paris*. Like so many of the most effective scenes in Mike Leigh, the fact that it happens in the apparently incongruous setting of a tiny bedroom in Enfield on a weekday afternoon alerts us to the vivacity, pathos and unexpectedness of life behind net curtains.

Domestic entrapment was another aspect of anorexia/bulimia that Horrocks worked into the role: 'As soon as you get away from the family, the problem starts to get better. Nicola only left the house to get cigarettes. Because of her paranoia, everything going on outside was huge, as huge as it was inside.' As in most families, the domestic atmosphere is replete with digs and parries, the matadorish array of passes and thrusts which Leigh distils into his familiar and distinctive poetry of comic retribution. Nicola's plight is summarised in a memorable, climactic encounter with her mother, a good example of how the mundane drizzle of family life can be transformed – as in a Greek tragedy – into the stuff of high dramatic tension and raw power. Horrocks scowls while Steadman's Wendy opens her maternal heart, eyes brimming with tears, and tells the sad, jobless wretch, who nearly died when she was little, how much they care: 'We love you, you stupid girl.' Nicola's tragedy, so recognisable because it is so common, is that she has made herself hard to get to know. The boyfriend is driven to distraction, and won't be hanging around for long. When Aubrey calls, early on, there is a wonderful moment of utter desperation and tension on both sides as Nicola, fiercely boxing against the inside of her 'Bollocks to the Poll Tax' T-shirt, stands unhelpfully in the hallway while Aubrey tries to maintain his act by pummelling a pineapple between his hands as if it were an American football.

Aubrey is a glorious misfit based on the one man on Spall's initial list of real people that he hoped Leigh wouldn't choose, a man whose name he could not remember but whom they privately christened 'Insane of Barclays'. This fellow was devoid of personality, 'a totally charisma-free zone'. So he affected a character that wasn't his own, and this was Spall's starting point. Aubrey is like a disc jockey, with a phoney transatlantic air about him and a misconception of his own image that has spiralled into grotesque parody. He comes from St Albans but he sounds like Kid Jensen. The man bringing *haute cuisine* to Enfield wears a baseball cap at what he thinks is a trendy angle and green spectacle frames that make him look not so much like Marco Pierre White as Christopher Biggins. His red convertible Triumph Spitfire is the wrong choice of car: he can hardly manoeuvre himself in and out, let alone create the desired impression of being a sex god: 'Aubrey is obsessed with shagging. It's the misguided, the self-deluded that Mike brings to life so brilliantly,' says Spall. 'Only Mike in all his perversion would have chosen him out of all the people I came up with. It would be impossible to just sit down and write someone like that.'

In the restaurant, Aubrey is assisted by a strange, silent girl (Moya Brady) in a white headscarf whom he is obviously aiming to seduce by way of teaching her how to play his drums. He gives her a few desultory tips as he prepares for the big night by cutting up some slippery grey lambs' tongues ('These tongues are a pain in the neck'). The menu of the Regret Rien is one of the master-pieces of modern culinary fiction, yet every single dish on it is totally plausible, however horrible. Aubrey, as Spall explains, had worked in lots of places as a sous-chef, and with lots of people who had experimented with food. 'The trouble is, they weren't in the Gavroche or Chez Nico; they were in the Copacabana, Ilford.' Thus the treats in store for unwitting patrons include tripe soufflé, king prawn in jam sauce, chilled brains, prune quiche, saveloy on a bed of lychees, pork cyst, liver in lager, duck in chocolate sauce, clams in ham and – Aubrey's 'pied de résistance' – grilled trotters on eggs over-easy. Very few of these items would look ridiculous on the menu of any fashionable restaurant. Spall and Leigh therefore drew the line at some of the more hilariously exotic dishes on their improvised shortlist: veal in marzipan, brawn in batter, turkey stomach in a Drambuie sauce, scrambled egg and tuna on a black fettucini base with a pumpkin garné, braised hearts with double cream and cinnamon stuffing, smoked salmon and banana salad, sparrows in treacle and fricassée of frogs' legs.

The whole doomed enterprise has an architectural splendour and pathos, because Spall's performance itself is conceived on a scale that is both grandly gestural and minutely observed. Aubrey's only friends are Wendy and Andy, and in the goodness of her heart, Wendy wishes him so well as to volunteer to help out on the opening night because his waitress has let him down (she's gone to liberated Prague with her boyfriend). As Aubrey, drinking heavily to steady his nerves, becomes drunk, and no one turns up, he takes to the pavement and rails against the world, and its horde of absentee 'working-class morons', like an absurd suburban version of King Lear. Tanked up and turned down, he makes a vulgar pass at Wendy, removes his trousers, blunders angrily around the empty tables, knocks most of them over, smashing all his crockery, and passes out in a quivering, sobbing gelatinous blob of disappointment.

Most critics were enthusiastic, but there were exceptions. Trying to match his dislike for *Life is Sweet* to a belated attack on Leigh's creative technique, David Sexton in *The Times Literary Supplement* said that 'the film never transcends sit-com and remains static and anecdotal, its unit the scene, not the complete story.' This is a patently incorrect deduction. The comedy achieves a kinetic vitality in a well-organised, systematic revelation of character linked organically to changes in fortunes and a series of well-timed narrative climaxes. Sexton also insists that the film is 'the product of an unresolved attitude to its subject matter and in particular of an uneasy relation to questions of class'. Again, one can only guess at the critic's own socio-political hang-ups. All the characters in *Life is Sweet* are conceived with an equal amount of detached affection and critical sympathy; that is how the quality, the timbre, of the comedy is forged. Philip French, reviewing the film in the *Observer*, had an effectively near-final word on this endless argument: 'Leigh has been called patronising. The charge is false. The Noël Coward/David Lean film *This Happy Breed*, evoked by Leigh in several panning shots across suburban back gardens, is patronising. Coward and Lean pat their characters on the back, give them little medals in their own honours list. Leigh shakes them, hugs them, sometimes despairs over them, but never thinks that they are other than versions of ourselves.'

The film was championed by Vincent Canby in the *New York Times*, and 'Thatcher's England' became a useful marketing phrase. Thin Man's American distributors were a new, small outfit called October Films operating out of an office in the Rockefeller Center in New York, run by Jeff Lipsky and Bingham Ray. 'We're called October,' says Lipsky, who started his career with John Cassavetes, 'because it's the month of revolution and both our birthdays are in October. And we formed the company to present *Life is Sweet* in America. Thanks to Mike and Simon Channing-Williams's organisational abilities, we got our company off the ground. Quite apart from all *that*, Leigh's Europe's best filmmaker at the moment, period.' October has since presented the New York premières of Pedro Almodovar's movies, Claude

Sautet's *Un Coeur en hiver*, Gérard Depardieu's *Balzac*, and many other high-quality European films.

When *High Hopes* opened in Los Angeles, Lipsky hired a carnival dunking booth. A cage was filled with water and a Mrs Thatcher lookalike sat on a seat beneath a target for sponge-throwers; when the target was hit, in she went. This stunt yielded three quarters of a page of editorial in the *Los Angeles Times*, a newspaper not so keen to promote Leigh, says Lipsky, as its New York counterpart: 'But it wasn't *just* the Thatcher element. Both *Life is Sweet* and *Naked* [which October did not promote; the price on Leigh had risen by then, and they were outbid] are rife with situations and recognisably American sensibilities. And *High Hopes*, for instance, is a perfect comment on the American yuppie experience, too, and on the class struggle, and on dysfunctional families; we have 'em here! We see all this on American chats and soaps every day. Bulimia was a great topic, too, for us, and the whole of *Life is Sweet* totally understandable, politically.'

Lipsky arranged menu T-shirts and a special screening for physicians of overweight people, 'though Weight Watchers were not too keen'. The same week as I visited Lipsky in New York in July 1994, the *New York Times* ran a front-page story reporting the fact that one in three adults in America is obese. Not just fat. Obese. *Life is Sweet* found some of this audience, but not nearly enough, though both that film, and *Naked*, were seen by more cinema-goers in the US than in Britain. Still, despite Leigh's ever-growing US reputation, no film of his has yet grossed $2 million there. Only 10 per cent of independent films exceed that figure each year. Lipsky says that to 'break through the envelope', you have to do $5 million at the box office, 'And now that figure's rising to $10 million. The problem with Mike is not audience appeal but the marketing hook. There isn't the sexual intensity of a *Piano*, or the violence of Tarantino.' In Los Angeles *Life is Sweet* won three critics' awards: Best Picture, Best Actress (Alison Steadman) and Best Supporting Actress (Jane Horrocks). New York responded in April 1992 when the film section of the Museum of Modern Art (MOMA) presented a retrospective, 'Life Could be Better: The Films of Mike Leigh'. Adrienne Mancia, who runs the MOMA films (with Jytte Jensen), says that the Leigh season was boosted by Terence Rafferty's enthusiasm for *Life is Sweet* in the *New Yorker*, and compares its impact – 'phenomenal' – on the New York public at MOMA with the first ever large Michael Powell season in the city, which she presented.

During this time, Channing-Williams was circulating producers and studios with Leigh's ideas for both 'Whingeing Poms', the proposed Australian emigrant saga, and 'Flight Attendants'. The latter, too, was a large-scale proposal with a nucleus of young women at its centre and an international auxiliary cast of at least seventy characters. Nothing about Leigh's way of working was to change, except that the film, a social comedy, 'not a disaster movie or a frivolous spoof', would be shot in separate segments, in Britain and abroad, and each shoot would be preceded by its own rehearsal period. Leigh was hardly surprised when producers enthused more, in so far as they enthused at all, over the aeroplane saga: 'First, Australia doesn't sound all that interesting to them. Second, all movie business people spend loads of time in planes and want to fuck the air stewardesses. The minute we mentioned it, you could see their hands were mentally up the skirts of the girls serving drinks.'

Eventually, at the end of 1991, a company called Mayfair Entertainment decided to put up two thirds of the proposed £3 million budget, with the rest coming from British Screen, Channel 4 and First Independent. British Screen had been set up by the government in the 1980s to promote and invest in British movies. The first chief executive was Simon Relph, who was succeeded by Simon Perry. These two formed the important relationship with first David Rose, and then David Aukin, at Channel 4, and this partnership was behind *High Hopes* (co-produced with Portman Films), *Life is Sweet* (co-produced with Palace Pictures) and *Naked* (co-produced with First Independent).

Mayfair wanted the film ready for Cannes in 1993, and they wanted some American involvement in the story-line. Leigh agreed to both conditions. But he was starting to have doubts about completing such a project in the time available. 'Actually, in my bones, I knew it could not be done. Come the spring of

1992, the contract had not been signed, and I walked away from it. The Channel 4 and British Screen money was still there, so we went to David Aukin and Simon Perry and said, "Can we do what we like with your bit of the money?" and they said yes. So we made *Naked*. The bleach bypass process [which gives the film its distinctive, blue and dead-of-night atmosphere] meant that *Naked* had to be lit in a very precise way, there was lot of shooting at night, and it was all very slow. At the end of the eight-week shoot, the film wasn't finished, but Channel 4 and British Screen were very good, Simon Channing-Williams was very clever, and we kept going. The cost shot up from just over £1.2 million to £1.6 million. Which is fuck-all in terms of *Schindler's List* but a helluva lot for a British film.'

While waiting for the contract on 'Flight Attendants' to come through, Leigh had been intrigued by a short script sent to him by his friend Jim Broadbent. *A Sense of History* was the confessional memoir of the fictional twenty-third Earl of Leete, spoken to camera, but on location, in the form of a documentary guide to the estate. As a holiday for himself, and to keep busy behind a camera, Leigh agreed to direct it for Thin Man and Channel 4. Broadbent himself played the Earl – who was not based on any particular real-life character – in a tweed suit and a bald pate. The twenty-eight-minute film was shot on the beautiful location of Highclere Castle, near Newbury, a site famous for its real-life Tutankhamen connection. The twenty-third Earl's father had hanged himself when he, the current Earl, was fourteen years old. At the age of seven, the Earl had paved the way to his succession to the title and the estates by killing his elder brother, knowing him to be dim and suspecting him to be homosexual, though he was only eleven at the time. Somehow, the responsibility that he keenly harboured for the estate must devolve to him. It was his duty not to flunk his heritage. He shot his brother under the chin at point-blank range.

When the war came, the Earl felt he could not take up arms against Adolf Hitler. He fell in love with a stable girl, and did away with his wife in the lake. His two sons of eight and six, possible witnesses of this event, he pulled towards him ('Come and help Daddy get Mummy out'), and drowned them too, acting out for the camera his blind and comic frenzy, making the whole incident look like a boating accident. The beautiful girl for whom he had done this he never saw again. Broadbent's performance, hard-boiled and rasping to start with, begins now to exert a curious fascination, and even toys with our sympathy. The Earl's frosty breath and cruel eyes are tinged with sadness, so that we witness not just the callous confessions of an old fool, but the tragedy of someone who was entirely wrong about what he believed to be the right course of action. For, deep down, he pulsates with appreciative passion for this property, this countryside, this England. Rather like the late John Osborne in his final country squire manifestation, the Earl has always fought, he says, to preserve his land against 'all the right people', who include 'the Euro bureau, Brussels sprouts, Communists, the Ramblers' Association and road-planners . . . It's so beautiful, my land, always here, and we've kept those other bastards out, and that's good, isn't it?' As the credits roll, he disappears inside with his dog and then pops his head round the door: 'If anything happens to me, I do want this film to be shown.' The spirit of crusty old England retreats and, we presume, blows out his pickled brains.

Carl Davis provided some beautiful spoof 'heritage' music almost overnight in a quick production turnaround, and Leigh and Dick Pope photographed the architecture, the landscape and the very sky itself with sharp, stunning and seductive clarity. A farmhand (played by the *Nuts in May* biker Stephen Bill) trundles by on a tractor, winking at the camera over the Earl's shoulder, to reinforce the mock-documentary element; the film cleverly combines the humour and the oddness of the narrative conditions while laying out a small, precisely composed feast of country snaps: in under half an hour, we have murder, mystery, travelogue, polemic, confession, lamentation and historical spoof. And a gem of a performance from the actor/writer.

The experience for Leigh was 'the joy of shooting without having been in prison', something akin to the fun of making commercials, about which he changed his mind a few years ago. 'I do them for the dosh. I used to be against adverts on principle but I've since been persuaded that it's so lucrative that this attitude is entirely eccentric. It's good to get behind a camera with no real pressure on.' Leigh's agent, Anthony Jones, says that directors like making advertisements partly because of the change in discipline, but mainly because of the money. 'People you'd never expect to do them, like [the late] Lindsay Anderson, Ken Loach and indeed Mike have no qualms at all, though of course Mike doesn't do very many. It's very good for them to work without huge commercial pressures.'

The McDonald's hamburger TV ads are often made by Ken Loach, but when he was unavailable in the summer of 1994, Leigh happily stepped in and filmed a couple. One was shot in the McDonald's branch in Chiswick High Street, west London, in July 1994. A small girl and her parents eat their burgers while Dad (played by Bob Mason, of *The Permissive Society* and 'Untitled 95', the latest Leigh film) parries his daughter's questions about burgers and eating without knives and forks. He answers them all patiently and then asks *her* a question she cannot answer: who won the FA Cup in 1978? (She doesn't know, and Dad doesn't tell her, that it was Ipswich Town, 1-0, against Arsenal.) Leigh quietly orchestrated the action and patiently supervised all the takes, Dick Pope on the camera, Heather Storr crouched at Leigh's elbow, Chris Rose, the first assistant director, converting Leigh's ideas about the movement of the background extras into specific commands, Lindy Hemming (costumes) and Chris Blundell (make-up) standing by. Leigh did not raise his voice all day, and when anything had to be said, he moved in closely and quickly and said it. No fuss, no camping around. There was no question, however, about who was in charge. And the mood was relaxed, efficient, good-humoured and painstaking; and so slow, my God, so *slow*. As Leigh is quick to point out, Mason must have eaten at least thirty-seven hamburgers in the course of several hours' filming. And I could have read the first half of *War and Peace*.

It was interesting to see the team in action, if only in slow motion and picking up a bit of spending money. Among the other extra-curricular activities of the same year was Leigh's visit to

Buckingham Palace to collect his OBE. It was the second time he had braved the red carpet to be publicly honoured. His honorary degree from Salford University was conferred in 1991, when he was welcomed by the Scottish Vice-Chancellor as an 'honorary graduand' wearing a mortar board, a black gown with blue facings and a fearsomely sombre expression. The Palace visit, in contrast, judging by the souvenir video, was a much more light-hearted affair. Leigh steps forward looking relaxed in a dark suit to be greeted by Her Majesty the Queen and invested as an Officer of the British Empire 'for services to the film industry'.

The subsequent conversation is animated and rather protracted. The trick in this is that the heritage film company (Bonham Carter Associates) which cooperates with the Palace shoots simultaneously on four cameras and joins up all four shots from end to end so the royal encounter is quadrupled in length. Actually, Her Majesty said to Leigh, 'I must indeed give you this,' followed by 'What exactly do you do?' to which Leigh replied that he made films, and Her Majesty countered with, 'Terribly difficult at the moment, isn't it?' to which Leigh replied, 'Yes, ma'am.' The Queen then held out her hand, Leigh shook it, backed away and, in his own words, 'buggered off'. Leigh's friend, the writer Jack Rosenthal, was disappointed by Leigh's account of the proceedings. He felt that when Her Majesty asked what exactly he did, he should have told her: 'Well, ma'am, I select a group of actors and then I go off with each in turn and discuss with him or her a dozen or so people, perhaps even more, that they know, and from that discussion I select one character who will form the basis for the development of that actor's role . . .' and so on. He could have been there until teatime.

Leigh probably has at least five or six major films still in him, with luck, more. His career spans a most extraordinary time of upheaval in the performing arts, and his struggle, survival and rise to eminence in that period is all the more extraordinary because of the singular, wilful and utterly committed way in which he has pursued and realised the consequences of his own muse. His output in the late 1960s and 1970s seemed odd, perhaps even unfashionable, because it lacked stridency and avant-garde trappings. But as he grew in wisdom and gathered experience, it became clear that he was uniquely dedicated to the science of acting; and to the idea of creating works of theatre and film which sprang from the liberation of an actor in a text on which he collaborated, not his imprisonment within one to which he was bound by traditional responses and ways of seeing. In that sense, every Leigh project was an antidote to the more critically approved output of the major subsidised theatres and the major film studios.

He puts a lot back into the profession he struggled so hard to join. Over the years, the institutions where he has taught include RADA, the Drama Centre, Webber Douglas, E15 Acting School, the Manchester Polytechnic Theatre School, the London Film School, the National Film School, the Royal College of Art film department, as well as the Australian Film and Television School and the National Institute of Dramatic Art in Sydney, and various workshops in Australia. Leigh thinks teaching is important, and learns a lot from doing it. On several occasions in the past ten years he has run a course for second-year National Film School students at Beaconsfield, where he has helped and advised students tackling a script, casting and crewing, going on location, right through to post-production. 'Film-making, like writing and paint-ing, can't really be taught. But there are things you can learn.'

Leigh makes no great statements of political propaganda or proscription. His friend Colin Cina remembers taking him to a symposium about cultural colonialism at the Institute of Contem-porary Arts in the mid-1980s. The novelist Antonia Byatt and the sociologist Stuart Hall were on the panel. 'It was all good stuff, and they were talking modern theory. It was clear that Mike hadn't immersed himself in any of that. He knew what they were talking about, but he found it absurd that they had to use these kinds of words, this kind of high-flown discourse. He is totally self-contained, and if he had any doubts, they would come from within himself. They wouldn't be doubts thrown at him by a new body of theory or new psychoanalytical or feminist critiques. He has not learned that language in order to talk back at people in it, because he doesn't need to. In that sense, he is one of the greats.

All great artists, when you think about it, have that intuitive sense of survival in the cultural stream.'

Leigh's job is to look at the world around him, and at the glorious variety of human endeavour and quirkiness, and to create, or recreate, a distinctive, idiosyncratic universe of reflecting images distorted by the controlling intervention of artistic interpretation. It took many years, and many artistic experiences, to convince himself, and others, of the way in which he wanted to operate. But having found that way, he has stuck to his guns and compelled the artistic establishment (part of it) and the available funding resources (a few) to dance to his tune. The rarity of this campaign ensures that he will never entirely succeed and will forever maintain the invaluable status of an outsider, while lesser talents and weaker men rise effortlessly to the top of public adulation and esteem. He's a truly brilliant and original creative artist. And he's an awkward customer. Long may he remain so.

EPILOGUE

In Victoria . . . and Chingford

Victoria, London, the penultimate Tuesday morning of June 1995. After two weeks of filming on 'Untitled '95', an hour's worth of rushes is being shown by Thin Man producer Simon Channing-Williams to David Aukin, head of drama at Channel 4, and Phillip Kenny, who works for CiBy 2000 out of Barcelona.

We are sitting in the basement cinema of the handsome new Channel 4 headquarters in Horseferry Road, five minutes from Victoria Station, behind the Army and Navy Stores. This wonderful new building, designed by Richard Rogers, is a modern temple of air, light, steel and space. Its external, transparent lifts are similar to those in Rogers' famous Lloyds Building in the City of London, visited by the despatch rider Cyril in *High Hopes*.

First big surprise of the morning: Aukin has changed his appearance since we last met, and has gone totally laid-back LA. The spruce, classically-attired lawyer-look has given way to the floppy-haired, centre-parting, designer T-shirt, 'Let me tell you how it is', casual-high-flying-film-executive rig-out. Kenny is canny and quiet, small and neat, non-committal. Channing-Williams is as large and bear-like as ever, clearly a man weighed down not just by his splendidly ample stomach, but also by many pressing responsibilities, many things to get done.

Second big surprise: Timothy Spall, in the few short scenes we see, is totally underplaying for once. And to devastating, heart-wrenching effect. The first sequence, the opening of the film, is at the funeral of a much-loved black woman. The establishing shots linger on some beautiful mock-classical Victorian statuary in Kensal Green Cemetery, and the camera pans slowly round the

231

assembled mourners, who are singing hymns as the coffin is laid in the earth. Marianne Jean-Baptiste, playing one of the film's chief characters, Hortense, is picked out in the crowd. An aerial shot of the floral tributes, a large one spelling out 'Mum'.

It is odd seeing a work in progress, by glimpses, in this way. Cut to Hortense riffling through some papers in a cardboard shoe-box in her mother's bedroom, while other characters squabble at the foot of the stairs. She visits the social services and tells the social worker that she has known since childhood that she was adopted. The film, one imagines, will in part be her quest to find, and get to know, her real mother, whom she learns is called Cynthia Rose Purley.

Other scenes introduce us to a married white couple, Maurice Purley, a photographer, played by Timothy Spall, and his wife Monica, played by Phyllis Logan. They are in bed. Maurice snuggles up under the blankets, Monica is deep in her book: 'I'll just finish this chapter; he's had his feet amputated.' In the living room, they drink wine and talk about a niece, Roxanne, they have not seen for over two years. Later, Monica is hoovering, slavishly. She sits on the loo and inserts a Tampax. Then we see the two of them in an otherwise empty restaurant – shades of the Chinese eatery in *Bleak Moments*, and of the disastrously underpopulated opening night of Aubrey's Regret Rien in *Life is Sweet*. Maurice sits fast asleep next to Monica, face down on the table.

Something is bubbling under, the relationship is not right, there are waves of tension and unhappiness emanating from Monica. Maurice absorbs them with benign tolerance. One thing for sure: Spall, bearded, sunnily-disposed and clear-eyed, is ditching his familiar yob/slob persona and outlining what promises to be a totally unexpected, and extraordinarily moving, performance. In moments of stillness and dignity, and of the quietest and clearest indication of inner thoughts, the actor resembles, both in the generosity of his physique and in the deft flickering of emotion, one of his most admired exemplars, Charles Laughton.

On the day of a wedding, Maurice is photographing a seemingly reluctant, almost tearful bride, in the middle-class opulence of her sitting room, her father hovering critically in the background. Maurice has a doctoral, bedside manner on the job, coaxing a response from his recalcitrant subject with his assurance that although she is under absolutely no obligation to do as he suggests, a little smile would not be a complete waste of everybody's time, nor a blight on the proceedings in general and this tiny task in particular.

In the photographer's office, Maurice and Monica – and Maurice's assistant, played by Elizabeth Berrington – are visited by Ron Cook as Stuart Christian. Cook, small and rat-like, with powerful, understated control, like Spall, over the slightest facial gesture or vocal inflection, presents a really desperate and unhappy character. The rushes show this scene four times over, the camera held on each of the four faces during Stuart's long speech: he had sold this photography business to Maurice and gone to Australia.

Things have not worked out well for Stuart. He has been living with his mother in Grays, Essex, but she died while he was in Bangkok. He misses his dead father a lot more. Australia was all very well if you were nine or ninety. Otherwise, they just don't want to know. And it's too hot there. It's too cold here. Stuart is climatically suspended in chill, unemployed middle-age, claiming assistance from Maurice, the odd job if he needs any help. Maurice says he does all the work himself, he doesn't want to be dependent on some tosser coming in and . . . Stuart explodes, accusing Maurice of calling him a tosser. He leaves in tears.

A few mines are being laid here which one assumes will explode fruitfully later in the film. The Channel 4 session ends with a delightful sequence of snapshots, almost mini-playlets, of Maurice once again at work, this time in his studio. An Asian boy is sending his photograph to the girls his aunt has marked down as suitable spouses. A nurse erupts in laughter. Paul Trussell and Wendy Nottingham – recycling the long and the short of their married relationship in *It's a Great Big Shame!* – present a delightful contrast between his grinning fatuity and her sour disapproval; she reacts to the suggestion that she should stand on a couple of volumes of Yellow Pages as if she had been asked to remove her underwear.

Gary McDonald shapes up ferociously as a champion boxer. Ruth Sheen and an irrepressibly hilarious gap-toothed, curly-headed 'husband' giggle uncontrollably. Angela Curran places her real-life two-year-old son on the sofa and he promptly starts picking his nose. Anthony O'Donnell sits with a huge black woman trying determinedly not to laugh, and gives in. Other customers not seen in this set of rushes include Alison Steadman and the floppy Leigh family dog, Bonzo.

One week later, Leigh is on location in Chingford, Essex. On a hot, sunny June day in the parish church of St Peter and Paul, a handsome, airy, light-filled Victorian building, he is shooting a wedding scene with Maurice Purley lurking in the back row. The parents of the bride, played by Bob Mason and Janine Duvitski, occupy the front row. There are several dozen extras, many of whom Tim Spall recognises from a wedding scene in a TV series he recently made; odd people, extras. Bob Mason tells me, without rancour, that his role has been truncated. Janine Duvitski is bursting out of a cerise suit and clutching a handbag that appears to be constructed from laminated Smarties.

Leigh is quiet, crouched, controlled. Simon Channing-Williams arrives at lunchtime and tells me that he has never seen Leigh so relaxed on a film, so generally at ease: 'He's really into this one. And he really is always this quiet. He hates a noisy set.' The filming is running reasonably on schedule, just a day or two to make up before the end of July and the wrap.

The pews are littered with copies of the marriage programme. No detail is spared. The date is right, the names of the couple – Darren Leslie Scott (played by Joe Tucker) and Zoe Simone Woodcock (Kate O'Malley) – are printed above the order of hymns. In between shots, Leigh shows me his personal shooting script: seventy-odd scenes, each pithily described in one line, are made up in green and white markings on a double-sided feather-weight piece of foamboard measuring approximately five inches by four inches – exactly the right size to fit into his top shirt pocket.

The quartet of bridesmaids is attired in mint green satin. The four young actresses all auditioned for the film and have been called back by Leigh, after not being cast, for a few days' work; each of them has developed a full character in a concentrated version of Leigh's rehearsal process. He quite often uses this way of working to find out more about new young actors and mark them down for possible future collaborations. Dick Pope, the cinematographer, has smoked out the apse and the nave to make the sunlight heavier, add texture to the shot (when I view these rushes a few days later, the composition and lighting look superb).

The exchange of vows is supervised by a vicar played by Richard Syms, who is a non-stipendiary clergyman. Two other British actors are similarly qualified – Tenniel Evans and James Roose-Evans, who taught Leigh at RADA. They became clergymen after becoming actors; uniquely, Syms is a clergyman-turned-actor. He knows the words of the liturgy, which saves a little time. The real-life vicar of the parish church stands behind the film crew and approves Syms's professional authority. Somebody wonders if the actors could indeed be really married when pronounced so by the acting vicar. Only in character, we conclude.

Tim Spall lumbers into the aisle with his tripod and takes a snap. The shot is repeated up and down the church, close in on Spall, not so close, behind the wedding party, and so on. The extras shuffle patiently in the pews, some of them more obviously acting than others. Spall tells me at lunch that he learned the trade with a professional photographer in Barking, Essex. He seems to know exactly where everything is. After each shot, Leigh re-runs the scene for his stills photographer, Simon Mein, to move in and snap away. With Spall hunched over his tripod and Mein closing in with his own camera, we are suddenly treated to a tense war of the lensmen.

Nothing much happens very slowly. The occasional parishioner arrives for a quick word with God but is dismayed to find the entrance barred. A glimpse of Mike Leigh is clearly no substitute for divine intercourse, and one elderly lady becomes quite agitated in frustration.

In mid-afternoon, the wedding party spills onto the steps of the church for the family album portraits, Spall shouting instructions at the extras in character and Leigh lunging up from behind the camera to move the bodies around, adjust the groupings, rearrange the line-up. Dick Pope is worried about a bright patch of sunlight on the grey stucco exterior. By the time the shot is lined up, the patch has all but disappeared. Leigh bids me goodbye and I wish him good luck before preparing to head off down the high street to the station.

It is now past five o'clock on a lovely summer afternoon. Rush-hour traffic builds up on the road alongside the pretty churchyard, where the camera on its dolly, light screens, sound booms, 'sparks', costume supervisors and make-up girls declare to the passing Chingfordians that a film is being made, not a true-life wedding enacted. Cars honk and hoot, schoolchildren shout ruderies.

Two local ladies linger in the middle distance among the gravestones:

'It's 'im, 'innit, that nice fat one in *Auf Wiedersehen, Pet* and *Frank Stubbs*.'

'He's filled out a bit, hasn't he?'

'Nah, he was always that fat. It's part of 'is character, innit?'

'Ooh, he's lovely. I'll just 'ave another little look before I go home and put the dinner on. D'you think 'e'd mind being my toy boy?'

They burst out laughing. Leigh softly says, 'Turn over.' The camera whirrs. The clapperboy shouts the scene's number and claps his clapper. Leigh says, 'Action.' The women, who do not know each other, giggle conspiratorially, briefly bonded. They go back down the churchyard path to resume their separate lives.

APPENDIX

The Works of Mike Leigh

PLAYS

(dates given are those of the first performance)

The Box Play
Midland Arts Centre, Cannon Hill, Birmingham, 18 December 1965. Designed by Mike Leigh.

My Parents Have Gone to Carlisle
Midlands Arts Centre, 13 May 1966. Designed by Mike Leigh.

The Last Crusade of the Five Little Nuns
Midlands Arts Centre, 2 July 1966. Designed (and music) by Steve Morris.

NENAA
RSC Conference Hall, Royal Shakespeare Theatre, Stratford-upon-Avon, summer 1967. With Gerald McNally (Gerald), Peter Rocca (Luigi), Edward Lyon (delivery-boy) and Mike Billington, C. G. Bond, Robert Davies, Peter Gordon, Roger Lloyd Pack, Louis Mahoney, Matthew Roberton, Richard Williams and David Weston (customers).

Individual Fruit Pies
E15 Acting School, Loughton, Essex, 3 July 1968. Designed by Mike Leigh. With David Atkinson (Ronald), Jane Briers (Mrs McAuley), Robert Putt (Andy), Sarah Stephenson (Betty), Mrs Briddon (Gwen Taylor), Peggy Goodson (Mary Brent), Edward Caswell (Gerald Swann).

Big Basil
Manchester Youth Theatre, Lesser Free Trade Hall, Manchester, 4 January 1969. Designed by Janet Payne.

Down Here and Up There
Theatre Upstairs, Royal Court Theatre, London, 1 August 1968. Designed by Mike Leigh. With Gerald McNally (Gerald), Robert Putt (Gus), Amaryllis Garnett (Kit), Gwen Taylor (Pat), David S. Boliver (Bert).

Epilogue

Sedgley Park College and De La Salle College joint drama department, Manchester, 27 June 1969. Designed by John Coupe and Mike Leigh.

Glum Victoria and the Lad with Specs

Manchester Youth Theatre, Renold Theatre, Manchester, 5 September 1969. Designed by Mike Leigh.

Bleak Moments

Open Space Theatre, London, 16 March 1970. Designed by Mike Leigh. With Anne Raitt (Sylvia), Sarah Stephenson (Hilda), Eric Allan (Peter), Joolia Cappleman (Pat), Mike Bradwell (Norman).

A Rancid Pong

Basement Theatre, Greek Street, London, 26 July 1971. Designed by Mike Leigh. With Joolia Cappleman (Marilyn), Reg Stewart (Arnold).

Wholesome Glory

Theatre Upstairs, Royal Court, London, 20 February 1973. Designed by Mike Leigh. With Alison Steadman (Candice-Marie), Roger Sloman (Keith), Geoffrey Hutchings (Dennis).

The Jaws of Death

Traverse Theatre, Edinburgh, 4 September 1973. Designed by Mike Leigh. With Alison Steadman (Brenda), Richard Ireson (Hack), Adrian Shergold (Young Man).

Dick Whittington and his Cat

Theatre Upstairs, Royal Court, 26 December 1973. Designed by Diz Marsh. With Paul Copley (Dick Whittington), Philip Jackson (his father/Stephen), Lavinia Bertram (his mother/Alice), Tim Stern (the Cat), Joolia Cappleman (the Cat's mother/Kim/Jackie), Peter Godfrey (Father Christmas), Roger Sloman (Mr Fitzwarren/Her Majesty's constabulary/motorist).

Babies Grow Old

The Other Place, Stratford-upon-Avon (later, the ICA, London), 27 August 1974. Designed by Judith Bland. With Anne Dyson (Mrs Wenlock), Sheila Kelley (Elaine), Eric Allan (Geoff), Matthew Guinness (Charles), Sidney Livingstone (Barry).

The Silent Majority

Bush Theatre, London, 24 October 1974. Designed by Mike Leigh. With Stephen Bill (Mr Clancy), Julie North (Mrs Clancy), Yvonne Gilan (Mrs Duffy).

Abigail's Party

Hampstead Theatre, London, 18 April 1977 (revived 18 July 1977). Designed by Tanya McCallin, costumes by Lindy Hemming. With Alison Steadman (Beverly), Tim Stern (Laurence), Janine Duvitski (Angela), John Salthouse (Tony), Thelma Whiteley (Susan). Harriet Reynolds played Susan in the revival.

Too Much of a Good Thing

BBC Radio 3, 1979 (broadcast July 1992). Produced by Liane Aukin, sound by Cedric Johnson and Julian Walther. With Lesley Manville (Pamela), Philip David (Graham), Eric Allan (Mr Payne).

Ecstasy

Hampstead Theatre, 26 September 1979. Designed by Alison Chitty, costumes by Lindy Hemming. With Sheila Kelley (Jean), Ron Cook (Roy), Rachel Davies (Val), Julie Walters (Dawn), Stephen Rea (Mick), Jim Broadbent (Len).

Goose-Pimples

Hampstead Theatre, 3 March 1981 (transferred to Garrick Theatre, 29 April 1981). Designed by Caroline Beaver. With Jim Broadbent (Vernon), Marion Bailey (Jackie), Paul Jesson (Irving), Jill Baker (Frankie), Antony Sher (Muhammad).

Smelling a Rat

Hampstead Theatre, 6 December 1988. Designed by Eve Stewart. With Eric Allan (Rex), Timothy Spall (Vic), Bríd Brennan (Charmaine), Greg Cruttwell (Rock), Saskia Reeves (Melanie-Jane).

Greek Tragedy

Belvoir Street Theatre, Sydney, July 1989; Edinburgh Festival, Church Hill Street Theatre, 13 August 1990; Theatre Royal, Stratford East 15, 3 September 1990. Designed by Stephen Curtis, costumes by Edie Kurzer. With Evdokia Katahanas (Kalliope), Stan Kouros (Alex), Nicholas Papademetriou (Perri), Christina Totos (Vicki), George Spartels (Larry) and Zoë Carides (Toni). Adam Hatzimanolis played Alex in the Edinburgh/Stratford East revival.

It's a Great Big Shame!

Theatre Royal, Stratford E15, 13 October 1993. Designed by Alison Chitty, music by Katherine Aughton. With Kathy Burke (Nellie Buckett), Ruth Sheen (Fanny Clack), Michael Gunn (Eli Finch), Paul Trussell (Jim Short), Joe Tucker (Jack Skegg), Wendy Nottingham (Ada Ricketts), Gregor Truter (Sholto Babbington, Esq/policeman), Katherine Aughton (Hon Augusta

Grabisham), Gary McDonald (Amos Churchill/Barrington), Michele Austin (Joy), Clint Dyer (Randall), Marianne Jean-Baptiste (Faith).

TELEVISION STUDIO RECORDINGS

The Permissive Society (1975)

BBC TV Second City Firsts. Produced by Tara Prem, designed by Margaret Peacock. With Bob Mason (Les), Veronica Roberts (Carol), Rachel Davies (Yvonne). 30 mins.

Knock for Knock (1976)

BBC TV Second City Firsts. Produced by Tara Prem, designed by Myles Lang. With Sam Kelly (Mr Bowes), Anthony O'Donnell (Mr Purvis), Meryl Hampton (Marilyn). 30 mins.

Abigail's Party (1977)

BBC TV Play for Today. Produced by Margaret Matheson. Cast as for the Hampstead Theatre revival. 104 mins.

FILMS

Bleak Moments (1971)

Autumn Productions/Memorial Enterprises/BFI Production Board. Produced and edited by Les Blair, photography by Bahram Manoochehri, designed by Richard Rambaut, sound by Bob Withey. With the cast of the stage play, and Liz Smith (Pat's mother), Malcolm Smith, Donald Sumpter (Norman's friends), Christopher Martin (Sylvia's boss), Linda Beckett, Sandra Bolton, Stephen Churchett (remedial trainees), Una Brandon-Jones (supervisor), Ronald Eng (waiter), Reg Stewart (man in restaurant), Susan Glanville (enthusiastic teacher), Joanna Dickens (stout teacher), Christopher Leaver (wine-merchant). 111 mins.

Hard Labour (1973)

BBC TV. Produced by Tony Garnett, photography by Tony Pierce-Roberts, sound by Dick Manton, edited by Christopher Rowlands, designed by Paul Munting, costumes by Sally Nieper. With Liz Smith (Mrs Thornley), Clifford Kershaw (Mr Thornley), Polly Hemingway (Ann), Bernard Hill (Edward), Alison Steadman (Veronica), Vanessa Harris (Mrs Stone), Cyril Varley (Mr Stone), Linda Beckett (Julie), Ben Kingsley (Naseem), Alan Erasmus (Barry), Rowena Parr (June), June Whitaker (Mrs Rigby), Paula Tilbrook (Mrs Thornley's friend), Keith Washington (Mr Shore), Louis Raynes (tallyman), Alan Gerrard (greengrocer), Diana Flacks (Mrs Rubens), Patrick Durkin (Frank). 75 mins.

The Five Minute Films (1975, broadcast 1982)

BBC TV. Produced by Tony Garnett, photography by Brian Tufano, sound by Andrew Boulton, edited by Chris Lovett. *The Birth of the 2001 FA Cup Final Goalie* with Richard Ireson (father), Celia Quicke (mother); *Old Chums* with Tim Stern (Brian), Robert Putt (Terry); *Probation* with Herbert Norville (Arbley), Billy Colvill (Sid), Anthony Carrick (Mr Davies), Theresa Watson (secretary), Lally Percy (Victoria); *A Light Snack* with Margaret Heery (Mrs White), Richard Griffiths (window-cleaner), Alan Gaunt (talker), David Casey (listener); *Afternoon* with Rachel Davies (hostess), Pauline Moran (teacher), Julie North (newly-wed). 25 mins.

Nuts in May (1976)

BBC TV. Produced by David Rose, photography by Michael Williams, sound by John Gilbert, edited by Oliver White, designed by David Crozier, costumes by Gini Hardy. With Roger Sloman (Keith), Alison Steadman (Candice-Marie), Anthony O'Donnell (Ray), Sheila Kelley (Honky), Stephen Bill (Finger), Richenda Carey (Miss Beale), Eric Allan (quarryman), Matthew Guinness (farmer), Sally Watts (farm-girl), Richard Ireson (policeman). 80 mins.

The Kiss of Death (1977)

BBC TV. Produced by David Rose, photography by Michael Williams and John Kenway, edited by Oliver White, designed by David Crozier, costumes by Al Barnett, music by Carl Davis, sound by John Gilbert. With David Threlfall (Trevor), Clifford Kershaw (Mr Garside), John Wheatley (Ronnie), Pamela Austin (Trevor's mum), Angela Curran (Sandra), Phillip Ryland (Froggy), Kay Adshead (Linda), Elizabeth Hauck (shoe-shop customer), Karen Petrie (policewoman), Frank McDermott (Mr Bodger), Christine Moore (Mrs Bodger), Eileen Denison (Mrs Ball), Marlene Sidaway (Christine), Brian Pollitt (doctor), Elizabeth Ann Ogden (bridesmaid). 80 mins.

Who's Who (1979)

BBC TV. Produced by Margaret Matheson, photography by John Else, edited by Chris Lovett, designed by Austen Spriggs, costumes by Robin Stubbs, sound by John Pritchard. With Simon Chandler (Nigel), Adam Norton (Giles), Richard Kane (Alan), Jeffrey Wickham (Francis), Souad Faress (Samya), Philip Davis (Kevin), Graham Seed (Anthony), Joolia Cappleman (April), Lavinia Bertram (Nanny), Francesca Martin (Selina), David Neville (Lord Crouchurst), Richenda Carey (Lady Crouchurst), Geraldine James (Miss Hunt), Sam Kelly (Mr Shakespeare), Catherine Hall (Samantha), Felicity Dean (Caroline), Angela Curran, Roger Hammond (couple in window). 80 mins.

Grown-Ups (1980)

BBC TV. Produced by Louis Marks, photography by Remi Adefarasin, edited by Robin Sales, designed by Bryan Ellis, costumes by Christian Dyall, sound by John Pritchard. With Philip Davis (Dick), Lesley Manville (Mandy), Brenda Blethyn (Gloria), Janine Duvitski (Sharon), Lindsay Duncan (Christine), Sam Kelly (Ralph). 90 mins.

Home Sweet Home (1982)

BBC TV. Produced by Louis Marks, photography by Remi Adefarasin, edited by Robin Sales, designed by Bryan Ellis, costumes by Michael Burdle, music by Carl Davis, sound by John Pritchard. With Timothy Spall (Gordon), Eric Richard (Stan), Tim Barker (Harold), Kay Stonham (Hazel), Su Elliott (June), Frances Barber (Melody), Sheila Kelley (Janice), Lorraine Brunning (Tina), Heidi Laratta (Kelly), Paul Jesson (man in dressing-gown), Lloyd Peters (Dave). 90 mins.

Meantime (1983)

Central Television/Mostpoint Ltd for Channel 4. Produced by Graham Benson, photography by Roger Pratt, edited by Lesley Walker, designed by Diana Charnley, costumes by Lindy Hemming, music by Andrew Dickson, sound by Malcolm Hirst. With Marion Bailey (Barbara), Phil Daniels (Mark), Tim Roth (Colin), Pam Ferris (Mavis), Jeff Robert (Frank), Alfred Molina (John), Gary Oldman (Coxy), Tilly Vosburgh (Hayley), Paul Daly (Rusty), Leila Bertrand (Hayley's friend), Hepburn Graham (boyfriend), Peter Wight (estate-manager), Eileen Davies (unemployment-benefit clerk), Herbert Norville (man in pub), Brian Hoskin (barman). 90 mins.

Four Days in July (1985)

BBC TV. Produced by Kenith Trodd, photography by Remi Adefarasin, edited by Robin Sales, designed by Jim Clay, costumes by Maggie Donnelly, music by Rachel Portman, sound by John Pritchard. With Bríd Brennan (Collette), Des McAleer (Eugene), Paula Hamilton (Lorraine), Charles Lawson (Billy), Brian Hogg (Big Billy), Adrian Gordon (Little Billy), Shane Connaughton (Brendan), Eileen Pollock (Carmel), Stephen Rea (Dixie), David Coyle (Mickey), John Keegan (Mr McCoy), John Hewitt (Mr Roper), Ann Hasson (midwife). 96 mins.

The Short and Curlies (1987)

Film Four/Portman. Produced by Victor Glynn and Simon Channing-Williams, photography by Roger Pratt, edited by Jon Gregory, designed by Diana Charnley, costumes by Lindy Hemming, music by Rachel Portman, sound by Malcolm Hirst. With David Thewlis (Clive), Alison Steadman (Betty), Sylvestra Le Touzel (Joy), Wendy Nottingham (Charlene). 18 mins.

High Hopes (1988)

Film Four International/British Screen/Portman. Produced by Simon Channing-Williams and Victor Glynn, photography by Roger Pratt, edited by Jon Gregory, designed by Diana Charnley, costumes by Lindy Hemming, music by Andrew Dickson, sound by Billy McCarthy. With Philip Davis (Cyril), Ruth Sheen (Shirley), Edna Doré (Mrs Bender), Heather Tobias (Valerie), Philip Jackson (Martin), Lesley Manville (Laetitia), David Bamber (Rupert), Jason Watkins (Wayne), Judith Scott (Suzi), Cheryl Prime (Martin's girlfriend), Diane-Louise Jordan (chemist-shop assistant), Linda Beckett (receptionist). 110 mins.

Life is Sweet (1990)

Thin Man/Film Four International/British Screen. Produced by Simon Channing-Williams, photography by Dick Pope, edited by Jon Gregory, designed by Alison Chitty, costumes by Lindy Hemming, music by Rachel Portman, sound by Malcolm Hirst. With Alison Steadman (Wendy), Jim Broadbent (Andy), Claire Skinner (Natalie), Jane Horrocks (Nicola), Timothy Spall (Aubrey), Stephen Rea (Patsy), David Thewlis (Nicola's lover), Moya Brady (Paula), David Neilson (Steve), Harriet Thorpe (customer), Paul Trussell (chef), Jack Thorpe Baker (Nigel). 102 mins.

A Sense of History (1992)

Thin Man/Film Four International. Written by Jim Broadbent, produced by Simon Channing-Williams, photography by Dick Pope, designed by Alison Chitty, music by Carl Davis, sound by Tim Fraser. With Jim Broadbent (23rd Earl of Leete), Stephen Bill (Giddy). 28 mins.

Naked (1993)

Thin Man/Film Four International/British Screen. Produced by Simon Channing-Williams, photography by Dick Pope, edited by Jon Gregory, designed by Alison Chitty, costumes by Lindy Hemming, music by Andrew Dickson, sound by Ken Weston. With David Thewlis (Johnny), Lesley Sharp (Louise), Katrin Cartlidge (Sophie), Greg Cruttwell (Jeremy), Claire Skinner (Sandra), Peter Wight (Brian), Ewen Bremner (Archie), Susan Vidler (Maggie), Deborah Maclaren (woman in window), Gina McKee (café girl), Carolina Giammetta (masseuse), Elizabeth Berrington (Giselle), Darren Tunstall (poster man), Robert Putt (chauffeur), Lynda Rooke (victim), Angela Curran (car owner), Peter Whitman (Mr Halpern), Jo Abercrombie (woman in street), Elaine Britten (girl in Porsche), David Foxxe (tea-bar owner), Mike Avenall, Toby Jones (men at tea-bar), Sandra Voe (bag lady). 126 mins.

Secrets and Lies (1996)

Thin Man/CiBY 2000/Channel Four Films. Produced by Simon Channing-Williams, photography by Dick Pope, edited by Jon Gregory, designed by Alison Chitty, costumes by Maria Price, music by Andrew Dickson, sound by George Richards. With Timothy Spall (Maurice), Phyllis Logan (Monica), Brenda Blethyn (Cynthia), Claire Rushbrook (Roxanne), Marianne Jean-Baptiste (Hortense), Elizabeth Berrington (Jane), Michelle Austin (Dionne), Lee Ross (Paul), Lesley Manville (social worker), Ron Cook (Stuart), Emma Amos (girl with scar), Brian Bovell and Trevor Laird (Hortense's brothers), Clare Perkins (Hortense's sister), Elias Perkins McCook (Hortense's nephew), June Mitchell (senior optometrist), Janice Acquah (junior optician), Keeley Flanders (girl in optician's), Hannah Davis (first bride), Terence Harvey (first bride's father), Kate O'Malley (second bride), Joe Tucker (groom), Richard Syms (vicar), Grant Masters (best man), Annie Hayes (mother in family group), Jean Ainslie (grandmother), Daniel Smith (teenage son), Lucy Sheen (nurse), Frances Ruffelle (young mother), Felix Manley (baby), Nitin Chandra Ganatra (potential husband), Metin Marlow (conjuror), Amanda Crossley, Su Elliott and Di Sherlock (raunchy women), Alex Squires, Lauren Squires and Sade Squires (triplets), Dominic Curran (little boy), Stephen Churchett, David Neilson, Peter Stockbridge and Peter Waddington (men in suits), Rachel Lewis (graduate), Paul Trussell (grinning husband), Denise Orita (uneasy woman), Margery Withers (elderly lady), Theresa Watson (daughter), Gordon Winter (grinning man), Jonathan Coyne (fiancé), Bonzo (dog), Texas (cat), and special guest appearances by Peter Wight (father in family group), Gary McDonald (boxer), Alison Steadman (dog owner), Liz Smith (cat owner), Sheila Kelley (fertile mother), Angela Curran (little boy's mother), Linda Beckett (pin-up housewife), Philip Davis (man in suit), Wendy Nottingham (glum wife), Anthony O'Donnell (uneasy man), Ruth Sheen (laughing woman) and Mia Soteriou (fiancée). 140 mins.

SELECT BIBLIOGRAPHY

Auty, Martin and Roddick, Nick, *British Cinema Now* (British Film Institute, 1985)

Boston, Richard, *Boudu Saved from Drowning* (British Film Institute, 1994)

Canter, David, *Criminal Shadows* (HarperCollins, 1994)

Chambers, Colin, *Other Spaces: New Theatre and the RSC* (Methuen, 1980)

Clements, Paul, *The Improvised Play* (Methuen, 1983)

Edgar, David, *The Second Time as Farce* (Lawrence & Wishart, 1988)

Gleick, James, *Chaos* (Heinemann, 1988)

Laprevotte, Gilles, *Mike Leigh* (Trois Cailloux, Amiens, 1993)

Leigh, Mike, *Abigail's Party and Goose-Pimples* (Penguin, 1983)

Leigh, Mike, *Smelling a Rat and Ecstasy* (Nick Hern Books, 1989)

Leigh, Mike, *Naked and Other Screenplays* (Faber, 1995)

Martini, Emanuela (ed.), *Mike Leigh* (British Council, 1993)

Pevsner, Nicholas, *The Buildings of England: South Lancashire* (Penguin, 1969)

Powell, Michael, *Million-Dollar Movie* (Heinemann, 1992)

Pym, John, *Film on Four* (British Film Institute, 1992)

Renoir, Jean (trans. Carol Volk), *Renoir on Renoir* (Cambridge University Press, 1989)

Thomson, David, *A Biographical Dictionary of Film* (André Deutsch, 1994)

Wesker, Arnold, *As Much as I Dare* (Century, 1994)

INDEX

Index

Index

Index

This is Orson Welles

Orson Welles and Peter Bogdanovich

This is the book that Welles ultimately considered his autobiography, but it's a memoir like no other. At once accessible, entertaining and revealing, Welles and Bogdanovich's collaboration is an unforgettable collection of penetrating, fascinating and often hilarious conversations undertaken over many years, on both sides of the Atlantic. With *This is Orson Welles* the master illusionist and self-confessed 'faker', in his own words, 'puts the record straight'.

'The Art of Bogdanovich's interrogation conceals itself in the ease of good friends talking, yet it elicits from Welles answers which show us his position and his character under the arc-light thrown upon them by his brilliant tongue . . . Such humorous charm is captivating'
Philip Glazebrook, *Spectator*

'This is a book you must beg, borrow or steal . . . Welles pulls no punches: reading it is like being a privileged guest at his table, savouring that inimitable voice, as the pearls drop in abundance'
Bryan Forbes, *Mail on Sunday*

'Fascinating. A treasure-trove of insights'   John Lahr

'Welles at his roaring best'   *New York Times Book Review*

ISBN 0 00 638232 0

Hollywood vs. America
Popular Culture and the War on Traditional Values

Michael Medved

This book has struck a raw nerve. Film stars, commentators and politicians joined the fierce debate fuelled by Michael Medved's trenchant critique of the film industry – the most provocative study of the moral implications of popular culture ever written. His condemnation of sex, violence, bad language, and the seemingly consistent attack on traditional values, has given rise to feverish discussions on both sides of the Atlantic. Jane Fonda has accused Hollywood of immortality. Sir Anthony Hopkins may not now recreate the monstrous role of Hannibal Lecter.

Why do so many films attack religion, glorify violence and undermine the family? What is the cost of big-screen brutality? Have we become impervious to the increasingly grotesque violence erupting from our cinema screens and high-street video shops?

Greeted both with cheers of support and howls of enraged dissent, *Hollywood vs. America* confronts head on one of the most significant issues of our time.

'Real dynamite . . . The author says his book will make him the most hated man in Hollywood. On the other hand, it might save an industry that seems bent on self-destruction.'   *Daily Mail*

ISBN 0 00 638235 5

k. d. lang

All You Get Is Me

Victoria Starr

'Elvis is alive, and is she ever beautiful'   Madonna

From the rolling wheat fields of Southern Alberta to the glitz and glam of Hollywood, from the days when she was destined to become an Olympic athlete to the moment she became the first openly lesbian artist to win an American Music Award, *k. d. lang: All You Get Is Me* traces k. d.'s path from college drop-out to pop superstar. Exhaustively researched and compellingly narrated, this is the story of Kathy Dawn Lang's meteoric rise: how her seemingly perfect childhood was shattered when her father walked out on the family; how she stumbled accidentally into country music; her work with Roy Orbison, Owen Bradley, Anne Murray and filmmaker Percy Adlon; and the night the most important man in her life, her friend, mentor and soul-mate, Drifter, died in a bar-room brawl.

Uncovering k. d.'s deepest emotions, from a commitment to animal rights that threatened to ruin her career to her coming to terms with a sexuality that made her an unwitting poster girl for the lesbian and gay community, *k. d. lang* is the definitive biography.

'Once in a while, someone comes along who refuses to be stuffed into the accepted pigeon-hole, who defies the limits of category, and who takes a popular form and stretches it beyond what was thought possible. Usually you can't get away with this unless you are very, very good. k. d. lang is very, very good'

Margaret Atwood

ISBN 0 00 638240 1